Statistics Explained

2nd Edition

Statistics
Explained

2nd Edition

- Perry R. Hinton

Routledge
Taylor & Francis Group

LONDON AND NEW YORK

First published 2004
by Routledge
27 Church Road, Hove, East Sussex BN3 2FA

Simultaneously published in the USA and Canada
by Routledge
29 West 35th Street, New York, NY 10001

Reprinted 2004
by Routledge
27 Church Road, Hove, East Sussex BN3 2FA
270 Madison Avenue, New York, NY 10016

Routledge is an imprint of the Taylor & Francis Group

Copyright © 2004 Routledge

Typeset in 11/13.5pt Times by Graphicraft Limited, Hong Kong
Printed and bound in Great Britain by TJ International Ltd, Padstow, Cornwall
Cover design by Anú Design

This publication has been produced with paper manufactured to strict
environmental standards and with pulp derived from sustainable forests.

British Library Cataloguing-in-Publication Data
A catalogue record for this book is available from the British Library

Library of Congress Cataloging-in-Publication Data
Hinton, Perry R. (Perry Roy), 1954–
    Statistics explained / by Perry R. Hinton. – 2nd ed.
        p.   cm.
    Includes bibliographical references and index.
        ISBN 0-415-33284-2 – ISBN 0-415-33285-0 (pbk.)
    1. Psychometrics–Textbooks.   I. Title.
BF39.H54 2004
519.5–dc22   2003027026

ISBN 0-415-33285-0 (pbk)
ISBN 0-415-33284-2 (hbk)

To Anna, Anthony and Emma

Contents

Please note the 'sums of squares' formulae are incorrectly presented on pages 117 and 118, the formulae should read: $\Sigma (X - \bar{X})^2$

9 Significance, error and power 95

10 Introduction to the analysis of variance 111

11 One factor independent measures ANOVA 125

12 Multiple comparisons 137

18 One factor ANOVA for ranked data

19 Analysing frequency data: chi-square

20 Linear correlation and regression

21 Multiple correlation and regression

Figures

FIGURES

Preface

This book sets out to explain the major statistical analyses used by undergraduate students in psychology. It should also satisfy many of the statistical requirements of students of social and life sciences, education, health, business and communication; indeed anyone with a need to understand statistical analysis. The examples in the book are varied but there is a focus on analysing data about people. The book examines many important statistical techniques, providing explanations of how and why they are used.

When I was an undergraduate myself I learnt the appropriate statistics to analyse my experimental data but was frustrated that the books I read simply told me to do this, do that, like a cookbook, with no explanation of why I was using such strange formulae or calculating numbers in the manner suggested. As a graduate student I needed a more detailed knowledge of statistics and there were some excellent books for the new researcher. The only problem was that they were very weighty tomes, as thick as an encyclopaedia and comprehensive to match. There were pages and pages of mathematical formulae that tended to make the heart quail.

I discovered that the apparently mysterious formulae and calculations actually made sense: indeed, they made common sense and the logic of statistical tests was no more difficult than understanding a theory in psychology. As a lecturer I noticed that there was a tendency for students to view statistical tests as difficult and esoteric. In part this was because they knew the formulae for calculating the tests but did not know 'how' or 'why' the tests were as they were. Over the years as a lecturer I have gained much satisfaction from students exclaiming: 'so that's what it means!' when an explanation is given. And often these are students who had the view that statistics was something they would not be able to understand. Yet this is not the case. Statistics are actually remarkably sensible – they make good sense. The key to understanding statistics is to understand how and why they were developed, what they set out to do, and how they do it. Unfortunately this is sometimes missing. Unlike many theories and explanations of human behaviour and experience which by their nature are the subject of fierce debate, statistics are simply techniques to be used where necessary. A statistical test is a tool, like any other, and so can be used wisely or foolishly. If we know what it is for we can use it well. Few of us would choose to use a fork to drink soup yet people choose inappropriate statistical tests to analyse data. But statistical tests are like spoons and forks. If you know what they can do and how to use them, there is no mystery, you just get on and use them. But like any other tool it does take a little while to understand how and why it works as it does, and then to get the hang of using it oneself. Once the tools have been mastered they becomes easier to use.

I hope that, for students facing the purchase of a statistics book, this book will be able to provide an account of statistical analysis where the mysterious formulae are explained, but without weighing down the reader!

I would like to thank Sue Wilkinson for encouraging me to write this book, Margaret Manning for many interesting statistical discussions and David French for helping me find the time to write it. I would especially like to thank Paul Hartmann for many helpful comments on the text. I have taught an undergraduate course on the *Analysis of Experiments* for a number of years and the feedback, questions and criticisms of the many students who have taken the course have helped me to understand the problems and delights of learning statistics. I have learnt a lot. This book is a response to that experience and I thank them too. Finally, I would like to thank Anna, Anthony and Emma, without whose support I could never have written this book.

Preface to the Second Edition

I have been very pleased with the success of the first edition of this book. I found it particularly gratifying when one of my students said that she could hear me speaking when she read the book. I hope other readers have felt like her, that the book reads like someone talking – hopefully a friendly, helpful voice – as I believe that the best way of learning is having someone explain the material to me clearly. Despite the wonders of new technology we should strive to maintain that personal contact between teacher and student, and writer and reader. I was therefore in a quandary when asked to do a second edition. I had received a number of complimentary letters and emails from lecturers and students so I felt the book was doing its job well. As the old adage says 'if it's not broken don't mend it' and the age of a book shouldn't undermine its value – indeed one of my own favourite books on statistics is Siegel (1956) despite the excellent new editions. However, there are changes I want to make based on the experience of the passing years along with the constructive comments of my readers. I have also produced, with colleagues, a companion volume on the computer statistics package SPSS, which informed some of my thoughts on the new edition (Hinton *et al.*, 2004). I hope my voice still comes through clearly and comprehensibly.

Since the first edition the debate has developed around the importance of significance testing (Wilkinson and Task Force on Statistical Inference,

1999). Most academic papers are only published if the findings within them are statistically significant. This may be giving a distorted picture of the overall outcome of research, as we do not know how many studies did not find a significant effect. So a greater prominence should be given to both confidence intervals and statistical power in the reporting of findings. The findings of one study showing a significant finding may in the long run be far less important than a broader understanding of the size of an effect that emerges with a number of studies. I have therefore gone into more detail in explaining 'power' in Chapter 9 and also introduced the calculation of confidence intervals into the book. However, I think that students need to understand the basics of significance testing first so that they are able to understand the issues and engage in the debate from a position of knowledge. I have, therefore, maintained the structure and explanation of significance testing from the first edition of the book.

I have also included a final chapter that introduces the reader to the general linear model. Whilst it is quite possible to happily undertake statistical analysis without knowing about the general linear model, I hope this chapter provides, for the interested reader, a bridge between a good understanding of the statistical techniques and a more in-depth understanding of the underlying principles of most of our statistical analyses. I have found that the assumptions of statistical tests often appear strange but that some appreciation of this underlying model reveals what the assumptions are all about.

I would also like to thank the many students (hundreds in fact) on the undergraduate course in *Research and Experimentation II* who, for seven years, were able to interrogate the author of their set textbook. I appreciated their (generally) kind comments and I am glad that the book helped a number of them to realise that statistics were not so alien after all. I have many happy memories of teaching on that course with my colleagues Victoria West and Alfredo Gaitan, who I would also like to thank. Thanks also to Ian Robertson for our many discussions on teaching and learning, especially on how to make topics clear and comprehensible. Finally, I would especially like to thank Charlotte Brownlow, Isabella McMurray and Bob Cozens, the other members of the *SPSS Explained* team, without whose enthusiasm, support and friendship I might not have taken on the task of writing this new edition.

Chapter 1

Introduction

R ESEARCH IS PERFORMED to find answers to questions: what events from their lives do people remember best?; can we judge people's occupations from the way they dress?; what effect does tiredness have on our performance of different tasks? To help us develop answers to these questions we often collect data. We distinguish between two types of data: quantitative and qualitative. Quantitative data concerns numbers or quantities that we have collected using measuring devices such as timers, performance tests or questionnaires. Qualitative data concerns accounts, descriptions and explanations – linguistic rather than numeric data. Most researchers focus on either quantitative or qualitative data collection analysis (and this book is exclusively concerned with the former) but ultimately it is a combination of the two that will provide the fullest insight into our research questions. Consider students undertaking an examination. We might collect information on how many hours they spend studying, how many books they have read and how well they perform in the examination (quantitative data) but we might also ask them for their own explanations of how well they studied, how motivated they were and why, along with what they thought about the experience of taking the examination (qualitative data).

Sometimes, but not often, it is possible to look at that research data and see what it is telling us. Usually, however, the implications of the data are not so obvious, especially when we have collected a large amount of data in numeric form. Simply looking at lots and lots of numbers is usually uninformative and possibly confusing. We need to draw from it the relevant information for the research question posed. This is where statistics can help us. A mass of data can be described and summarised or different sets of data can be compared by the calculation of appropriate statistics. Thus statistical analysis should not be seen as either incomprehensible or esoteric, but as a useful technique for helping the researcher in finding answers to the questions set.

Much of this book is about the various statistics we calculate. Whilst we shall see in Chapter 5 that it has a technical definition, a statistic is essentially a number that has been systematically obtained. A 'total' is a statistic. We can find a total for the number of apples in a bowl or children in a school: we just add them up. Some statistics are easy to obtain (such as the number of fingers on my left hand) whereas others are a little more difficult to work out (such as the F-ratio in the analysis of variance – something we shall be looking at later in the book). However, the purpose of calculating these statistics is to tell us something we want to know: are girls performing better than boys at school?; which of two types of cola do people prefer? It is not the calculation of statistics that is intrinsically interesting (we have computers to do this) but what the statistic tells us about the questions we are interested in. However, the ability to choose the appropriate statistic, and the ability to see whether our calculations are correct or not, are both crucial factors in obtaining a valid answer to our questions, rather than making an error: we don't want to do the statistical equivalent of asking the time and being told it's Tuesday.

We invariably need to calculate statistics when we undertake certain forms of research and having an understanding of what they are and why we calculate them can make us much better able to critically analyse the work of others. If someone informs you that the statistical analysis of their research shows that pigs can fly, and people sometimes do make wild claims as a result of their research, then you might be sceptical about their choice or use of statistics. However, there are many cases where the claims are not so obviously in error yet a simple knowledge of statistical analysis can reveal a flaw.

The purpose of this book is to explain the logic behind statistical techniques, when you would use them and how you would calculate them. Often the latter tends to dominate one's experience, and there is a desire to just get the thing worked out, but with calculators and computers it is easy to put data into an analysis but less easy to know we have done it correctly. It is understanding why one is calculating a particular statistic that is of crucial importance to data analysis.

The book begins with an explanation of the statistics that help us to describe data, examining what 'frequency distributions' can show us and which summary statistics we can calculate. It then moves on to the importance of the 'normal distribution' and hypothesis testing. The difference between populations and samples is considered along with the use of information from samples to estimate the details of populations. Subsequently the various techniques are introduced that allow us to compare data from different samples.

The book can be read straight through to see the way in which the statistical tests have been developed. These tests all have a logical basis, and explanations are provided for the particular formulae that we use for our calculations. Alternatively, the book can be dipped in and out of, providing enough information on each test so that readers requiring a specific analysis can see why it has been developed and undertake an analysis on their own data by following the worked examples provided.

The final chapter provides an introduction to the model underlying many of our statistical tests. In the explanation of this model we can see why many statistical tests require a particular set of assumptions. Whilst this chapter does not contain any new statistical techniques to learn it is hoped that the reader who does tackle this chapter will gain a deeper understanding of the principles underlying statistical techniques which can lead to a greater appreciation of what in practice is happening when carrying out a statistical analysis.

Descriptive statistics

A MAJOR REASON FOR CALCULATING statistics is to describe and summarise a set of data. A mass of numbers is not usually very informative so we need to find ways of abstracting the key information that allows us to present the data in a clear and comprehensible form. In this chapter we shall be looking at an example of a collection of data and considering the best way of describing and summarising it.

One hundred students sit an examination. After the examination the papers are marked and given a score out of one hundred. You are given the results and asked to present them to a committee that monitors examination performance. You are faced with the following marks:

22	65	49	56	59	34	9	56	48	62
55	52	78	61	50	62	45	51	61	60
54	58	59	47	50	62	44	55	52	80
51	49	58	46	32	59	57	57	45	56
90	53	56	53	55	55	41	64	33	0
38	57	62	15	48	54	60	50	54	59
67	58	60	43	37	54	59	63	68	60
46	52	56	32	75	57	58	47	45	52
55	51	50	50	69	63	64	49	56	52
37	60	71	26	30	57	56	55	58	61

Fortunately, you are told the sort of questions the committee might ask:

- Can you describe the results of the examination?
- Can you give us a brief summary of them?
- What is the average mark?
- What is the spread of scores?
- What is the highest and lowest mark?
- Here are last year's results, how do this year's compare?

You sit looking at the above table. The answers to the questions are not obvious from the 'raw' data, that is, the original data before any statistics have been calculated. We need to do something to make it clearer. The first thing that we can do is to list the data in order, from lowest to highest:

0	9	15	22	26	30	32	32	33	34
37	37	38	41	43	44	45	45	45	46
46	47	47	48	48	49	49	49	50	50
50	50	50	51	51	51	52	52	52	52
52	53	53	54	54	54	54	55	55	55
55	55	55	56	56	56	56	56	56	56
57	57	57	57	57	58	58	58	58	58
59	59	59	59	59	60	60	60	60	60
61	61	61	62	62	62	62	63	63	64
64	65	67	68	69	71	75	78	80	90

With this ordering certain things are more apparent: we can now see the lowest and highest scores more easily, with the scores falling between 0 and 90.

Another thing we can do to improve our presentation is to add up the number of people who achieved the same mark. We work out the frequency of each mark. For example, 5 people scored 52 and only 1 scored 69. When we do this it allows us to see that the most 'popular' mark was 56 with a frequency of 7. We should not forget that there are a number of possible marks that no one achieved: no one scored 8 or 35 for example, so each of these marks has a frequency of 0.

We can present this information in graphical form if we convert it to a histogram, where the frequency of a mark is represented as a vertical bar. In the histogram, shown in Figure 2.1, we list out all the possible marks that a

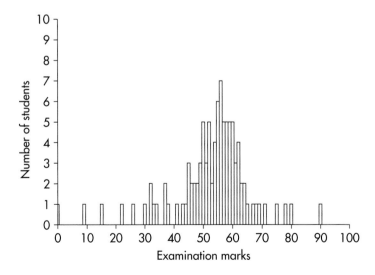

FIGURE 2.1 Frequency distribution of the examination results

student could get, 0 to 100, and draw a bar above each mark, with the length of the bar corresponding to the frequency of the mark in the set of results. For a mark of 55 we draw a bar of length 6 (as 6 students obtained a mark of 55) and for 64 we draw a bar of length 2. This gives a clear visual presentation of the results.

This histogram is called a frequency distribution, as we can see how the marks are distributed across the range of possible marks. Frequency distributions are very important in statistical analysis as they provide the basic representation of our information. The frequency distribution is a clear infor-mative chart, providing us with a way of showing the pattern of the marks we obtained: their distribution across the range of possible values. We might wish to present the frequency distribution to the committee as it provides us with a graphical representation of the marks. But what it doesn't do is provide us with a summary of the findings.

Measures of 'central tendency'

Is there a single mark that best represents the results? Can we provide the committee with a typical mark to summarise the findings? The most reason-able mark to use here is a central or middle mark. In statistical terms we are trying to find a measure of central tendency. The question we are now faced with is: what is the central position in our frequency distribution?

One answer is simply to select the most frequent mark, the longest bar in the histogram. This statistic is called the mode. As you can see from Figure 2.1 the longest bar is at the mark of 56, where seven people obtained this result in the examination. In this case 56 appears to be a reasonable estimate of a central mark. However, the mode is not often used as a measure of central tendency for a number of reasons. First, what do we do if there were two marks each having the same high frequency? What if seven people had scored 52 and seven 56, which one would we choose? Second, there will be occasions where the mode clearly does not represent a central mark. Imagine that we had ten very weak students who all scored zero in the examination, yet the rest of the distribution was the same as in Figure 2.1. Even though there would be a clustering of the marks in the 50s our mode would be zero. In this case the mode would be a poor measure of central tendency.

Another measure of central tendency that is used more often than the mode is the median. This is the score that comes in the middle of the list when we have ordered it from lowest to highest. If we had nine students in all then the median would be the fifth mark in the list. However, we have one hundred students and, with an even number, there is no middle mark. The middle lies halfway between the fiftieth and fifty-first marks. In our example the fiftieth and fifty-first marks are both 55, so the median is 55. (If the fiftieth and fifty-first marks had been different the median would be halfway between them. We would simply add them up and divide by two to get our median value.[1])

The median is a good measure of central tendency as it picks up the score in the middle position of the distribution. Its weakness, if indeed it is a weakness, is that, like the mode, it does not use all the information given by the marks. The median is simply the score where we cut our list into two halves. The marks either side of the median could be anything below or above the median respectively. If we found that someone who had had been given a mark of 9 in the examination really had a mark of 29 or 39, correcting this score would not change the median as 55 would still be the middle mark in the list. The median would stay the same even if a number of marks were changed (as long as a mark below the median was not changed to a value higher than the median or vice versa). The median doesn't take account of the values of all the scores, only the value of the score at the middle position.

Whilst we might regard the median as a better choice of a central value than the mode, as it finds the score at the middle position rather than the most frequent score, there is a third measure of central tendency that is used far more often than either of the above two measures. This is the mean.

We express the formula for calculating the mean using special symbols. We use the Greek letter μ (pronounced 'mu') for the mean, the Greek letter capital sigma, Σ, to mean 'the sum of' (or 'add up'), X to indicate a score (in our example, an examination mark) and N for the number of scores. The symbols ΣX means 'add up all the scores'. The mean, μ is the sum of the scores divided by N:

$$\mu = \frac{\sum X}{N}$$

When we talk of an 'average' we are usually referring to the mean (although the word 'average' is often used much more loosely than the word 'mean' which has its statistical definition). To calculate the mean we add up all the marks and divide them by the number of students. Adding up all the marks we arrive at 5262. Dividing this by 100 gives us a mean of 52.62.

One way of thinking about the mean is by analogy with a see-saw. Imagine that the horizontal axis of our frequency distribution is a beam of wood going from 0 to 100 in length. Each of the marks is a student sitting on the beam at the position specified by their mark (so there are seven students sitting on the beam at 56 and one at 75 etc.). Where would you have to put a supporting post under the beam to make a perfectly balanced see-saw? The answer is at the mean position. We can see it as the value that balances the scores either side of it. Any change in the marks (we move a student along the beam) results in a change in the mean (the see-saw will tip to one side unless we move the supporting post to a new position to restore balance). So the mean is a statistic that is sensitive to all the scores about it, unlike the median, as we saw above.

There is another point about the mean that we can see from the see-saw analogy; that is, the mean is very sensitive to extreme values. A very large score or a very small score will have a greater effect on where the support post ends up than a mark in the middle of the distribution. If you have a number of people sitting on a balanced see-saw it tips up much more easily if a new person sits on an end rather than near the middle. Thus, the mean position, like the supporting post of a see-saw, is determined both by the number of scores and also by their distance from it.

Comparing measures of central tendency

In our example we now have three measures of central tendency, a mode of 56, a median of 55 and a mean of 52.62. Which do we choose? The answer is: whichever we want. We simply choose the one that best represents a central value in our distribution, for our purpose. Usually this results in us picking the mean as it takes into account all the scores but there are occasions when we choose the mode or median.

The mode is quick and easy to determine once we have created the frequency distribution, so we might use it as a 'rough and ready measure' without the need for further calculation. Also we cannot calculate the median or mean with some types of data. For example, if I am planning a trip for a group of friends and I suggest a range of places to visit, I'll probably select the place chosen by the largest number. Note that we cannot calculate a mean or a median here as the names of places cannot be put in numeric order or added up.

We use the median when we have an abnormally large or small value in our frequency distribution, which would result in the mean giving us a rather distorted value for the central tendency. As an example, six aircraft have the following maximum speeds: 450 km/h, 480 km/h, 500 km/h,

530 km/h, 600 km/h and 1100 km/h. We can see that most have a maximum speed around 500 km/h but the inclusion of the supersonic aircraft with a speed of 1100 km/h gives us a mean of 610 km/h. This number might not be appropriate to use as a central value as 610 km/h is faster than five out of the six aircraft can fly. If we take the median, which is 515 km/h (halfway between 500 and 530) we have a more representative value for our central point.

However, in most cases of data collection the mean is the measure chosen. We shall see further reasons for the importance of the mean in Chapter 5.

Measures of 'spread'

So far we have charted our data on a frequency distribution and found measures of central tendency. Another useful statistic for summarising the data is a measure of 'spread'. It is important for a number of reasons to find out how spread out the scores are. Two groups of students taking the same examination could produce different frequency distributions yet the means might be the same. How then can we express the difference in the distributions? It is almost certain that the marks for one group of students are more spread out than the other. A small spread of results in a study is often seen as a good thing, as it indicates that all the people (or whatever produces the scores) are behaving similarly, and hence the mean value represents the scores very well. A large spread may be a problem as it indicates that there are large differences between the individual scores and the mean is therefore not so representative. Thus, we want a statistic that gives us a small number when the scores are clustered together and a large number when the scores are spread out.

The range

The simplest measure of spread is the range. The range is the difference between the highest and lowest scores. In our example the highest score is a mark of 90 and the lowest is 0. The range is therefore 90.

This measure is a little crude, it sets the boundaries to the scores but does not tell us anything about their general spread. Indeed, even if our marks were evenly spread between 0 and 90 rather than clustered in the 50s, our range would still be 90. The range uses information from only two scores, the rest could be anything between, so it is rather limited in what it tells us.

Quartiles

Another way of looking at the spread is to calculate quartiles. We saw earlier that the median cuts the ordered data into halves; the quartiles simply cut the ordered data into quarters. The first quartile indicates the score one quarter of the way up the list from the lowest. The second quartile indicates the score two quarters up the list. It does not take very much to realise that the second quartile is halfway up the list and is therefore the median. The third quartile is the score three quarters up the list. The fourth quartile is all the way to the end of the list and so it is the highest score.

From our ordered list of examination results, one quarter along the list of a hundred scores lies between the twenty-fifth and the twenty-sixth person's marks, so the first quartile is midway between 48 and 49, which is 48.5. We already know that the second quartile (between the fiftieth and fifty-first person's marks) is 55 as we worked out the median above. The third quartile is three quarters along the list so is between the seventy-fifth and seventy-sixth person's marks: this is 59.5.[2] And of course the fourth quartile is 90, as it's the highest score. If we use the symbol Q for quartile, we have $Q_1 = 48.5$, $Q_2 = 55$, $Q_3 = 59.5$, $Q_4 = 90$.

A slightly more sophisticated measure of spread than the range is the interquartile range: that is the difference between the third and first quartile, $Q_3 - Q_1$. In our example this is $59.5 - 48.5 = 11$. This is the range of half the scores, those in the middle of the distribution. The reason why the interquartile range is used is that, unlike the range, it is not going to be affected by one particularly high or low score and may represent the spread of the distribution more appropriately. (Some people use the semi-interquartile range, which is simply half the interquartile range. In our example this is 5.5.)

Calculating quartiles is quite useful as it can tell us a few interesting things about the distribution, in particular whether the distribution is symmetric about the median within the interquartile range. $Q_2 - Q_1$ tells us the range of the quarter of scores below the median and $Q_3 - Q_2$ tells us the range of the quarter of the scores above the median. In our example the first is 6.5 and the second is 4.5. We have the scores bunched closer together in the quarter above the median than in the quarter below the median, as 4.5 is a smaller range than 6.5, for the same number of scores.

It is worth noting here how each new statistic tells us something different about the data. It may be something we already know by looking at the distribution but often the statistic makes it clearer and more explicit, with a number attached. However, these statistics do not miraculously appear. They have been created by people attempting to find ways of best describing their data. When we wish to describe our data we choose the most appropriate statistic for our purposes.

Variation

Calculating quartiles does not use all the information available from the scores in the data, and again, as in our discussion of the median, some scores could be different and we would still end up with the same interquartile range. The question therefore is whether we can devise a measure of spread that takes into account each and every score. It is in answer to this question that a number of measures of spread have been developed. The common feature of them is that they all begin with the mean (once again indicating the importance of the mean). Their logic is as follows. If we take the mean as our 'central' position then we can compare each of the scores with the mean and find out how far each score varies or deviates from it. If we add up the deviation of each of the scores from the mean we will have a measure of the total variability in the data. If we want to we can then divide this total by the number of scores to find the average deviation of a score from the mean.

We can calculate the deviation of a score from the mean by simply working out $X - \mu$, where X is a score and μ is the mean. We can do this for every score. However, we have a problem: when we add them up to find the total variability, the deviations tend to cancel each other out. In our example, a mark of 55 gives a deviation from the mean of $55 - 52.62 = +2.38$ and a mark of 50 gives a deviation from the mean of $50 - 52.62 = -2.62$. If we add up these deviations we get 2.38 plus −2.62, which equals −0.24. Due to the minus sign, two scores, both over two marks from the mean, end up giving a deviation of less than one when added up. We do not want this; it is not a statistic that reflects the variability as it really is. Indeed, as the mean is the position of 'balance' in the scores, adding up all the deviations will give us a total of zero as all the positive deviations exactly cancel out the negative deviations. As the sum of the deviations of our scores always turns out to be zero whatever scores we have, it is useless as a statistic as it certainly does not provide us with a measure of how spread out the scores are.

When we consider it, all that the minus sign of a deviation is telling us is that the score is lower than the mean. We are not actually interested in whether the score is higher or lower than the mean only how far away it is from the mean. What we need to do is to find a way of adding up the deviations so that they do not cancel each other out, so that we end up with a reasonable estimate of the real variability of the scores. There are two solutions:

1 Absolute deviation

We can solve our problem by ignoring the minus sign altogether and treat all the deviations as positive. If we get a deviation of −2.62 we call it +2.62. We put two vertical lines round a formula to indicate that we take the absolute value, that is, ignore a minus sign in the solution and treat it as positive. Absolute deviation is $|X - \mu|$. We add up the deviations for all the scores. To find the average deviation we divide it by the number of scores, denoted by N. We call this the mean absolute deviation and represent it by the following formula:

$$\text{Mean absolute deviation} = \frac{\sum |X - \mu|}{N}$$

For our examination results the mean absolute deviation is 9.15.

2 Variance

An alternative solution to taking absolute values is to square the deviations, as the square of a number is always positive. The square of −2.16 is +4.67. We then add up the square of each of the deviations to produce a sums of squares: $\sum(X - \mu)^2$. This formula can be can be translated into English as: 'find the deviation of each score from the mean, square each deviation, then add up the squared deviations'. We can then divide this figure by the number of scores (N) to find the average of the squared deviations. This value is called the variance.

$$\text{Variance} = \frac{\sum(X - \mu)^2}{N}$$

In our example the variance is 176.52.

The variance gives us a figure for the average variability of the scores about the mean, expressed as squared deviations. It also does what we want: gives us a large figure for scores that are spread out and a smaller one for scores that are closer together. Interestingly, as it is dealing with squared deviations, the variance gives more weight to extreme scores. For example, a score that deviates by 2 from the mean will contribute 4 to the variance but a score 4 away from the mean will contribute 16 to the variance, so even though the second score is only twice as far from the mean as the first it contributes four times as much to the variance.

If we just wanted a measure of variability then variance is fine. However, note that the figure we calculated of 176.52 cannot be placed on the frequency distribution as a distance from the mean. This is because the variance is the average of the <u>squared</u> deviations, rather than the average deviation. To bring the statistic back to the terms we started with we need to find the square root. (As we squared the deviations earlier to get rid of the minus signs we need to 'undo' this now it has served its purpose.) We call this statistic, the square root of the variance, the <u>standard deviation</u> and represent it by the symbol σ (the lower case Greek letter sigma).

$$\text{Standard deviation, } \sigma = \sqrt{\frac{\sum(X - \mu)^2}{N}}$$

A simple example will show how we calculate the standard deviation. Imagine that we only had 4 scores 2, 2, 3, 5 in our data. The mean is 3. We work out σ as follows:

Score X	Deviation $X - \mu$	Squared deviation $(X - \mu)^2$
2	−1	1
2	−1	1
3	0	0
5	2	4
		$\sum(X - \mu)^2 = 6$

Dividing the sums of squares ($\sum(X - \mu)^2 = 6$) by the number of scores ($N = 4$) gives a variance of 1.5. Taking the square root of 1.5 gives us a standard deviation of $\sigma = 1.22$. In the examination example the standard deviation of the one hundred marks is 13.29.

The standard deviation gives us a measure of spread about the mean. In many cases most of the scores (about two-thirds) will lie within one standard deviation less than and one standard deviation greater than the mean, that is, in the range $X - \sigma$ to $X + \sigma$. The standard deviation gives us a measure of the 'standard' distance of a score from the mean in this set of data.

W A R N I N G ! The above formulae for variance and standard deviation are used when are interested in these data *only*. When our data is a subset or a sample of a larger set of data that we want it to *represent* then we use slightly different formulae, the same as the above except that we would divide the sums of squares by the degrees of freedom *df*, rather than the sample size *n*, where $df = n - 1$. If it was the case that our one hundred students were not the complete set we were interested in but were a sample drawn from one thousand students taking the examination then we would use the different formulae:

$$\text{Variance} = \frac{\sum (X - \mu)^2}{n - 1}$$

$$\text{Standard deviation, } \sigma = \sqrt{\frac{\sum (X - \mu)^2}{n - 1}}$$

The reason for the difference is explained in Chapter 5 when we consider samples. Most of the time we use the formulae with $n - 1$ (the degrees of freedom) rather than n (the sample size) as most of the time we wish to use our samples to generalise to a wider population rather than treating our data as all that we are interested in.

Comparison of measures of spread

As with the measures of central tendency, the measure of spread that is most useful depends on the reasons for calculating it.

The range and interquartile range are both easy measures to calculate, giving a limited but potentially adequate measure of spread. Their weakness is that they do not take into account all the scores in the data and may be limited in their ability to represent the true variability of the scores. The range, in particular, may not reflect the general spread of results very well if there is one very low or very high score.

The variance is a good measure of the variability in the data. It uses all the scores and will give a small number if all the scores cluster round the mean and a large number if they are spread out. As we shall see in the chapters on the analysis of variance this statistic is extremely important in some statistical analyses. However, when we are describing a set of data the variance may not be particularly useful as a description of the spread of scores as the number it produces is not of the same order as the scores. It is expressed in terms of the squared deviations from the mean. In our example the variance of 176.52 appears large but this may be because it is expressed in terms of marks squared, not marks.

The mean absolute deviation and the standard deviation are both good descriptive statistics of the spread of a set of scores. They both use the information from all the scores and both produce a number that expresses an 'average' deviation from the mean in the terms we want (in our example: marks). As they are expressed in the same terms as the scores they are easy to understand. We can, if we wish, plot these figures as a distance from the mean on the frequency distribution, so they can be graphically represented as well.

Why is it that the spread of a set of results is almost always expressed, in research reports, as the standard deviation and rarely as the mean absolute deviation? If the data we are describing is all we are interested in then there is not a compelling argument. However, there is a distinct advantage of using the standard deviation when our data is a sample of a larger set (a population) that we wish it to represent. In our example, the 100 students were the only ones we were interested in. If, however, 1000 students had taken the examination and our 100 were a representative sample then we would want to use the standard deviation. The reasons, which are dealt with in Chapter 5, concern samples representing populations and the use of sample statistics to estimate population values.

Describing a set of data: in conclusion

When describing a set of data we want to summarise the frequency distribution by two measures, one indicating a central value indicating the 'average' score and a second to indicate the spread of the scores. The two most commonly used statistics for these measures, because of their usefulness, are the mean and the standard deviation. We can summarise the examination results by the following statistics: mean = 52.62 marks, standard deviation = 13.29 marks.

Comparing two sets of data with descriptive statistics

Summary statistics neatly and briefly describe the data but in most cases people want to use the information to make certain points. In our example a committee member might be concerned about possible falling standards or the effect of a change in the student selection procedure. The summary statistics can then be used to help make a decision about such questions. Notice that the points raised by the committee member both require a comparison with the previous year's results. The calculation of statistics is often used to go beyond description to allow us to answer specific research questions and this invariably involves comparing different sets of results.

For our example, the previous year's results for the same examination, where 100 students also sat the examination, are shown below. Note that it would not be easy to see any similarities or differences between the results for the two years very well by simply looking at the two tables of raw data. Both years have a mixture of marks in them and, whilst we might be able to pick out certain interesting results, such as the highest and lowest, the tables do not provide a good way of allowing us to make any comparisons between the two sets of data.

24	56	54	56	55	43	55	52	45	58
54	52	65	50	60	57	47	62	7	58
51	60	53	81	59	61	56	63	57	49
68	61	39	59	49	63	54	60	57	60
66	53	36	50	59	52	37	70	66	30
61	50	55	55	65	58	51	22	68	57
87	64	50	35	56	54	60	72	58	51
46	62	56	15	63	59	39	60	58	76
65	36	4	59	57	53	49	69	64	53
38	58	48	58	66	62	56	54	61	63

Again, if we order the data and create a frequency distribution we might begin to see where any differences lie. Figure 2.2 shows the frequency distribution of last year's results. We can compare Figure 2.2 with Figure 2.1 by eye. The distribution of results looks similar over the two years. This in itself might be useful evidence indicating a year on year consistency in performance. However, simply looking by eye cannot really tell us how similar the two distributions are, as we may miss subtle differences between them. This is where statistics can help.

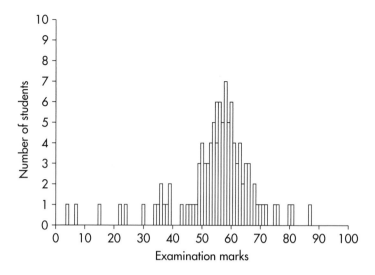

FIGURE 2.2 Frequency distribution of last year's examination results

If we consider measures of central tendency first, we can compare the two years directly:

	Last year	This year
Mode	58	56
Median	56.5	55.0
Mean	54.25	52.62

We can see that all three measures have dropped a little since last year. The mode could easily change by the effect of just a few students and so in this case is not the most useful statistic. The median does indicate that the central point was higher last year. The mean value shows a drop of 1.63 from last year to this. It may not seem a lot but remember the mean takes into account all the students, so there is a reduction of 1.63 marks per student. Now this could be due to a number of factors that are worth further investigation, such as: are there less able students this year or is it a harder examination this year? Before we do that we want to eliminate a simple alternative reason. Maybe last year there were a few particular good students or this year a few poor ones. These occur now and again and do not indicate that the general standards are changing. The way we can look at this is by considering the spread: maybe the spread was wider in one of the two years indicating a greater mixture of student ability in that year?

We can compare the various measures of spread:

	Last year	This year
Range	83	90
Interquartile range	10.5	11.0
Mean absolute deviation	8.82	9.15
Variance	169.93	176.52
Standard deviation	13.04	13.29

There was a narrower range last year with no one scoring as low as 0 or as high as 90, but there was not much difference in the interquartile range and, more particularly, the standard deviations are not very different from each other. It might be worth investigating further to see why there was the reduction in the mean performance. Notice that these results alone cannot distinguish between reasons for a difference, they can only be used to argue that one has occurred. The reason for the slightly lower marks, be it lower ability students, a harder paper, stricter marking or whatever, requires the skill of the researcher to find out.

As can be seen from the above figures, the mean and the standard deviation are generally the most informative statistics for a particular distribution. These are the statistics that are most commonly chosen, but there may be occasions when you think that other statistics are more appropriate or will tell you more accurately what you want to know. This leads to an important point: it is NOT worth calculating statistics until you know why you are doing it and what you want the statistics to show. It could be that the raw data tells you all you need to know, so do not bother calculating statistics. However, most of the time it is not possible to see the important characteristics of the data without some further analysis. Calculating the appropriate statistics can help you decide the answers to the questions you are asking. The difficulty in describing and analysing data is NOT calculating the statistics (we have computer programs that do this) but in knowing the questions you wish to find answers for, and the statistics that help inform those answers.

Note also that calculating statistics only gives you information. It is up to you how you interpret and use that information. A difference in means, or standard deviations, might be useful information, but that is all. Calculating statistics will not explain similarities and differences between distributions. What the statistics do is to provide us with pieces of information we can work with: they are tools to be used for our own purposes. After that we must use our judgement.

> Details on how to produce statistics to describe a set of data using the SPSS computer statistical package can be found in Chapter 3 of Hinton *et al.* (2004).

Some important information about numbers

Up to now we have been calculating statistics using sets of examination results. This is fine as examination results are the types of number that it makes sense to calculate means and other statistics on. But this is not the case for all types of number. We need to know what type of data we have before we know what statistics we are able to calculate.

Nominal data

Sometimes numbers are used like names. For example, in a sports squad of 22 players the number 15 on the back of a player's shirt simply allows us to identify him or her during play. It does not mean that player number 15 is better than players 1 to 14 or worse than players 16 to 22. It is meaningless to calculate statistics on these numbers as they are only nominal, used as names.

When we categorise someone or something we can use numbers to label the categories. For example, if we classify people by eye colour we might choose to label brown as 1, blue as 2, green as 3 and so on. Notice that the numbers are arbitrarily assigned to colours: we could have chosen other numbers or assigned the same numbers in a different way. The use of these numbers is nominal. We cannot use these numbers to calculate statistics: it is nonsense to say that the mean of a brown eyed person (1) and a green eyed person (3) is a blue eyed person (2)!

Ordinal data

We can use numbers to define an order of performance. For example, Susan is the best chess player in the class, followed by Robert, Marie and Peter. We can give Susan the top rank of 1, Robert 2, Marie 3 and Peter 4. These numbers tell us the rank order but little else. They do NOT tell us that the difference between 1 and 2 (Susan and Robert) is the same as the difference between 3 and 4 (Marie and Peter) despite there only being one place between them in the ranks. Susan could be the best player for her age in the country whereas the other three might not be as good as others of their age from nearby schools. Because of this we cannot calculate means and standard deviations on ordinal data. Chapter 16 discusses ordinal data further and considers how we can calculate statistics with it.

Interval and ratio data

Time, speed, distance and temperature can all be measured on interval scales and we have clocks, speedometers, tape measures and thermometers to do it. They are called interval scales because the differences between the consecutive numbers are of equal intervals: the difference between 1 and 2 is the same as the difference between 3 and 4 or 10 and 11. Unlike an ordinal scale where these could be different, on an interval scale they are all the same. For example, the difference between 6 and 7 minutes is the same as the difference between 20 and 21 minutes, it is 1 minute in both cases. When our numbers come from a scale with equal intervals then we can calculate means and standard deviations.

Ratio data is a special kind of interval data. With interval data the zero value can be arbitrary, such as the position of zero on some temperature scales: the Fahrenheit zero is at a different position to that of the Celsius scale, whereas with ratio data zero actually indicates the point where 'nothing' is scored on the scale, such as zero on a speedometer when there is no movement, and so this zero means the same thing regardless of whether we are measuring in miles per hour or kilometres per second. We can illustrate the difference in the following example. In an examination there are 100 questions of equal difficulty and students are required to get at least 50 correct answers to pass the examination. The examiner could choose to label the pass mark as zero. A score of 0 indicates 50 correct answers, +1 indicates 51 correct answers, −1 indicates 49 correct answers and so on. This is an interval scale with an arbitrary zero: the examiner chose where to put it. Now let us consider the same examination where zero indicates no correct answers and the pass mark is given a score of 50. This time the zero is nonarbitrary as it specifies a score of 'nothing' in terms of examination performance. Here the interval scale becomes a ratio scale.

Only on a ratio scale, with a genuine zero, can we make claims to do with ratios, such as: Susan's score is twice as good as John's, Robyn's score is one third of Peter's. If Susan had scored 80 and John 40 on a ratio scale examination then her score really is twice John's score. On an interval scale with zero set arbitrarily at 50 their scores are 30 and −10. With the interval scale we would not have been able to make the ratio judgements appropriately.

Many of our statistics require interval or ratio data. In the majority of the book (up to Chapter 16) we shall be considering only data that is interval or ratio as these types of data allow us to perform the largest range of statistical tests. For this reason, researchers often choose to collect interval or ratio data for analysis. With human subjects research often focuses on how fast or how accurately a task can be performed, where both *speed* and *accuracy* can be measured on ratio scales.

Standard scores

Comparing scores from different distributions

If you received a mark of 58 in an examination would you know how well you had done relative to the other candidates? Were you the best in the class or the worst? Clearly this is a case where you need further information. With the mean and standard deviation you can begin to answer these questions. If the mean is 52 and the standard deviation is 5 then your score is one of the best. If, however, the mean is 59 and the standard deviation is 3 then you are a little below average but as the scores are clustered around 59 there are likely to be a lot of students with similar results.

If you took two examinations and received a 58 for Psychology and a 49 for Statistics, which would you be most pleased with? You might want to use these results to help a decision on which subject to major in. You could choose the 58 because it is numerically higher. But if you found out that everyone else who took the Psychology examination scored over 60 and all the others who took the Statistics examination scored under 45 then you might change your mind. Even though you received a higher mark for Psychology the distributions of the two sets of scores are different. It could be that the Statistics examination is especially hard this year and 49 is a very high mark compared to the rest of the class, whereas 58 in Psychology might be a relatively low mark.

You then find out that, for the Statistics examination, the mean is 45 and the standard deviation is 4, and for Psychology the mean is 55 and the standard deviation is 6. This at least tells you that you are above average in both subjects but it doesn't tell you which yielded the higher class position.

To compare two scores that come from different distributions we need to standardise them. We do this by calculating a statistic called, not surprisingly, a standard score (or z score). This expresses the score relative to the mean in terms of the standard deviation. Thus a score of 58 is 3 away from a mean of 55. With a standard deviation of 6, this distance is 3/6th of the standard deviation. The score is half a standard deviation from the mean. Essentially the standard score tells us how many standard deviations the score is from the mean of the distribution. We calculate the standard score using the following formula:

The standard score, $z = \dfrac{X - \mu}{\sigma}$,

where X is the score to be standardised, μ is the mean and σ is the standard deviation of the distribution.

Standard scores can be compared, because, no matter what your distribution is like to start with, converting scores to z scores always results in a distribution of z scores with a mean of 0 and a standard deviation of 1. If the examination scores are converted to standard scores then we can compare them and see which examination result gives the higher class position.

In Psychology, $X = 58$, $\mu = 55$, $\sigma = 6$:

$$z = \frac{X - \mu}{\sigma} = \frac{58 - 55}{6} = \frac{3}{6} = 0.5$$

In Statistics, $X = 49$, $\mu = 45$, $\sigma = 4$:

$$z = \frac{X - \mu}{\sigma} = \frac{49 - 45}{4} = \frac{4}{4} = 1.0$$

In Psychology you are half a standard deviation above the mean and in Statistics you are one standard deviation above the mean. The higher z score for Statistics means that you are higher in the class results for Statistics than you are for Psychology.

In the previous chapter we compared two sets of examination results, from this year and last year. Notice that this year a score of 59 gives the following z score:

$$z = \frac{59 - 52.62}{13.29} = \frac{6.38}{13.29} = 0.48$$

For last year's distribution a score of 59 produces the following z score:

$$z = \frac{59 - 54.25}{13.04} = \frac{4.75}{13.04} = 0.36$$

From these two z scores we can see that a score of 59 is higher up the distribution this year ($z = 0.48$) than last year ($z = 0.36$), so 59 is a better score this year than last, possibly because the examination is harder this year (or one of the other reasons cited earlier).

The Normal Distribution

If I decided to collect data on, say, women's heights I might initially measure the height of a large number of women and plot the results as a frequency distribution on a histogram. What would the distribution look like? I start by choosing the steps for my histogram, i.e. deciding on the range of values to include for each bar. I'll choose 5 centimetre steps and include in the same bar all the women whose height falls within a particular 5 cm band. (To stop overlapping bands, the band includes heights from the lowest point of the band up to but not including the highest point of the band: for example, the band 160 cm to 165 cm covers the women's heights from 160 cm up to but not including 165 cm, so the woman whose height is exactly 165 falls into one band only – the 165 cm to 170 cm band.) When I have collected the data and added up all the women whose height falls within each 5 cm band I would find lots of women whose height was between 160 and 165 cm, or between 165 cm and 170 cm but not many between 135 cm and 140 cm or between 185 cm and 190 cm. There are not as many very short or very tall women compared to those in-between. In fact, the distribution would probably look like the histogram in Figure 3.1. Notice the distribution has a hump in the middle and tails off symmetrically either side.

If I then kept on measuring more and more women and also made my steps smaller and smaller (instead of 5 cm I choose 2 cm bands, then I plot

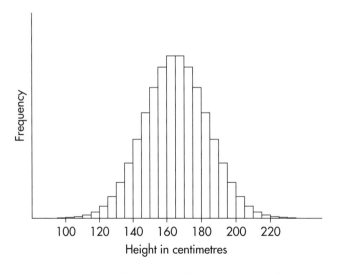

FIGURE 3.1 The distribution of women's height: histogram

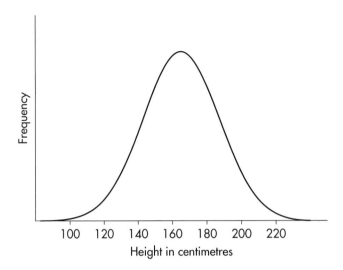

FIGURE 3.2 The distribution of women's height

the heights within 1 cm bands, then 0.5 cm and so on until my bands become extremely small) I would end up with a very large number of women's heights plotted on a histogram with very small steps. Eventually my histogram would become a smooth curve, as in Figure 3.2.

It is remarkable how many times we end up with this same bell-shaped curve, irrespective of which variable we are studying, be it women's heights, the foot size of ten year old boys or the gestation period of babies. As the curve is produced so often it is called the <u>Normal Distribution</u>. The interesting and very useful feature of this curve is that it is actually quite simple to express mathematically and can be calculated using only the mean and standard deviation. That is, we can work out the formula for a normal distribution precisely with only the knowledge of the mean and standard deviation.[3]

The normal distribution is very important for statistical analysis for the following reasons.

1   Many of the things we study and measure in our research (although not all) are assumed to be come from a population of scores that are normally distributed (such as women's heights). If we took all the men in the population we would expect to get normal distributions for height, weight, foot size, etc. We would expect normal distributions for the women's data as well.

2   Many of the statistical tests that we shall be examining in the course of the book make the assumption that the distributions they are investigating are normally distributed. Indeed these tests rely on this assumption: without it the logic of the test fails.

3   Interestingly, even if a distribution is not a normal distribution, when we take a large number of samples of the same size and plot their means on a frequency distribution this distribution tends to become a normal distribution. This again is extremely useful for statistical analysis.

These points are examined further in Chapter 5 when we consider samples, but the important thing to note here is that we have a lot of useful information when we know the mean and standard deviation of a set of scores and also that the distribution of the scores is a normal distribution.

The Standard Normal Distribution

As it is such a useful distribution people have drawn up tables of the normal distribution. However, the values would be different for all the various means and standard deviations we could get, and we would end up with lots and lots of different tables. So the values in the table are for a normal distribution with a mean of 0 and a standard deviation of 1. This normal distribution is called the Standard Normal Distribution.

If scores come from a normal distribution (such as height, weight) then converting the scores to standard scores (z scores) converts the distribution to the standard normal distribution. When we convert a score from a normal distribution to a z score we can then look up the z score in the standard normal distribution tables. This is given in Table A.1 of the Appendix. This information can be remarkably useful in statistical analysis.

The table tells us how many scores in the distribution are higher than the score we are examining. It does this by providing us with a figure for the area under the standard normal curve beyond the z scores, shown in Figure 3.3. The area underneath the whole curve is 1 (we have one whole area, like a whole cake before we cut it into portions) and the z score (like the knife cutting the cake) cuts it into two portions and the table tells us what proportion of the whole area we have cut off beyond the z score. If we subtract this value from 1 we know how much of the area is below the z score. Also, as the curve is symmetrical the mean value cuts the area into halves (so there is 0.5 of the area above the mean and 0.5 below).

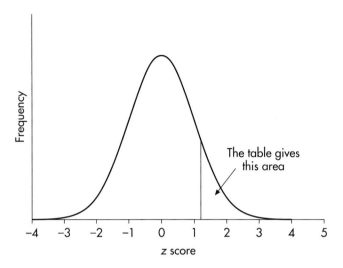

FIGURE 3.3 The Standard Normal Distribution

In this case, proportions are linked to <u>probability</u>. I am a 180 cm tall man. Let us assume, for the sake of this example, that the proportion of men taller than me in the population is a fifth. Now one fifth is 1 divided by 5, which equals 0.2, so we can express the proportion of men taller than me as 0.2 of the whole population. From this information I also know that the chance or probability of finding a man taller than me in the population is also one in five or 0.2. The area under the standard normal distribution curve is linked to probability in this way. The whole area under the curve (1) is linked to the probability of 1. Probability values range from 0 to 1. A probability of 1 is a certainty that something is the case. There is a certainty that any man I find will have a height somewhere on the men's height distribution so the whole area (1) is certain to include him. A probability of 0 is a certainty that something is not the case. The probability of finding a man twice my height (360 cm!) is so small as to be virtually zero. As we move from a probability of 0 to a probability of 1 we go from taking none of the area to taking larger and larger portions until we have the whole area.

When people talk about the chances of something happening they do not often talk in terms of probabilities ('the probability of me passing the examination is 0.5'), rather they prefer to use percentages ('I've a 50 per cent chance of passing the examination'). There is a simple relationship between probabilities and percentages, a percentage is a probability multiplied by 100. Thus, a probability of 0.3 is the same as a 30 per cent chance.

By looking at the area under the standard normal distribution curve above or below a z score we are able to obtain the probability of finding a score from the distribution larger or smaller than the score we have selected. In this way we are able to work out a whole range of interesting probabilities concerning scores from a normal distribution.

An example of using the standard normal distribution table

The distribution of scores in a Statistics examination is a normal distribution with a mean of 45 and a standard deviation of 4. You receive a mark of 49.

(a) What is the probability of someone scoring higher than you?
(b) What percentage of people are above the mean but lower than you?

As we have a normal distribution, the calculation of z scores will convert the distribution to the standard normal distribution. The score of 49 gives a z score as follows:

$$z = \frac{x - \mu}{\sigma} = \frac{49 - 45}{4} = 1$$

The standard normal distribution table (Table A.1 in the Appendix) will give us the probability of a score greater than a z score of 1. We look up the z score of 1.00 in the table and get a figure of 0.1587, so the probability of a score greater than 49 is 0.1587. (This means that you are in the top 16 per cent of the class, as $0.1587 \times 100 = 15.87$ per cent of the scores are better than yours.)

We know the area above the mean is 0.5 (half of the area) and the probability of a score greater than a z score of 1.00 is 0.1587, so if we subtract 0.1587 from 0.5 we will find the probability of a score above the mean and below your score: $0.5 - 0.1587 = 0.3413$. If we multiply this by 100 we will obtain the percentage: $0.3413 \times 100 = 34.13$ per cent. There are 34.13 per cent of the scores lower than your score but above the mean.

z scores of less than zero

If you calculate a z score and it turns out to be a minus number, all this means is that the score is less than the mean. As you can see from the standard normal distribution table you cannot look up negative z scores. However, as we have seen, the normal distribution is symmetrical so the proportion of scores *greater than*, say $+1.52$, is the same as the proportion of scores *less than* -1.52. If you wish to look up a minus number in the table ignore the minus and look up the number. The figure you get from the table now tells you the probability of a score *less* than the z score. To find the proportion of scores greater than the z score subtract the table figure from 1. For example, if we calculated a z score of -1, this means the score is below the mean. We cannot look up -1 in the tables. We ignore the minus and look up 1 in the table. The probability value is 0.1587. This tells us that the probability of a score *lower* than a z score of -1 is 0.1587 and the probability of a z score *greater* than -1 is $1 - 0.1587 = 0.8413$.

Chapter 4

Introduction to hypothesis testing

IN THE BOOK SO FAR we have seen that frequency distributions can be described by choosing appropriate statistics, usually the mean and standard deviation. Furthermore, we can compare scores from different distributions by the use of standard scores. Finally, if scores are normally distributed we can find out additional information about probability values through the use of the standard normal distribution. Now we need to see how we can exploit this information to help us answer the questions we wish our research to answer. In this chapter we move from simply describing data to seeing how we can use it to test hypotheses.

Testing an hypothesis

An hypothesis is a supposition: we state something we suppose to be the case and then collect evidence that bears upon it. For example, we are sitting talking with a group of friends about intelligence and one friend, Peter, makes the surprising claim that his 'genius' is due to being *hothoused* as a boy. Everyone laughs at this claim of genius but he continues seriously. Hothousing, he explains, is where children are provided with lots of information even before they can speak. He tells us that his mother used to show him flashcards with pictures of different types of cars, buildings, and even politicians and describe to him what they were as he gurgled back. Children have untapped potential for learning at that age that is not exploited, he argues. He even begins to get some of the sceptics to start to be swayed by his view of the development of the intellect. Everyone is now interested so we decide we want to test out Peter's claim.

To do this we need to use a procedure called hypothesis testing. This procedure underlies all the statistical tests that we shall be looking at in this book. Hypothesis testing follows a logical sequence of stages from proposing the hypothesis to deciding whether to accept or reject it.

The first problem we face is putting the hypothesis in a form that we can test. There is no genius meter that we can attach to Peter to see if he gives a genius reading. We have to find a way of expressing our hypothesis in a form that can be tested. We might decide that intelligence can be measured by the ability to solve mathematical problems or write essays on the current political situation. On this occasion we decide to operationally define intelligence in terms of an Intelligence Quotient (IQ) test. Our operational definition is a redefinition of the original concept in terms of *something we can measure*, geniuses being those people who score very highly on an IQ test. You might believe that this is a poor definition of genius (given the criticisms of IQ tests) and you may be right. I would then demand that you provide a more appropriate measure so we could continue. This problem occurs often in research, different experimenters arguing for different operational definitions. Clearly, we must use our judgement to produce a suitable definition. In this case, Peter agrees that an IQ test is an acceptable measure of his genius.

Peter's argument is that hothousing enhanced his intellect; without the hothousing he would not be so intelligent. Similarly, the rest of us who have not had the advantage of being hothoused are not as intelligent as we would have been had we had it. Therefore, the hypothesis we are testing is that being hothoused (in the way Peter was) increases IQ. This is called the research hypothesis. Note that we are being very specific here, there may be different ways of being hothoused but we are only concerned with the form that Peter experienced.

To decide whether this hypothesis is true or not all we need to do is to compare two distributions: the distribution of IQ scores for everyone without the benefit of Peter's hothousing, which I'll call the 'usual-IQ' distribution, and the distribution of IQ scores for everyone with the benefit of Peter's hothousing, which I'll call the 'hothouse-IQ' distribution. If we find that the hothouse-IQ distribution is further up the IQ scale than the usual-IQ distribution, giving a higher mean, then we can say that hothousing does increase IQ scores. (We might not know why but we have shown that it does.) In Figure 4.1 the two distributions are positioned to show an effect of hothousing resulting in an IQ enhancement of 30 points, thus, in this example, the research hypothesis is supported as hothousing shifts the usual-IQ distribution up the scale to produce the hothouse-IQ distribution.

If we found that hothousing had no effect then the hothouse-IQ distribution would be identical to the usual-IQ distribution. As a final possibility, if hothousing actually resulted in a decrease of IQ then the hothouse-IQ distribution would be lower on the IQ scale than the usual-IQ distribution (to the left of it rather than the right as in Figure 4.1). Note that we have identified three possibilities here: the hothouse-IQ distribution can be higher, the same or lower than the usual-IQ distribution. Only if we found the first of these would we accept Peter's hypothesis, whereas if either of the other two occurred we would reject it.

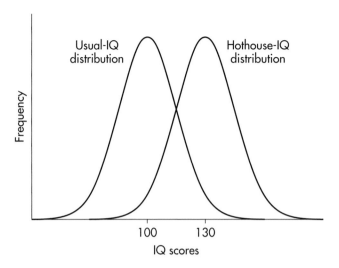

FIGURE 4.1 A hothousing effect of 30 IQ points

This is all apparently very easy but of course impossible! How are we going to find the hothouse-IQ distribution, given that this is the distribution of IQ scores for everyone after they had been hothoused as a child like Peter. The answer is we cannot. This distribution is something we simply cannot find out. Indeed, we can only find out one score from this distribution and that is Peter's score when we give him an IQ test.

Can we find out the usual-IQ distribution? It is simply too difficult to give everyone an IQ test, so what can we do? One assumption we can make is that IQ scores are normally distributed. If we do this then we will have a distribution we know a lot about. We can justify the assumption on the following grounds. First, as noted above, many human statistics are normally distributed so why not intelligence, and, second, believing this to be the case the creators of IQ tests deliberately constructed them to produce a normal distribution of scores with a mean of 100 ($\mu = 100$) and a standard deviation of 15 ($\sigma = 15$).

Note that we either have to test everyone we are interested in to find a particular distribution of scores (as in the examination example of Chapter 2) or make assumptions about the shape of the distribution. In the examination example there were only 100 scores but in many cases we are considering distributions comprising vast numbers of scores that are impossible to obtain, such as IQ scores for the adult population of the country. Hence we have to make assumptions about the distribution or else we cannot continue, and as we shall see in Chapter 5, assuming a normal distribution is often quite valid.

We now have one distribution we know about and one we do not. Unfortunately, without the hothouse-IQ distribution we are unable to test our research hypothesis. However, we are able to offer another hypothesis, the null hypothesis. The null hypothesis predicts that the two distributions are the same, that is, hothousing has no effect on IQ scores. Given that we know what the usual-IQ distribution looks like we can assume that the hothouse-IQ distribution is the same. If the null hypothesis is true then Peter's IQ score comes from the same distribution as the usual-IQ distribution.

We give Peter his IQ test and his score comes out at 120. We can find the position of this score in the distribution by finding the z score.

$$z = \frac{X - \mu}{\sigma} = \frac{120 - 100}{15} = 1.33$$

As we are assuming that the distributions are normal, we can look up this z score in the standard normal tables (Table A.1 in the Appendix) to find the probability of an IQ score higher than Peter's. A z score of 1.33 gives a probability of 0.0918. Given that we are assuming the distributions are the same, this means that 9.18 per cent of the usual-IQ distribution, who have not been hothoused, score higher than Peter who had. Can we use this evidence to support the null hypothesis that the distributions are the same or does the evidence supoprt the view that the distributions are different and Peter is from a distribution higher than the usual-IQ distribution? The fact that over 9 per cent of the usual-IQ population have higher IQ scores than Peter's doesn't convince me of the effect of hothousing. I would expect geniuses to be rarer than 9.18 per cent which is equivalent to 1 person in every 11 from the usual-IQ distribution scoring higher than Peter. On this evidence I accept the null hypothesis and say that we have not found evidence to support Peter's view of hothousing.

Now imagine that Peter had scored 145 instead of 120. This gives a z score of 3 and a probability of 0.0013 of a score higher than Peter's. This means that only 0.13 per cent of the usual-IQ population score are better than Peter. This small percentage, 0.13 per cent, tells us that only 1 person in every 769 from the usual-IQ distribution scores higher than Peter. On this evidence, if the two distributions are the same Peter is very unusual indeed. A score as high as Peter's score is so rare in the usual-IQ distribution that it seems more likely that it belongs to a different, higher, distribution. Here, the chances are that the null hypothesis is false. So I reject the null hypothesis and accept the hypothesis that Peter's score comes from a hothouse-IQ distribution higher up the IQ scale than the usual-IQ distribution.

Thus, hypothesis testing is a gamble on the basis of probabilities. If the probability of Peter's score coming from a distribution the same as the usual-IQ distribution is very low I reject the null hypothesis, if the probability is not very low I accept it.

If I accept the null hypothesis when the probability is 0.0918 and reject it when the probability is 0.0013 then where is my dividing line, at which probability do I switch from acceptance to rejection? The answer is: where ever I choose! However, it has been agreed for reasons discussed in Chapter 9, to conventionally reject the null hypothesis when the probability is less than or equal to 0.05 (written as: '$p < 0.05$' or 'significant at $p = 0.05$'). This means that when a score from the unknown distribution could only arise from the known distribution (i.e. the distributions are the same) with a chance of less than 5 times in 100 then we reject the null hypothesis and say that the score really does come from a different distribution. Essentially we are gambling on the probability that a score (such as Peter's IQ) comes from a unknown distribution (hothouse-IQ) identical to the known distribution (usual-IQ). When the chances are 1 in 20 or less (that is, a probability of 0.05 or less, as 1 divided by $20 = 0.05$) we switch our gamble and bet that the distributions are different. Thus, the probability of 0.05 is called the significance level. If the probability of Peter's score is greater than or equal to the significance level we accept the null hypothesis and if it is lower than the significance level then we reject the null hypothesis.

The significance level of 0.05 means that we are more than 95 per cent certain that we are correct in accepting that the distributions are different. We are allowing ourselves to get it wrong, and claim there is a difference in the distributions when there is not, on 5 per cent or fewer occasions, as such an extreme score could only arise by chance (i.e. come from a distribution identical to the known distribution) 5 per cent or less of the time. Sometimes we want to be even more certain that we are correct in claiming a difference between the distributions. In these cases we take the significance level of $p = 0.01$, accepting only 1 chance in 100 or less that we have got it wrong. With this level of significance we can be 99 per cent or more certain that we have made the right choice in claiming a difference in the distributions.

A summary of the hypothesis testing

We tested the hypothesis that the hothousing Peter received produced his genius by the following steps:

1   We chose IQ as a measure of performance on which intelligence could be judged. This is our operational definition.

2   We set up a research hypothesis: hothousing of the form Peter experienced increases a person's IQ.

3   We set up the null hypothesis: hothousing of the form Peter experienced does not affect a person's IQ.

4   We cannot test the research hypothesis as we do not know both distributions. We can test the null hypothesis as we know the usual-IQ distribution and the null hypothesis assumes that the unknown hothouse-IQ distribution is the same.

5   We gave Peter the IQ test and obtained his score.

6   We worked out the probability of a score as high or higher than Peter's from the usual-IQ distribution by looking up the z score in the standard normal distribution table. We can only do this because we have assumed that the usual-IQ scores are normally distributed.

7   If the probability of a score as high or higher than Peter's is very small, smaller than the significance level, then we say that it is very rare for a score as high as Peter's score to come from a distribution the same as the known usual-IQ distribution and we reject the null hypothesis, concluding that the hothouse-IQ distribution is different, higher up the IQ scale. If the probability is not smaller than the significance level then we accept the null hypothesis and do not conclude that there is a difference in the distributions.

The logic of hypothesis testing

Despite the variety of statistical tests that we examine in this book they all follow the same basic logic. A research hypothesis predicts a difference in distributions whereas a null hypothesis predicts that they are the same. If we have the details of the two distributions we simply compare them. Usually we do not have these details. However, we can continue the analysis when one of the distributions is known and one unknown. One is known because we are able to make the assumption that it is normally distributed and we know about normal distributions. We select a significance level. This is our decision criterion for accepting or rejecting the null hypothesis. This is conventionally set at $p = 0.05$ or $p = 0.01$. We select the significance level before we collect the data. It is like betting on a horse race. We don't place a bet until we know the odds. We collect the data that provides a score from the unknown distribution. We look up the probability of a score such as this arising from the known distribution to decide whether to accept the null hypothesis and conclude that the distributions are the same. If the probability is lower than the significance level we reject the null hypothesis and say that the chances favour the score coming from a different distribution to the known distribution. If the probability is not lower than the significance level then we accept the null hypothesis.

One- and two-tailed predictions

Hypothesis testing is about deciding whether an unknown distribution is the same or different to a known distribution. There are three possible arrangements of the two distributions:

1   The unknown distribution is the same as the known distribution.
2   The unknown distribution is higher up the scale than the known distribution.
3   The unknown distribution is lower down the scale than the known distribution.

We always test the null hypothesis (1, above) that the distributions are the same but our research hypothesis can take a number of different forms. Our research hypothesis could predict 2 (above). In fact this was the prediction about the hothousing-IQ distribution, that it was higher up the scale than the usual-IQ distribution. Alternatively, we might predict 3, that the unknown distribution is lower than the known distribution. Imagine another friend David had a serious head injury through a car accident. In this case we might predict that this type of injury leads to a lower IQ than would have been achieved without it. Finally, there are occasions when we predict either 2 or 3. Here we are predicting that the unknown distribution will be different to the known distribution but leaving open the possibility that it will be higher or lower. A third friend Susan grew up eating her grandmother's special diet. We might predict that this diet affected her intellectual performance. However, we might not be sure whether to predict that the special diet improves IQ (maybe Susan was getting just the right mix of foods for intellectual growth) or reduces IQ (maybe Susan was missing out on important vitamins).

In the hothousing and brain injury examples we are predicting a direction to the difference in the distributions as the research hypothesis is stating in which direction along the scale the unknown distribution will be shifted in relation to the known distribution. These predictions are called one-tailed predictions. If you look back to Figure 4.1 you can see that the hothouse distribution is expected to overlap with only the higher end of the usual-IQ distribution, only one tail of the known distribution. If the hothouse-IQ distribution turned out to be the same as the usual-IQ distribution or even resulted in lower IQ scores then our hypothesis would not be supported. Only if the distribution is at the one-tail we are interested in, the upper end of the usual-IQ distribution, is our hypothesis supported (as in Figure 4.1). We infer this by observing whether Peter's IQ score occurs so far into the end of the upper tail (the top 5 per cent) of the usual-IQ distribution that we can claim that his score comes from a different distribution, higher up the scale.

The brain injury example is also a one-tailed prediction as it follows the same logic as the hothouse example, but here we are interested in the lower tail of the known distribution. Only if David's IQ falls into the bottom 5 per cent of the usual-IQ distribution would we accept the hypothesis that the brain-injury-IQ distribution is lower than the usual-IQ distribution.

The diet example is a two-tailed prediction as we are hedging our bets, we are saying that Susan's diet might have reduced her IQ or enhanced it. The diet-IQ distribution could overlap the lower tail of the usual-IQ distribution or the higher tail, either outcome supports our hypothesis of a difference in distributions. Only if the two distributions are the same do we accept the null hypothesis.

There are many instances where we are unable to make specific directional, one-tailed predictions. For example, in an experiment on stress and job satisfaction we might predict that a certain type of stress reduces job satisfaction as it produces anxiety. However, it could also increase job satisfaction if it results in interest and excitement. Where there is not enough evidence to decide which hypothesis to follow, the experimenter might decide to do a two-tailed test first of all, to see whether this type of stress has any effect at all, be it positive or negative. In this case any difference in the distributions would support the hypothesis.

Significance level and two-tailed predictions

When we undertake a one-tailed test we argue that if the test score has a probability lower than the significance level then it falls within the tail-end of the known distribution we are interested in. We interpret this as indicating that the score is unlikely to have come from a distribution the same as the

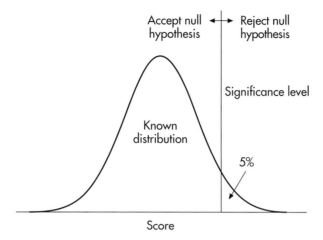

FIGURE 4.2 A one-tailed prediction and the significance level

known distribution but from a different distribution. If the score arises anywhere outside this part of the tail cut off by the significance level we reject the research hypothesis. This is shown in Figure 4.2. Notice that this shows a one-tailed prediction that the unknown distribution is higher than the known distribution. As an exercise try drawing this figure for a one-tailed prediction where the unknown distribution is predicted to be lower than the known distribution. (When you have tried this, look at Figure 6.1, which shows a prediction of this kind.)

With a two-tailed prediction, unlike the one-tailed, both tails of the known distribution are of interest, as the unknown distribution could be at either end. However, if we set our significance level so that we take the 5 per cent at the end of each tail we increase the risk of making an error. Recall that we are arguing that, when the probability is less than 0.05 that a score arises from the known distribution, then we conclude that the distributions are different. In this case the chance that we are wrong, and the distributions are the same, is less than 5 per cent. If we take 5 per cent at either end of the distribution, as we are tempted to do in a two-tailed test, we end up with a 10 per cent chance of an error, and we have increased the chance of making a mistake.

We want to keep the risk of making an error down to 5 per cent overall (our fixed amount of risk) as otherwise there will be an increase in our false claims of differences in distributions which can undermine our credibility with other researchers, who might stop taking our findings seriously (one mustn't cry wolf too often!). When we gamble on the unknown

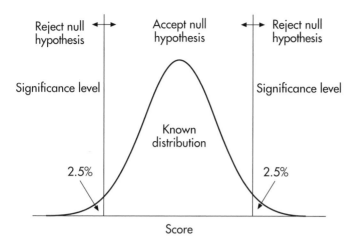

Score

FIGURE 4.3 A two-tailed prediction and the significance level

distribution being at either tail of the known distribution, to keep the overall error risk to 5 per cent, we must share out our 5 per cent between the two tails of the known distribution, so we set our significance level at 2.5 per cent at each end. If the score falls into one of the 2.5 per cent tails we then say it comes from a different distribution. Thus, when we undertake a two-tailed prediction the result has to fall within a smaller area of the tail compared to a one-tailed prediction, before we claim that the distributions are different, to compensate for hedging our bets in our prediction. This is shown in Figure 4.3.

Hypothesis testing, as described here, where we are using a chosen significance level to make our decision is often referred to as significance testing. Whether we perform a one-tailed or a two-tailed test, the decision to reject (or not to reject) the null hypothesis depends on which side of the significance level our score falls. Significance testing has been extremely useful in analysing research findings, as I hope you appreciate from the example of Peter's 'genius' above. However, we need to be aware of its advantages and limitations, and these issues will be examined on page 71 and in Chapter 9.

Chapter 5

Sampling

Populations and samples

In the book so far we have been looking at what we call populations, that is the complete set of the things we are interested in. The frequency distributions have included all the scores we are interested in, such as the scores of all one hundred students who took the examination this year, the example from Chapter 2. A population need not be a collection of people, even though we are used to hearing the term used in this way, such as the population of Britain. A population can be a complete set of anything. In statistics it refers to a complete set of scores, such as the number of pages of each book in a library, the IQ scores of fifteen year old girls living in London, the number of goals scored in each football league match on a particular Saturday, the times to complete a jigsaw by members of the Robinson family, the number of food pellets eaten by each rat in an animal learning experiment. The population is simply every member of the particular category we wish to study.

Often, through the sheer size of the population we cannot study it all. In this case we select a sample. A sample is a subset of a population. Usually, we want to know about populations rather than samples yet we are almost always only able to test samples. This is the fundamental problem of statistical analysis. When and how can information from a sample give us information about a population? The following sections will deal with this key question. But first an example to illustrate the difficulty.

A doctor wishes to know the incidence of respiratory problems in British men over the age of 50 years. This is a large population and extraordinarily difficult to test them all. A sample must be tested instead. But the doctor is not interested in the sample *per se* but what it tells him or her about the population. If it is not possible to estimate details of the population from the sample it is not worth studying it. What this doctor, and researchers in general need to find is sample information that is useful for estimating details of the population.

Selecting a sample

One of the difficulties of using samples to represent populations is the selection of sample members. In most cases we want our sample to truly represent the population so we can generalise our findings to the population and claim the population will perform like the sample. If we have a sample with the same characteristics as the population we will have a <u>representative sample</u>. If the characteristics of the sample are different to those of the population then any findings based on the sample could be biased and not be generalisable to the population. Opinion pollsters will sometimes try to get a representative sample of the voting population to question, making sure that they have, for example, the same proportion of men and women in the sample as there are in the population.

Consider the example of respiratory problems. Most people would agree that a sample of men under 50 or a sample of women over 50 is clearly not representative of the population we wish to generalise to. However, will any group of men over 50 be acceptable? If we took all our men from a hill top village where the air is clear, or from a coal mining town polluted with coal dust we are likely to have a biased sample, as not all members of the population live in a hill top village or a coal mining town. We would need to take the sample from a range of locations, or from a place where there is not a specific bias due to the location. We would need to consider age as well. If our sample contained only men between 50 and 60 years old could we generalise to a population where there are many men older than 60 in the population?

Any difference between the sample and the population could lead to a problem of generalisation: location, age, occupation, class, whether they smoke or not and so on. It is almost impossible to obtain a truly representative sample, where every characteristic of the sample matches the population characteristics. Rather than giving up, researchers do the best they can with the available resources and try to be aware of any differences between the sample and population. Here the judgement is not entirely statistical but also depends on the researcher's expertise in the subject. A medical practitioner will know that certain factors are important with respect to respiratory problems, so will try to select a sample representative of the population on these key factors, such as whether the person is a smoker or not, but not on factors unlikely to be relevant to the study, such as a person's hair colour. It requires the professional judgement of the researcher (rather than statistical knowledge) to make the decision on which characteristics the sample must match the population on and which factors can be ignored.

An alternative way of selecting a sample to represent a population is through random selection. With a <u>random sample</u> the sample members are selected at random from the entire population, with each member of the population having an equal chance of being selected. If I take 100 ping pong balls and write the numbers 1 to 100 on them, put them in a sack, shake them up, then take five out without looking, I have a random sample of five numbers from the population of numbers 1 to 100. Similarly, if I am doing a survey, I might select names at random from the telephone directory to select people to send the survey to. I have no idea who those people will be, I am leaving it up to chance. By random selection I am not deliberately biasing my sample, so any differences between the sample and the population should be random and, therefore, not systematically influencing my data in any way.

However, even so-called random sampling might not be quite so random after all. If I am randomly selecting passers by in the street for a survey, I am excluding all those people not passing by. If I perform my survey at 3 pm then I will not get anyone whose occupation keeps them at work at this time. I may not have a random selection of the population I am interested in. Selecting numbers at random from a telephone book excludes all those people not listed in the directory. If my population is 'people listed in the telephone book' then it is fine, otherwise I need to be careful. Often it is hard to collect a truly random sample of the population we are interested in but, once again, we must do the best we can by deciding on the key factors and selecting randomly within these factors.

In many cases it is not possible to be truly representative or random but a good researcher will make it clear how the sample was selected so that other researchers can decide if there was a systematic bias on an important factor. Finally, there are a couple of useful points concerning a pragmatic approach to sampling that many researchers adopt.

1   This is the only sample I have, or am able to test, so even though there may be sampling problems I'll test the sample anyway. If the results are interesting I can investigate further, aware of the potential difficulties in sampling.

It is called an <u>opportunity sample</u> when we simply select an available sample. There are many experiments in psychology that use samples of psychology students, who may not be representative of people in general. However, often they are available for testing and if it turns out that something intriguing comes up then other non-student samples can be tested as well. Furthermore we might decide that there is no serious reason to assume that the students will perform differently to the general population on this experiment.

2   If I don't find what I am interested in with a sample biased in my favour then it is not worth spending more resources finding a more representative sample.

If I am testing the hypothesis that people in Britain prefer the television to radio I might deliberately be perverse and select a group of people who have just bought a new radio. One might expect these people to be more favourable to radio than the general population and if I found that they preferred radio it would not be surprising. However, if I found that even these people preferred the television despite my bias in favour of radio in the sample selection then it is not unreasonable to infer that the general population would also prefer the television.

Sample statistics and population parameters

Statistics and parameters

At this point is worth explaining some terminology. To make the distinction between sample details and population details, the word statistic is used to refer to a sample figure and parameter for the population figure, so the sample mean is a statistic but the population mean is a parameter. (In the earlier chapters I have referred to a 'statistic' when I really should have been using the term 'parameter'. I did this because we are all familiar with the term statistic but not parameter. It is only at this point in the book that I believe the distinction should be made.) The term parameter for population characteristics explains why the tests we shall be looking at until Chapter 16 are referred to as parametric tests. In these tests we use sample statistics as estimators of population parameters. The two most important of these sample statistics are the sample standard deviation and the sample mean.

Sample standard deviation

Of the various measures of spread the mean absolute deviation and the standard deviation both use information from all the scores. However, it has been found that the sample mean absolute deviation is an <u>unstable</u> estimator of the population figure, that is, there is no consistent relationship between the sample statistic and the population parameter. On the other hand the standard deviation of a sample is a much more reliable estimator of the population value. Because of this, when we do not know the population standard deviation, we can use the sample standard deviation to estimate it. This is a key reason for the preference for the standard deviation in statistical analysis.

The formula for a standard deviation of a population was given in Chapter 1 and was designated by the symbol σ. However, if we apply that formula to the sample scores we end up with a sample standard deviation that <u>underestimates</u> the population value. To improve the estimate we change the formula and always calculate a sample standard deviation by the formula:

$$\text{Sample standard deviation } (s) = \sqrt{\frac{\sum (X - \bar{X})^2}{n - 1}}$$

Notice we use 's' rather than σ to indicate it is a sample standard deviation rather than a population standard deviation. We also use the lower case 'n' for the sample size (the number of scores in the sample) and $\bar{X}$ for the mean of the sample (to distinguish it from the population parameter μ).

The reason why we use $n - 1$ instead of n in the formula is a little complicated but it helps when we consider the different purpose of the sample and population standard deviations. In the latter case we are simply seeking an average deviation and divide by the number of scores N. In the former case we are seeking a good estimate rather than an average. This estimate is more accurate when it is based not on the number of scores but on the <u>degrees of freedom</u>, $n - 1$. Degrees of freedom concern the scores that contain new information. As we have calculated the sample mean from the sample scores we have used up some of the information in the scores. The number of scores with new information, the degrees of freedom, is $n - 1$.

A simple example illustrates this fact. If I have a sample of four scores ($n = 4$) with a sample mean of 5, how many scores must I tell you before you can work out the rest? With 4 scores and a mean of 5 the total of the scores is 20. If we label the four scores as X_1, X_2, X_3, and X_4 then:

$$X_1 + X_2 + X_3 + X_4 = 20$$

I tell you that one score is 6, $X_1 = 6$, this gives us:

$$6 + X_2 + X_3 + X_4 = 20$$

$$X_2 + X_3 + X_4 = 14$$

The other three scores could be any three numbers that add up to 14, there is some freedom in what they could be. I now tell you that another score is 4, $X_2 = 4$:

$$4 + X_3 + X_4 = 14$$

$$X_3 + X_4 = 10$$

It is still not certain what the other two scores are, they still have some freedom, although now you know they add up to 10. The third score is 2, $X_3 = 2$. Given this information you can work out that the fourth score must be 8:

$$2 + X_4 = 10$$

$$X_4 = 8$$

There is no freedom for this last score to vary. The final score can only be 8 because we know that the mean is 5. As we started with the knowledge of the sample mean then only three $(n - 1)$ of the scores give us any new information, so there are only three $(n - 1)$ degrees of freedom in this sample.

In words, the sample standard deviation is the square root of the <u>sums of squares</u> divided by the <u>degrees of freedom</u>. We shall meet these terms often in our statistical analyses. The sums of squares, $\sum(X - \bar{X})^2$, requires us to calculate the sample mean first. However, we know that $\bar{X} = \dfrac{\sum X}{n}$ (which is the formula for the sample mean – add up all the scores in the sample and divide by the sample size). If we replace $\bar{X}$ by $\dfrac{\sum X}{n}$ in the sums of squares formula we end up with an equivalent formula for the sample standard deviation that does not require us to calculate the mean first:

$$\text{Sample standard deviation } (s) = \sqrt{\dfrac{\sum X^2 - \dfrac{(\sum X)^2}{n}}{n - 1}}$$

In the formula $\sum X^2$ refers to the sum of the squared scores (we square each of the scores first then add them up), whereas $(\sum X)^2$ refers to the square of the sum of the scores (we add up the scores before we square the total).

Notice that dividing by the degrees of freedom, $n - 1$, rather than the sample size, n, makes less difference when the sample size is large but has a much larger effect when the sample size is small. Dividing by 99 rather than 100 will not change the calculation very much compared to dividing by 9 rather than 10. As we see below, small samples are not as good for estimating population values as large samples.

Sample mean

We also want to know what a central figure is in the population but when we only have a sample, rather than details of the population, we have to estimate it with a statistic from the sample. Of the various measures of central tendency (mode, median, mean), the sample mean is the best estimate of the population value, again for reasons of stability. But how good an estimate of μ is the sample mean $\overline{X}$? It depends a lot on the size of the sample, the larger the sample the better the sample mean is as an estimate of the population mean. It also depends on the specific sample that we pick. We can see this in the following example.

The population of IQ scores is normally distributed with a mean of 100 and a standard deviation of 15. If we took a sample of 20 people's IQ scores would our sample mean be 100? The answer is probably not. The reason is that we might have a sample with a number of clever people in it and so the sample mean would be higher than 100. Alternatively if we had some less able people in the sample the mean would be lower. So sample means will have a range of different values dependent on the scores we select for our sample.

Imagine for a moment that we were able to select every possible sample of 20 IQ scores and work out their sample means: what range of values would we get and with what frequency? What would be the mean of all these sample means?

So far we have only looked at the frequency distributions of scores, but now we are interested not in the individual scores but in the mean of every sample of size 20. If we plot this information as a frequency distribution, the curve determined by the number of sample means at each value, we get the distribution of sample means. It turns out that the distribution of sample means has some very interesting and useful characteristics.

First, we find that, as we obtain more samples, the mean of the sample means gets closer to the population mean. When we have selected all possible samples we find that the mean of sample means is the same as the population mean. Thus, if we collect the means of samples of 20 IQ scores, then the mean of all the sample means will be 100. We refer to the mean of sample means by the symbol $\mu_{\bar{X}}$. We use the Greek letter μ to show that it is still a population mean and the subscript $\bar{X}$ to show that it is the mean of a population of sample means.

Second, the distribution of sample means will tend to be a normal distribution. If the population of scores is normally distributed then the distribution of sample means will definitely be normally distributed. Even if the population of scores is not normally distributed the distribution of sample means will still look rather like a normal distribution with a hump in the middle and tails off to either side. The larger the samples we select the closer the distribution approaches the normal distribution. This can be shown by a mathematical proof, called the central limit theorem. Even though the distribution of scores is not normally distributed, the distribution of sample means will end up as a normal distribution as long as the samples are large enough. When the sample size is 30 or more the sampling distribution is almost exactly a normal distribution, regardless of whether the original distribution was normally distributed or not. This is an extremely useful piece of information for our statistical analysis as we now see.

Third, as the distribution of sample means is either normally distributed or approximately normally distributed, we can work out the probability of finding a sample with a particular mean value by calculating a z score for our sample mean and looking up the probability in the standard normal distribution tables.

Finally, we can easily work out the standard deviation of the distribution of sample means by a simple formula using the standard deviation of the individual scores. We call this new standard deviation the standard error of the mean and refer to it by the symbol $\sigma_{\bar{X}}$. The standard error provides us with the standard deviation of a sample mean from the population mean.

$$\text{Standard error, } \sigma_{\bar{X}} = \frac{\sigma}{\sqrt{n}}$$

where σ is the standard deviation of the population and n is the sample size.

The standard error of the mean is precisely that, the standard distance, or error, that a sample mean is from the population mean. In our statistical tests we want to know how good an estimate the sample mean is of the population mean. The standard error tells us just that. Notice, as the sample size (n) gets larger so the standard error gets smaller. Again this illustrates that larger samples give better estimates of the population mean than smaller samples.

The distribution of sample means turns out to be something we now know a lot about without having to laboriously calculate means for all the samples. The distribution of the sample means will be a normal distribution (or similar to it) with a mean, $\mu_{\bar{X}}$, the same as the population mean, μ, and a standard deviation, $\sigma_{\bar{X}}$, the standard error of the mean, equal to the population standard deviation divided by the square root of the sample size.

In the IQ example the distribution of sample means for samples of 20 scores will be a normal distribution with a mean of 100 and a standard error of $\dfrac{15}{\sqrt{20}}$, which is 3.35. As we have a normal distribution and we know its mean and standard deviation we can calculate z scores and work out probability values, just as we did for a score and a population in previous chapters, but now we can do it with a sample mean and a population of sample means (the sampling distribution of the mean).

Summary

To recap, we want to know about populations rather than samples but usually we can only test samples. We want our sample to tell us about the population. We therefore have to be careful in selecting our sample because we would like to generalise from the sample to the population.

The sample mean and the sample standard deviation are the best estimates of the population parameters but we use degrees of freedom rather than sample size in calculating them as that improves their estimation. Larger samples provide better estimations of population figures than smaller samples. Degrees of freedom make more of a difference to the estimation when the sample size is small than when it is large.

We can compare our sample to the population by calculating the sampling distribution of the mean. This tells us what the distribution of sample means would look like if we took every sample the same size as our own (n) from the population and worked out their means. The sampling distribution of the mean turns out to be a distribution we know about because it is almost certainly normally distributed and has a mean the same as the population mean and a standard deviation, the standard error of the mean, equal to the population mean divided by the square root of the sample size.

As the distribution is normal and we know its mean and standard deviation we can calculate z scores and work out probability values. This is exactly what we need for hypothesis testing.

We shall see in the following chapters how the distribution of sample means is extremely useful to hypothesis testing when we consider a sample rather than a single score.

Chapter 6

Hypothesis testing with one sample

An example

There was a leak of the gas Cyadmine[4] at a chemical works and the gas cloud hung over the town of Newtoncastle for a number of days before dispersing into the atmosphere. There were some complaints of sore throats amongst the townspeople but the chemical company assured the public that there are no adverse effects of Cyadmine on the human body. However, a scientist who worked on the Cyadmine project has gone on record as saying that Cyadmine could have an effect on pregnant women and their unborn children. The company has dismissed the scientist's claim as nonsense, noting that the scientist was unable to specify what problems could arise. There is not a universal confidence in the chemical company and there is some concern in the affected areas especially from parents of young children. A doctor in the large maternity hospital has been keeping an eye on babies born in the nine months after the cloud passed over the town. She has noted that the babies appear healthy on all the usual checks but is suspicious that the Cyadmine could have affected their birth-weights as many of the babies appear rather small at birth. The doctor is worried about any long-term effects and wants to test whether the 'Cyadmine babies' are smaller at birth than usual. Essentially, the doctor is making a one-tailed prediction: the distribution of the birth-weights of the Cyadmine affected population will be different to the distribution of the birth-weights of the unaffected population with the overlap of the distributions occurring at the lower end of the unaffected distribution.

To test this hypothesis we need details of the two birth-weight populations. Comparing the two distributions will tell us whether there is a difference between the two, specifically whether the mean of the Cyadmine-affected population is lower on the birth-weight scale than the unaffected population. The problem is collecting the details of the two populations.

We may be lucky here, in that medical records are very detailed and let us assume in this case that there are detailed records of birth-weights. We find from the records that, for babies born in this country, the mean birth-weight is 3.2 kg and the standard deviation is 0.9 kg. These are the details we take for the population unaffected by Cyadmine.

The problem now is to collect details of the Cyadmine-affected population. Essentially what we want to know is how the unaffected population would be affected by Cyadmine were they to be affected by it, as the doctor's prediction is that the effect of Cyadmine is to shift everyone's birth-weight down the scale by a fixed amount. We can never get details of this population, all we have are the babies of Newtowncastle who were in the womb at the time of the leak. This is only a sample of the second population. Not only that, but our sample is not necessarily representative or random. We are unable to select freely from the Cyadmine-affected population. Our sample could be influenced by other factors as well as, or instead of, Cyadmine, such as a hospital inducing babies early, which might also lead to lower birth-weights.

We decide to select one hundred of these babies, balancing home births and hospital births, selecting a range of foetal ages when the cloud appeared, and so forth, to try to select a sample that will not be systematically influenced by factors such as hospital practice, foetal age, etc. We may not be able to account for all systematic differences, bar the Cyadmine effects, between the sample and the unaffected population but we can do our best to control for key confounding variables (see Chapter 7 for further explanation of 'confounding'). If we do find differences between Cyadmine babies and unaffected babies it will be worth investigating further to ascertain whether it is really due to Cyadmine or some other reason. If we find no difference we might decide we need investigate no further.

We obtain the birth-weights for the sample of Cyadmine babies and calculate the <u>sample mean</u>. This turns out to be 3.0 kg. Can we compare this mean with the population mean for the unaffected babies? The answer is no, because we are not comparing like with like and this allows for the possibility of bias. To explain this, let us consider the unaffected population for a moment. Not all babies have the same birth-weight, some will be lighter than others due to the normal spread of birth-weights. It is quite possible that if you selected a sample of unaffected babies you might find their sample mean lower than the population mean. By chance we might have selected a group of babies with relatively low birth-weights despite the fact that they come from a population with a higher mean birth-weight – we could have just selected small babies. (I'm sure that you can see that, equally, by chance, we might select a sample with a mean birth-weight higher than the population mean.) Even though our sample of Cyadmine-affected babies gave a sample mean lower than the unaffected population mean, we cannot take this as evidence for the effect of Cyadmine on birth-weight. It might not be due to a difference in populations but simply due to the nature of sampling.

If we cannot compare our sample mean with a population mean what can we do? Recall that we can compare a score with a population of scores, so we need to compare a sample mean with a population of sample means. If we select all possible samples of size 100 from the unaffected population and work out their sample means we can create a distribution of sample means. In this way we are creating a 'known distribution', the distribution of the mean for samples of size 100 from the unaffected population and an 'unknown distribution', the distribution of the mean for samples of size 100 from the affected population. Now we can compare these two populations of sample means. If they are different, with the affected distribution having a smaller mean, this will support the doctor's hypothesis. Unfortunately, we don't have the details of these populations yet, in fact we only have one value from the unknown population: the mean of our sample of 100 affected babies.

Do we have details of the distribution of sample means for samples of size 100 from the unaffected population? Here the answer is yes. Fortunately, as we saw in the previous chapter, we don't need to go out and select every possible sample of size 100 from the unaffected population as we know about sampling distributions – with a sample size greater than 30 the distribution of sample means will almost certainly be a normal distribution. Also, the mean of a sampling distribution, $\mu_{\bar{x}}$, is the same as the population mean, μ, so it will be 3.2. And the standard deviation of the sampling distribution, $\sigma_{\bar{x}}$, the standard error, will be the population standard deviation ($\sigma = 0.9$) divided by the square root of the sample size ($n = 100$), so will be $\dfrac{0.9}{\sqrt{100}} = 0.09$.

We have now created a logically identical framework for hypothesis testing to the one we had in Chapter 4. We have a 'score' from an unknown distribution, in this case our affected sample mean of 3.0, and we have a known distribution, the sampling distribution of unaffected samples of the same size. The distribution is known to be normally distributed with a mean of 3.2 and a standard deviation of 0.09. All we need to do is choose a significance level for the doctor's hypothesis, find the z score, look up the probability and make our decision as to whether the affected sample comes from the same distribution as the unaffected samples or a lower one.

We find out how likely it is to get a sample of 100 unaffected babies with a sample mean of 3.0 by working out the z score. Recall that a z score is a score minus a population mean divided by the population standard deviation. Here the sample mean $\overline{X}$ is our 'score', the mean of the sampling distribution, $\mu_{\overline{x}}$, and standard error, $\sigma_{\overline{x}}$, are the mean and standard deviation of the distribution we are interested in, so

$$z = \frac{\overline{X} - \mu_{\overline{x}}}{\sigma_{\overline{x}}} = \frac{\overline{X} - \mu}{\dfrac{\sigma}{\sqrt{n}}} = \frac{3.0 - 3.2}{\dfrac{0.9}{\sqrt{100}}} = \frac{-0.2}{0.09} = -2.22$$

We can look up the probability of the z score in the standard normal distribution tables as our sampling distribution is normally distributed. Remember the minus sign simply tells us that the score is lower than the mean of the distribution. From the Table A.1 in the Appendix a z score of 2.22 gives a probability of 0.0132. Thus, the probability of obtaining a sample mean as low or lower than 3.0 kg from a sample of 100 unaffected babies is only 0.0132. This is well within the bottom 5 per cent of the unaffected sampling distribution, well below the significance level of $p = 0.05$. We can conclude that a sample mean of 3.0 kg is so rare in the unaffected population that our affected sample mean of 3.0 kg indicates that the affected distribution is <u>not the same</u> as the unaffected distribution, and we reject the null hypothesis, concluding that Cyadmine-affected babies do have a lower birth-weight than unaffected babies. This is shown graphically in Figure 6.1.

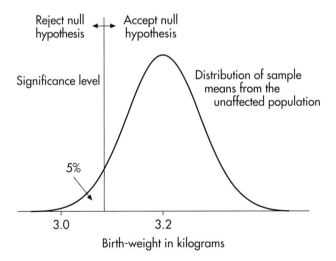

FIGURE 6.1 Hypothesis testing with a sample of Cyadmine-affected babies

In summary

When we have a sample from an unknown population we cannot compare it to a known population. We must find the sample mean, $\overline{X}$. Then we find the sampling distribution of the mean for all samples of the same size from the known population. This distribution is usually a normal distribution with a mean, $\mu_{\overline{X}}$, equal to the population mean μ, and a standard deviation (or standard error), $\sigma_{\overline{X}}$, equal to the population standard deviation, μ, divided by the square root of the sample size, $\sqrt{n}$.

Using this information in our example we tested the hypothesis that the unknown distribution is lower on the scale than the known distribution. As the known distribution is a normal distribution we worked out a z score to find the probability of finding a sample mean from the known distribution as small or smaller than the sample mean from the unknown distribution. As the probability was smaller than the significance level we rejected the null hypothesis and concluded that the unknown distribution is lower on the scale than the known distribution: Cyadmine-affected babies do have a lower birth-weight than unaffected babies.

When we do not have the known population standard deviation

The average number of purchases in a supermarket is 25 items. The company would like to increase this figure and introduces an advertising campaign to encourage shoppers to buy more products in the store. In the week after the campaign a sample of 50 shoppers are tested to see if the number of purchases has increased.

The following number of purchases were recorded:

```
30  44  19  32  25  30  16  41  28  45
28  20  18  31  15  32  40  42  29  35
34  22  30  27  36  26  38  30  33  24
15  48  31  27  37  45  12  29  33  23
20  32  28  26  38  40  28  32  34  22
```

The mean number of purchases for this sample is 30 items and the sample standard deviation is 8.43.

Has the advertising campaign had an effect? As we saw above we cannot compare the sample mean of the post-advertisement shoppers

(30 items) with the population mean of the pre-advertisement shoppers (25 items) as one is a sample and the other a population. To compare a sample mean with a distribution of sample means we must calculate the sampling distribution of samples of size 50 from the pre-advertisement shoppers. This distribution has a mean of $\mu_{\bar{X}} = 25$ ($\mu_{\bar{X}} = \mu$, the same as the population mean) and a standard error of $\sigma_{\bar{X}} = \dfrac{\sigma}{\sqrt{50}}$, where σ is the standard deviation of the pre-advertisement population.

Our sampling distribution is almost certainly normally distributed so we can look up a z score in the standard normal distribution table to find the probability of finding a sample mean as large as 30 from the pre-advertisement shoppers.

$$z = \frac{\overline{X} - \mu_{\bar{X}}}{\sigma_{\bar{X}}} = \frac{\overline{X} - \mu}{\dfrac{\sigma}{\sqrt{n}}} = \frac{30 - 25}{\dfrac{\sigma}{\sqrt{50}}}$$

Unfortunately, we are stuck, as in this case we do not know σ, the standard deviation of the pre-advertisement shopper population. In order to continue we have to make an estimate of σ. We assume that the effect of the advertising campaign is to shift the whole distribution of purchases up the scale: that is, after the campaign the population mean is higher (people buy more items) but that the standard deviation stays the same (the spread in the number of purchases stays the same). The only standard deviation we have is the post-advertisement sample standard deviation, s. Sample standard deviations are quite stable estimates of the population figure so we could use this to estimate the post-advertisement population standard deviation. As we are assuming that the post-advertisement population has the same standard deviation as pre-advertisement we can use our sample standard deviation, s, as an estimate of the pre-advertisement population standard deviation. (We are predicting that the effect of the advertisement will be to shift the distribution up the scale but not change the shape of the distribution in any way, so the standard deviation will remain the same.) In order to use our sample standard deviation as an estimate of the population parameter we must assume that our sample is not biased in any way, such as made up only of wealthy shoppers, or it will not be a good estimate. So we assume that our sample is randomly chosen from the post-advertisement population. If this assumption is met then our sample standard deviation should be a reasonable estimate of the pre-advertisement population figure.

To distinguish the fact that we do not have the population standard deviation σ but are using s as an estimate, instead of calling the statistic z, we call the new statistic t:

$$t = \frac{\overline{X} - \mu}{\dfrac{s}{\sqrt{n}}}$$

As we saw in the previous chapter a sample standard deviation has the following formula:

$$s = \sqrt{\frac{\sum X^2 - \dfrac{(\sum X)^2}{n}}{n - 1}}$$

replacing s by its formula in the formula for t we get a new formula for t:

$$t = \frac{\overline{X} - \mu}{\sqrt{\dfrac{\sum X^2 - \dfrac{(\sum X)^2}{n}}{n(n - 1)}}}$$

Notice that t is influenced by the degrees of freedom of the sample $(n - 1)$. This is because t is not the same as z but an estimate of it. When the degrees of freedom are small the t distribution is similar to a normal distribution but flatter and more spread out. As the degrees of freedom get larger the t distribution gets rapidly closer to a normal distribution and when the degrees of freedom are infinite it is identical to the normal distribution. Figure 6.2 shows three t distributions for 1, 10 and infinity degrees of freedom. Even at 10 degrees of freedom the t distribution is very similar to a normal distribution and at 30 degrees of freedom and above the differences are so small as to be irrelevant.

We always look up a z score in the standard normal distribution tables. We cannot do this with t as it is not a normal distribution. However, like the standard normal distribution tables, the values of the t distribution have been worked out. Indeed these have been worked out for the different t distributions corresponding to the different degrees of freedom. We can look up our calculated value of t in the table for the appropriate distribution and find the probability of this value arising from the known distribution.

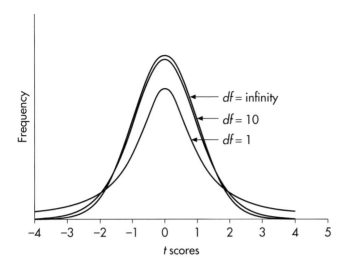

FIGURE 6.2 Examples of the *t* distribution

We can compare this value with our significance level and make a decision whether to accept or reject the null hypothesis. Thus we are able engage in hypothesis testing with a sample even when we do not know the standard deviation of the known population.

In order to perform a *t* test we have to make three assumptions:

1   The known population is normally distributed. This is important as (like a *z* score) we need our sampling distribution to be normally distributed. If it is not then the *t* distribution in the table might not provide us with the appropriate figures for our decision on the significance of the *t* value we calculate. However, it is often stated that the *t* test is 'robust': this is statistical jargon for saying that even if the underlying sampling distribution is not normal the *t* test might still provide a reasonably good figure for comparison. Certainly when the sample size is 30 or more the sampling distribution will be very close to normal, whatever the underlying population distribution.

2   The sample is randomly selected from the (unknown) population. We want our sample standard deviation to be an unbiased estimate of the population standard deviation, and hence a suitable estimate to use. Otherwise it will affect our calculation of *t*.

3   The standard deviation of the unknown population is the same as the known population. Only if we make this assumption can we take

the sample standard deviation as an estimate of the standard deviation of the known population.

Returning now to our example, the above assumptions are reasonable to make here, as long as we have no reason to believe our sample 50 shoppers was selected in a biased manner. We can now calculate t to find the probability of finding a pre-advertisement sample with a mean as large as 30 items:

$$t = \frac{\bar{X} - \mu}{\sqrt{\dfrac{\sum X^2 - \dfrac{(\sum X)^2}{n}}{n(n-1)}}} = \frac{30 - 25}{\sqrt{\dfrac{48482 - 45000}{2450}}} = \frac{5}{1.1922} = 4.19$$

We must also work out the degrees of freedom: $n - 1 = 50 - 1 = 49$.

If we look at the table of t values given in Table A.2 of the Appendix we note that, unlike the standard normal table, it does not have the figures for the whole distribution. Otherwise we would have table after table, giving all the values for each different t distribution. What the table shows is the key values for each distribution, where the key values are the values of t at the significance levels we commonly choose, i.e. which t value cuts off exactly 5 per cent and which value cuts off 1 per cent of the tail of the t distribution.

We have a one-tailed test (we are predicting the advertising campaign will result in more purchases). Using a significance level of $p = 0.05$, we look down the $p = 0.05$ column and along the row for 49 degrees of freedom and we find the t value is not there! There is a figure of 1.684 for 40 degrees of freedom and 1.671 for 60 degrees of freedom. The reason for this is that, again, if every figure was listed the column would go on for ever. We can see that there is there not much difference in these values (0.013) so we know roughly what our value for 49 degrees of freedom will be: somewhere between the two (1.671 and 1.684). We can find it out by a process called linear interpolation, which is easier than it sounds! Between 40 and 60 is a gap of 20 and between 1.684 and 1.671 there is a gap of 0.013. So for every degree of freedom between 40 and 60 the difference in the table is 0.013/20, which is 0.00065. For 9 degrees of freedom the gap is 9×0.00065, which is 0.00585. Therefore 49 degrees of freedom has a table t value of $1.684 - 0.00585$, which is 1.67815. (If you don't want to do a linear interpolation just take the larger of the two values in the table: 1.684.)

As a *t* value of 1.67815 cuts off exactly 5 per cent of the tail of the *t* distribution with 49 degrees of freedom, our value of *t* being larger will cut off less of the tail and the probability of getting a *t* value of 4.19 from the known distribution is less than 5 per cent, so we can reject the null hypothesis and argue for a difference in the two distributions.

More simply we can conclude that, as our calculated value of *t* of 4.19, with 49 degrees of freedom, is larger than the table value of 1.67815 for a one-tailed test, at the $p = 0.05$ level of significance there is a significant increase in the number of items purchased after the advertising campaign. Notice that it is also significant at the more conservative $p = 0.01$ level of significance and we would usually report the finding at the smaller significance level to indicate how unlikely it is that the effect could have occurred by chance. (See if you can work out by linear interpolation the table value of *t* for 49 degrees of freedom for the $p = 0.01$ level of significance. You should get a value of *t* of 2.40815.)

Confidence intervals

The *t* test is a test of significance and we seek evidence for a statistically significant difference between populations based on the sample information we have. An alternative approach is to use the sample information to estimate the population parameters. Now you may say that we have already done that by using our sample mean value as an estimate of the population value. That is true but we can be a little more sophisticated by working out a confidence interval for the mean. Rather than choosing a single value for the population mean we can specify a range of values within which we are confident that the value lies. We choose a level of confidence, usually either 95 per cent or 99 per cent confident, and then work out the range of values. With a 95 per cent confidence interval we are saying that if we worked out the confidence interval for 100 different samples from a population then 95 per cent of those confidence intervals would contain the population mean value. So our confidence interval is a good estimate of where the true mean lies.

In the above example we can work out the 95 per cent confidence interval quite easily as we use the information we produced for the *t* calculation to work it out. This is because for the *t* test the confidence interval (CI) is specified as follows:

CI = Sample mean ± (critical *t* value × standard error of the mean)

In this case the critical t value is the one that 'captures' the central 95 per cent of the distribution, leaving only 5 per cent outside the range, so is the two-tailed t value from the tables at $p = 0.05$, as this cuts off 0.025 from each end of the distribution.[5] We have 49 degrees of freedom so we can now find the critical t value from the tables, which is 2.0116 (by linear interpolation between the values for $df = 40$ and $df = 60$). We know the sample mean is 30 and we know that the (estimated) standard error of the mean is 1.1922 (as it is the bottom part of the t test formula).

So we have:

$$95\%CI = 30 \pm 2.0116 \times 1.1922 = 30 \pm 2.3982$$

which gives

$$95\%CI = (27.6018, 32.3982)$$

This gives us a helpful indication of the position of the true population mean. The narrower the confidence interval the more specific our estimate of the population mean. Here we are confident that the population mean lies between 27.6018 and 32.3982. Even the lowest of the two limits, 27.6018, is still well above the 25 value for the pre-advertising purchases.

We can extend our confidence interval analysis to give the confidence interval of the <u>difference</u> between our post- and pre-advertisement mean values $(\overline{X} - \mu)$. We use the same formula but replace the sample mean with the difference in means:

$$CI = \text{Difference in means} \pm (\text{critical } t \text{ value} \times \text{standard error of the difference in means})$$

The critical t value and the standard error are the same as in the previous calculation and we know the value of μ so:

$$95\%CI = (30 - 25) \pm (2.0116 \times 1.1922)$$

$$95\%CI = (2.6018, 7.3982)$$

This provides us with a range of values that we are confident (95 per cent of the time) contains the real difference in the populations. Notice that in the 'worst case' (the lower limit) we still predict 2.60 more purchases after the advertisement so we can be confident that it has had an effect. Had the lower limit been zero or even negative we would not be able to assume a definite effect of the advertisement as the true difference could have been zero.

The general structure of a confidence interval

The above confidence intervals have been worked out using the sample statistic (the mean, or the difference in means), sample information (the standard error) and the appropriate statistical distribution for the data (the *t* distribution). We can calculate confidence intervals for many statistical analyses using the same structure as above, but we write the general statement as follows:

CI = Value of statistic ± critical value of appropriate distribution × standard error of the statistic

We then need to select the appropriate statistic, critical value and standard error to calculate the confidence interval. As we saw above, we work out the statistic and the estimate of the standard error from our data, choose the level of confidence we want (e.g. 90 per cent or 95 per cent) and then select the correct critical value for that confidence level.

Significance and confidence intervals

Significance tests and confidence intervals are both attempting to answer the same question: what does our sample information tell us about the population values and what can we conclude from it? In the first case, a significance test, we are seeking whether the sample statistic exceeds a particular criterion (the $p = 0.05$ significance level) to claim statistical significance (and reject the null hypothesis). In the second case, confidence intervals, we are seeking to find the range within which we can be confident that the population value lies. If we look at confidence intervals of a difference we can examine this range in relation to zero to give us an indication of whether we think the difference is important or not. If the confidence interval contains zero then the difference for the population values could well be zero and hence any difference we found in the sample means is not important.

Significance tests have been traditionally used in data analysis in a number of fields of study. However, confidence intervals are increasingly used.

This is because significance tests provide an 'either–or' outcome – either the null hypothesis is rejected or it is not at a particular significance level – whereas the confidence interval provides a range of values that provide a useful estimate of the size of the difference.

In a real sense significance tests and confidence intervals are complementary in that together they reveal a clearer picture of the data than they might on their own. In many cases (with a highly significant finding, for example) the conclusion is clear but where the finding is 'close' to significance (with a probability of 0.06, for example, which we would say is not significant) confidence intervals can help us evaluate the worth of further investigation, particularly if, as we shall see in Chapter 9, there are a number of factors that influence our statistical outcome.

Hypothesis testing with one sample: in conclusion

The same logic applies whether we are testing a sample or we are testing an individual score. However, with a sample the 'score from the unknown distribution' becomes the sample mean from the unknown sampling distribution and the 'known distribution' we compare it to is the distribution of sample means from the known population for samples of the same size. Once we have the details of the 'score' and the 'known distribution', then the procedures are identical: we work out the z score and find the probability in order to decide whether to accept or reject the null hypothesis. It is a little more complicated if we do not have the standard deviation of the known population but as long as we make the appropriate assumptions we can use the sample standard deviation to estimate it. We then calculate t instead of z. As the t distributions have all been worked out we can look up the critical value of t, with the appropriate degrees of freedom, for our chosen level of significance. If our calculated value is larger than the table value we can reject the null hypothesis.

Confidence intervals provide an alternative way of representing our findings as they provide a range of values within which we are confident that the population value lies. We may choose this as an alternative to our significance test or as supplementary information to it.

Chapter 7

Selecting samples for comparison

HYPOTHESIS TESTING with a single sample is used when we know about a particular population and wish to decide whether the sample comes from a different population or not. In most research we do not have details of any populations at all. All we know about are the samples we can obtain. In the majority of cases hypothesis testing is about comparing samples rather than comparing a sample mean with a sampling distribution. In the Cyadmine example considered in the previous chapter we had the details of a birth-weight population unaffected by the gas. More usually we will not have this information and can only collect a sample of babies affected by the gas and a sample of babies unaffected by it for comparison. We, of course, increase the problems of sample selection when we have two samples rather than one, as each is required to represent a population. Indeed, it is the fact that we want to use our samples to estimate populations that causes problems in sample selection, for we do not want to introduce biases that make our samples untypical of their population.

When we have two samples, not only do we wish them to represent their respective populations but we also want them to be comparable. For example, if we are comparing forty year old men and women on their degree of fitness we would not select women who were athletes and men who were taxi drivers as the samples are not comparable. Any difference in fitness could be due simply to occupation rather than gender. It is this problem of comparability we consider now.

Designing experiments to compare samples

The reason we undertake experiments is to test hypotheses. A major cause for concern is whether the experiment is really examining the hypothesis we wish it to test, to the exclusion of all others, or whether we have introduced a bias in some way. Poor sample selection can lead to an ambiguous experiment if we are unable to decide whether, say, a difference in fitness is due to occupation or gender.

Experimental variables

All experiments look at the effects of <u>variables</u> or <u>factors</u>, the terms are used synonymously. Variables are, not surprisingly, things that vary! Temperature, reaction time, teaching methods, gender, class, drinking habits, accuracy of performance are just a few examples.

In the simplest case of hypothesis testing we want to know whether a single score comes from a known population distribution or from a different population distribution. An example is comparing the reaction time of someone after a head injury with the population of reaction times from the uninjured population. We can also compare a sample mean with a known distribution of sample means. As an example we might compare the mean IQ score of a group of children taught by a new teaching method with the distribution of means of samples of the same size of children taught by the traditional method. In both these cases we need a known distribution.

More usually we will compare two or more samples of subjects to decide whether they come from the same or different populations, for example do men and women differ on their memory for faces? Note the word <u>subject</u> in this context simply refers to a member of a sample. A subject could be anything. Quite often it will be a person but it could be an animal (if we are studying rats learning mazes or dogs learning tricks) or indeed anything we want to study (bolts made by one machine in one sample and bolts made by another machine in a second sample). The use of the term 'subject' has been criticised in the study of psychology when referring to people who agree to take part in research. The modern terminology for such a person is <u>participant</u> as it is viewed as more respectful of these helpful individuals, without whom there would be little psychological research. However, in statistical analysis we refer to 'between subjects' and 'within subjects' for particular types of designs or calculations, so the term continues to have currency in this context. Where it is clear that it is people taking part in a study I will refer to them as participants rather than subjects.

In the examples we have considered so far each experiment has at least two factors. In the Cyadmine gas example we have the variable *Cyadmine*, varying between 'affected' and 'unaffected' and *birth-weight*, varying between the individuals we are measuring. In the memory experiment above we have *gender*, either 'men' or 'women', and *memory for faces*, which we vary along the scale devised to measure it.

In an experiment there can be one or more <u>independent variables</u>. These are the variables for which the experimenter selects the values in advance. With the variable *Cyadmine* we chose to look at two values: affected and unaffected (rather than looking at, say, badly affected, moderately affected and slightly affected). With the variable *gender* we selected men and women (rather than boys and girls). The experimenter controls the values of the independent variables and the samples are selected so that they differ on these values.

As well as independent variables there is also the dependent variable in an experiment. This is the variable we measure and on which we obtain the scores. Whilst the researcher selects what factor will be the dependent variable in the experiment (birth-weight, reaction time, IQ score, memory for faces) the researcher cannot control the values of that variable. We do not know in advance what the scores will be on this variable. This is the point of performing the experiment. Let us consider another example of the two sample case: two groups of children engage in different methods of learning a second language. Is one method better than the other? In statistical terms we want to find a suitable dependent variable (such as amount learnt) that is dependent (i.e. influenced by) the independent variable (learning method) to see if the values of the dependent variables differ in our two samples to such an extent that we can conclude that the sample scores come from different distributions, and one method leads to a greater amount learnt than the other.

The problem of equivalent conditions

Experiments are all about predicting relationships between independent and dependent variables. A research hypothesis is a prediction that the dependent variable will vary with (depend on) changes in the independent variable.

Imagine we set up an experiment to test whether girls are better than boys at map reading. The first problem is deciding what we mean by 'map reading'. Reading a road map to get into town? Reading an ordnance survey map to cross a moor? There is not an easy answer to the question. We must make a choice and state it clearly. As we saw in Chapter 4, we must operationally define *map reading ability* for the purpose of our experiment, such as 'the time it takes a child to get from a specific church, across the fields to a specified post office, using an ordnance survey map only'. We have to attempt to arrange the conditions equally for the children, such as making sure that they are all unfamiliar with the route. And this highlights a second problem.

What if we find a difference between the boys and the girls on map reading ability: can we infer a relationship between gender and map reading ability? Not necessarily; the reason being the difficulty of arranging equivalent conditions for the boys and girls. If the girls had undertaken the task in bright daylight and the boys in the dusk we would not be surprised if the boys were worse. In this case the independent variable *gender* was confounded by another variable *daylight*. Likewise, if all the boys were from an orienteering club and the girls had never seen a map before then a difference between them would not necessarily indicate a relationship of map reading ability to gender but to *experience*.

Confounding is an example of a systematic error. The experimental conditions are consistently different for the two samples due to other independent variables as well as the one under test. In addition to systematic errors influencing an experiment we also have random errors. These occur in an unsystematic way: a gust of wind makes it temporarily hard for one boy to read his map, a road is busy when one girl tries to cross but is quiet for another.

As it appears that we can never produce equivalent conditions for all the participants in the study should we abandon experimentation altogether? Unfortunately there is no research method without problems and there are ways of dealing with these difficulties. Systematic errors can be avoided when we are aware of them and it is the skill of the researcher to spot them. We can deliberately select our participants so that they are matched on a confounding variable. In our example, for each boy that has some map reading experience we match him with a girl who has had the same amount of experience. In this way the samples no longer differ on *experience* and it should no longer bias our results in favour of one sample. We can also monitor the *daylight* and make sure that the children perform in similar daylight conditions. By being a little more sophisticated in the design and operation of the experiment we can remove relevant systematic errors.

It is unlikely that we would match the children on hair colour as this is a factor we would not expect to influence this experiment. In matching we take account of only the factors we believe to be relevant. Again we can see it is one's expert knowledge of one's own discipline rather than statistical knowledge that guides these judgements. This is why an experiment should always be accurately reported, stating how the samples were matched. Another researcher might argue that an important confounding factor was not controlled for in the experiment.

We cannot control for random errors. However, our statistical tests are deliberately designed to help us decide if there is a difference between our samples above the level of any 'background noise' caused by these random errors, and we set a significance level to do this. We do not expect every boy to get the same score, nor every girl. We expect a distribution of scores: not every boy runs at the same speed, not every girl trips up on the way. Random errors produce a distribution of scores across each sample. Statistical tests look for systematic differences between samples due to the independent variable above the random variation within a sample.

Related or independent samples

Sometimes, as in the map reading experiment, there are different participants in each sample. This is not surprising for the variable *gender*, as most children are either a boy or a girl, not both. In other experiments it is possible use the same participants in each sample. An example of this might be an experiment on the effect of temperature on reading comprehension where we test the participants' comprehension at two different temperatures. When a participant contributes a score to only one sample the experiment is called an unrelated, independent or between-subjects design and when the participants contribute a score to each sample the experiment is called a related, repeated measures or within-subjects design.

Consider an experiment where a researcher is trying to find out whether it is harder to understand the writing of Joseph Conrad (reputed to be difficult) compared to Charles Dickens. The researcher might select pieces written by the two authors (matched on length at least) and give them to a group of participants to read, followed by a comprehension test. This is a related design, as each person is in both samples. This has the advantage of matching the participants with themselves, so reducing possible errors due to differences between individuals (we will not have all the English enthusiasts in one sample). However, there are other problems to watch for. If the participants read the Dickens piece first followed by the Conrad they might perform worse on the Dickens, not due to comprehensibility, but because they read it first and it is not so fresh in their minds. We have introduced the confounding factor *memory time* into the experiment. To overcome this we must counterbalance the order of presentation, so half the participants read the Dickens first and half the Conrad. By this counterbalancing we will have controlled for confounding factors such as memory time, tiredness, boredom, experience of the test, etc.

The advantage of an independent design is that there are no carry-over effects from one sample to the next, whereas the disadvantage is that there may be systematic differences between the samples and therefore we must take care in our sample selection. In many cases we have to have an independent design as we are testing an independent variable such as *gender* or *occupation* where participants can only be a member of one sample: people are normally working as either a doctor or a nurse but not both.

The interpretation of sample differences

Essentially, in designing experiments, we would like to select our subjects randomly from the largest population possible. If we do this then our results have the greatest generalisability. However we also have the greatest chance of confounding. Researchers compromise (as they must using any methodology) and lose some generalisability in favour of greater control over the variables involved. In the Cyadmine example we considered babies born in a single town where the gas cloud rested. This sample might not generalise to all Cyadmine-affected babies. Maybe there is something specific to the location that influenced the impact of the gas in some way. Yet this should not stop the researcher carrying out the test. Important information can still be found and it would also need to be demonstrated that the location does have an influence on the effects of Cyadmine.

Finally, in this section, we wish to design experiments that actually test out the hypothesis we are interested in! (It is amazing how many do not.) If we wish to test whether a reading scheme improves children's reading performance we cannot simply test them before and after they have taken part in the scheme. Any differences might be due to the fact that the children are older rather than the reading scheme as such. We have the confounding factor of *age*. To overcome this we match two groups of children on reading ability and then give one, the experimental group, the reading scheme but not the other, the control group. If the performance of the experimental group improves more than that of the control group then we may be able to relate it to the reading scheme as we have controlled for the effects of age by the selection of the control group.

In all experiments we are trying to establish relationships between the independent and dependent variables, controlling for extraneous variables that could influence this relationship. We must be careful when we do find a relationship that our interpretation is not in error. Experiments do not establish causal relationships, they only support or do not support testable hypotheses. For example, we might hypothesise that men and women differ on a certain factor. If we find a significant difference it supports our hypothesis but does not tell us why. The answer may be genetic, social or even a confounding factor that we have not taken account of.

The reason for undertaking experiments is to give us some systematic data on which to base our judgements and test our ideas. The more we learn about experimental methods the more sophisticated our judgements can be in assessing the worth of our findings. And it is the statistical analysis which helps us to decide what we have actually found out.

Hypothesis testing with two samples

A TEACHER READ ABOUT a new reading scheme introduced in another country and wondered whether it could be used here. There were reports in the educational literature of the other country that the New Scheme resulted in better reading performance from the children. The problem was that these data were for another language. The teacher wanted to find out if the New Scheme was better than the Old Scheme currently being used in the classroom in this country.

The teacher decided to teach half the class on the New Scheme and half on the Old Scheme on the next class intake. The children were randomly allocated to the two schemes, to avoid biasing the samples due to factors such as intelligence. In this way the two samples were assumed to systematically differ only on the variable under study: *reading scheme*. The teacher can now compare the samples. Yet the teacher is not really interested in the samples as such but the population of children these samples are drawn from. Is the New Scheme better for children of this age rather than just this class? The question is whether the population distribution for the New Scheme is higher up a scale of reading performance than the distribution for the Old Scheme. This is a one-tailed prediction that the New Scheme will result in better performance than the Old Scheme. Unfortunately the teacher has no details of these populations, they are both unknown.

How can these samples be used to test the hypothesis? First of all we can ask whether the samples are representative of the populations we want to generalise to. How are the pupils selected for this school? What social groups do they come from? These factors might limit the generalisation. Second, we can look at the performance of the two samples on a test of reading. If the difference between the samples is small we might be sceptical of a difference in populations but if the difference is big we might decide that the finding indicates a likely difference in the populations. The problem we face is: how big must a difference be before we reject the null hypothesis and decide the samples really do come from populations with different distributions.

We can attack the problem in the following way. Let us assume that the two samples really do come from the same distribution, the null hypothesis is true and there is no difference in reading performance between the populations. What differences would we expect between two samples

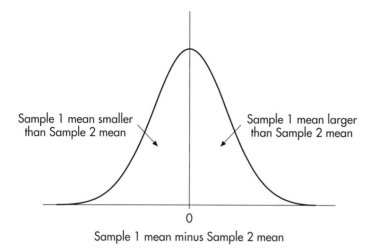

Sample 1 mean smaller than Sample 2 mean

Sample 1 mean larger than Sample 2 mean

0

Sample 1 mean minus Sample 2 mean

FIGURE 8.1 The distribution of the difference between sample means

simply by chance alone? We can find this out if we take the mean of every possible sample, of the size we are interested in, and compare it with the mean of every other possible sample of this size. These differences (in sample means) will tell us what differences we would expect when the null hypothesis is true. If we plot these differences we get the distribution of differences between sample means. Like the distribution of sample means this will tend to be a normal distribution as it is a sampling distribution. This will be especially the case if our sample size is large. The mean of this distribution will be zero because, when we take samples from the same distribution the differences will pile up around zero as there will be little or no difference between most sample means. Only occasionally will there be a large difference, say, when one sample has all the good readers and the other all the bad readers. The distribution of differences between sample means when the null hypothesis is true is shown in Figure 8.1.

Now, lo and behold, we have a known distribution: a normal distribution with a mean of zero. We also have a score to test: 'the difference in our sample means'. Hypothesis testing is all about comparing a score with a known distribution. If the probability is high that our difference in sample means comes from this distribution then the chances are that the null hypothesis is true. If there is a low probability of finding a difference such as ours from this distribution then the chances are that our samples come from different population distributions, and the null hypothesis can be rejected. All we need to do now is to construct a z score for the 'score' (the difference between our sample means) and we can find the probability of this score coming from the 'known distribution' (the distribution of differences between sample means) to find the probability of the null hypothesis being true.

A z score needs a score, a mean and a standard deviation. Our 'score' is the difference in sample means. If we call the mean of Sample 1 $\overline{X}_1$ and the mean of Sample 2 $\overline{X}_2$ then the difference in sample means is $\overline{X}_1 - \overline{X}_2$. The mean and standard deviation of the distribution of differences in sample means, when the null hypothesis is true, are given the following symbols: $\mu_{\overline{X}_1-\overline{X}_2}$ and $\sigma_{\overline{X}_1-\overline{X}_2}$, respectively. (As it is the standard deviation of a distribution concerning sample means we must remember that $\sigma_{\overline{X}_1-\overline{X}_2}$ is a standard error. It gives us the standard distance of a difference in sample means from the mean of the differences in sample means.) And we so can write the following formula for z:

$$z = \frac{(\overline{X}_1 - \overline{X}_2) - \mu_{\overline{X}_1-\overline{X}_2}}{\sigma_{\overline{X}_1-\overline{X}_2}}$$

Now we know that $\mu_{\overline{X}_1-\overline{X}_2} = 0$, so we can write z as follows:

$$z = \frac{(\overline{X}_1 - \overline{X}_2) - 0}{\sigma_{\overline{X}_1-\overline{X}_2}} = \frac{\overline{X}_1 - \overline{X}_2}{\sigma_{\overline{X}_1-\overline{X}_2}}$$

All we need to do now is look up the z score in the standard normal table to find the appropriate probability value. The problem is that we do not know $\sigma_{\overline{X}_1-\overline{X}_2}$. We will have to estimate it. How do we estimate the standard error of the distribution of differences between sample means when the null hypothesis is true? We have to use our samples. We replace $\sigma_{\overline{X}_1-\overline{X}_2}$ in the formula with $s_{\overline{X}_1-\overline{X}_2}$, which is the standard error of the difference between our sample means. It may look a little different to the one we created in Chapter 6 but we have the t statistic once again, as an estimate of z by using sample information to estimate the population standard error. The difference is only in the appearance of the formula: we still have a 'score' $(\overline{X}_1 - \overline{X}_2)$ minus a mean (which in this case is zero) divided by an estimated standard error $(s_{\overline{X}_1-\overline{X}_2})$:

$$t = \frac{\overline{X}_1 - \overline{X}_2}{s_{\overline{X}_1-\overline{X}_2}}$$

Recall from Chapter 6 that we know all about the t distribution so we are able to find probability values in the tables. We must not forget that the t distribution is influenced by the degrees of freedom of the samples, as the larger the samples the closer the distribution approximates the normal distribution. We must work out the degrees of freedom of our samples if we are to compare our calculated t value to the correct t distribution.

We now have a statistic we can work out using the information from our samples and we will be able to use it to make decisions concerning the population distributions: just the thing for hypothesis testing using two samples. Essentially, $s_{\bar{X}_1 - \bar{X}_2}$ is (an estimate of) how much we would expect our means to differ by chance (when they come from the same distribution) whereas $\bar{X}_1 - \bar{X}_2$ is the actual difference in means. $(\bar{X}_1 - \bar{X}_2)/s_{\bar{X}_1 - \bar{X}_2}$ tells us how much bigger our difference in means is relative to the difference expected by chance alone. The larger this ratio the greater our confidence that the mean difference is not due to chance but due to two different population distributions. The tricky thing is working out $s_{\bar{X}_1 - \bar{X}_2}$ but in subsequent sections we will see how this is done.

The assumptions of the two sample *t* test

The basic assumptions of the t test are the same whichever t test we are undertaking. We require the sampling distribution to be normally distributed so we usually assume that our samples come from normally distributed populations. Fortunately, the t test is robust so that even if the distributions are only vaguely normal: humped in the middle and tailing off to the sides, then the t test is still likely to be valid. This is especially true for large samples (greater than 30). Again, we must assume that the samples are randomly chosen from their populations so that we can use sample statistics (mean, standard deviation) as unbiased estimates of the population parameters. Finally, we assume that the two samples come from populations with equal variances (and equal standard deviations as one is simply the square root of the other) to allow us to use the sample information to estimate population standard deviations. Thus, we are assuming that any effect of the independent variable is to shift the distribution of the dependent variable along the scale (i.e. alter the population mean) but not change its shape (its variance, or standard deviation).

Related or independent samples

As we saw in the previous chapter, related samples involve subjects providing scores for both samples, whereas with independent samples each subject contributes a score to only one sample. The way we calculate the two sample t test depends on whether the two samples are related or independent: there are different formulae that take account of the various differences this entails. For example, if we have 10 subjects in our two samples, for related samples we require only 10 different subjects as they are used twice, whereas with independent samples we require 20 subjects, 10 for each sample. The details of the different formulae are shown below.

The related *t* test

We start with our formula for t:

$$t = \frac{\overline{X}_1 - \overline{X}_2}{s_{\overline{X}_1 - \overline{X}_2}}$$

We can work out $\overline{X}_1 - \overline{X}_2$ easily enough. The difficulty is to work out $s_{\overline{X}_1 - \overline{X}_2}$. Recall that the standard deviation of a distribution of sample means is called a standard error of the mean. $s_{\overline{X}_1 - \overline{X}_2}$ is still a standard error, as it is still based on sample means, and so can be expressed as the standard deviation of the difference between the scores divided by the square root of the sample size:

$$s_{\overline{X}_1 - \overline{X}_2} = \frac{s_{X_1 - X_2}}{\sqrt{n}}$$

We now need to work out the standard deviation of the difference in sample scores, $s_{X_1 - X_2}$. The difference in sample scores is easy to calculate with related samples. For each subject we can calculate a difference score d simply by subtracting the subject's score in Sample 2 from their score in Sample 1: $d = X_1 - X_2$. We can legitimately do this as the samples are related. Consider the example of comparing the length of a night's sleep. If a person sleeps 8 hours on Monday and 7 hours on Tuesday the difference for that person is 1 hour of sleep. The difference score for the participant is $8 - 7 = 1$. We then find the standard deviation of the difference scores:

$$s_{X_1-X_2} = s_d = \sqrt{\dfrac{\sum d^2 - \dfrac{(\sum d)^2}{n}}{n-1}}$$

Here we have the usual standard deviation formula. With n subjects in each sample there are n difference scores. We can now produce a formula for $s_{\overline{X}_1-\overline{X}_2}$, the standard error, by dividing the above formula by $\sqrt{n}$:

$$s_{\overline{X}_1-\overline{X}_2} = \sqrt{\dfrac{\sum d^2 - \dfrac{(\sum d)^2}{n}}{n(n-1)}}$$

And now finally we have our formula for the two sample related t test:

$$t = \dfrac{\overline{X}_1 - \overline{X}_2}{\sqrt{\dfrac{\sum d^2 - \dfrac{(\sum d)^2}{n}}{n(n-1)}}}$$

Note that, whilst the formula looks very different to the z formula, it is still a score $(\overline{X}_1 - \overline{X}_2)$ minus a population mean (0) divided by a standard deviation, although in this case it's rather a complex standard deviation: the estimate of the standard error of the difference in sample means.

A worked example

A teacher believed that the children in her class were better at their work in the morning than in the afternoon. She decided to test this out by using a mathematics test as this required the children to concentrate. If there was a post-lunch dip in performance the test should pick it up. She chose a random sample of 8 children from the class and gave them two tests matched on their difficulty. The samples were balanced on the two versions of the test, and at what time they were tested first, to control for carry-over effects. The tests gave a score out of 10, the higher the score the better the performance. The results were as follows:

Participant	Morning	Afternoon
1	6	5
2	4	2
3	3	4
4	5	4
5	7	3
6	6	4
7	5	5
8	6	3

This is a related two sample t test as all participants contributed a score to both samples.

We must now find the values to fit into the formula:

$$t = \frac{\overline{X}_1 - \overline{X}_2}{\sqrt{\dfrac{\sum d^2 - \dfrac{(\sum d)^2}{n}}{n(n-1)}}}$$

We can now relabel the columns, with Sample 1 for Morning and Sample 2 for Afternoon and find the means ($\overline{X}_1$ and $\overline{X}_2$), the difference scores (d), the sum of the difference scores ($\sum d$), the square of the sum of the difference scores ($(\sum d)^2$), the squared difference scores (d^2), and the sum of the squared difference scores ($\sum d^2$). The number of participants in each sample is n.

Participant	Sample 1 X_1	Sample 2 X_2	Difference d	Squared d d^2
1	6	5	1	1
2	4	2	2	4
3	3	4	−1	1
4	5	4	1	1
5	7	3	4	16
6	6	4	2	4
7	5	5	0	0
8	6	3	3	9
$n = 8$	$\overline{X}_1 = 5.25$	$\overline{X}_2 = 3.75$	$\sum d = 12$ $(\sum d)^2 = 144$	$\sum d^2 = 36$

Inserting the figures into the t formula we get:

$$t = \frac{5.25 - 3.75}{\sqrt{\dfrac{36 - \dfrac{144}{8}}{8(8 - 1)}}} = \frac{1.50}{\sqrt{\dfrac{36 - 18}{56}}} = \frac{1.50}{\sqrt{0.321}} = \frac{1.50}{0.567} = 2.65$$

The degrees of freedom (df) for a related t test is always $n - 1$, so $df = 7$.

This is a one-tailed test as the prediction was that the children would perform <u>better</u> in the morning, and the prediction is that the scores in Sample 1 are larger than in Sample 2. As can be seen from the means this is the case but we need to test the significance of the difference. At the $p = 0.05$ level of significance, we find from the t distribution tables (Table A.2 in the Appendix) that $t = 1.895$, $df = 7$ for a one-tailed test.

The calculated value of t of 2.65 being greater than the table value of 1.895 allows us to reject the null hypothesis, at the $p = 0.05$ level of significance, and conclude that the pupils did perform significantly better on the mathematics test in the morning compared to the afternoon.

Sometimes we find that the calculated t has a minus sign. This simply indicates that the mean of Sample 1 is smaller than the mean of Sample 2. If we had found a minus sign in the above example we could have rejected the one-tailed prediction straight away as it would have meant better scores in the afternoon. If we had predicted that Sample 2 has the larger scores, or made a two-tailed prediction, we simply ignore the minus sign when comparing the calculated value with the table value.

The independent t test

We again start with our formula for t: $\dfrac{\overline{X}_1 - \overline{X}_2}{s_{\overline{X}_1 - \overline{X}_2}}$. The difficulty with independent samples is working out $s_{\overline{X}_1 - \overline{X}_2}$. How we do this is explained below. Now this does include some rather horrible formulae, so, if you wish, do not worry about following the derivation of the formula for the independent t test, feel free to skip the mathematics. If you understand the logic that we have to find a formula for $s_{\overline{X}_1 - \overline{X}_2}$ and that this formula, though rather cumbersome, is still an estimated standard error of the difference in sample means then that's fine.

We cannot produce difference scores as we did for the related t test. (If the samples are unrelated we cannot work out a difference score. If one person sleeps 8 hours on Monday and another person sleeps 7 hours on Tuesday it is meaningless to subtract one from the other as they are from different participants.) Indeed we may have different numbers of subjects in the two samples (n_1 and n_2). We are helped out in this case by a mathematical finding called the *Variance Sum Law*, which provides us with a relationship between $s_{\bar{X}_1 - \bar{X}_2}$ and the standard deviations of the two samples (s_1 and s_2):

$$s_{\bar{X}_1 - \bar{X}_2} = \sqrt{\frac{s_1^2}{n_1} + \frac{s_2^2}{n_2}}$$

The importance of this is that we cannot work out $s_{\bar{X}_1 - \bar{X}_2}$ but we can work out s_1 and s_2. Thus, we are able to produce a formula for the independent t that we can calculate.

Our problems are not over yet in developing the formula for t. We know that a sample standard deviation is a better estimate of the population parameter the larger the sample size and also that the t test assumes that the samples come from populations with equal standard deviations. From this we can infer that when we have samples of different sizes the larger one is likely to provide a better estimate of the population standard deviation than the smaller one. What we do is to weight the contribution of the two sample standard deviations by their sample size (more accurately, their variances by their degrees of freedom) and produce a population estimate based on the weighted average of the sample standard deviations, s_w:

$$s_w^2 = \frac{(n_1 - 1)s_1^2 - (n_2 - 1)s_2^2}{(n_1 - 1) + (n_2 - 1)}$$

Now, instead of using the sample standard deviations in the formula for $s_{\bar{X}_1 - \bar{X}_2}$ we replace them both with s_w:

$$s_{\bar{X}_1 - \bar{X}_2} = \sqrt{\frac{s_w^2}{n_1} + \frac{s_w^2}{n_2}} = \sqrt{s_w^2 \left(\frac{1}{n_1} + \frac{1}{n_2} \right)}$$

We now expand s_w in the formula:

$$s_{\bar{X}_1 - \bar{X}_2} = \sqrt{\left(\frac{(n_1 - 1)s_1^2 - (n_2 - 1)s_2^2}{(n_1 - 1) + (n_2 - 1)} \right) \left(\frac{1}{n_1} + \frac{1}{n_2} \right)}$$

Finally, we replace s_1 with $\sqrt{\dfrac{\sum X_1^2 - \dfrac{(\sum X_1)^2}{n_1}}{n_1 - 1}}$ and s_2 with

$\sqrt{\dfrac{\sum X_2^2 - \dfrac{(\sum X_2)^2}{n_2}}{n_2 - 1}}$, the standard deviation formulae for two samples.

After a little tidying up, we obtain the formula for calculating $s_{\bar{X}_1 - \bar{X}_2}$:

$$s_{\bar{X}_1 - \bar{X}_2} = \sqrt{\left(\frac{\sum X_1^2 - \dfrac{(\sum X_1)^2}{n_1} + \sum X_2^2 - \dfrac{(\sum X_2)^2}{n_2}}{(n_1 - 1) + (n_2 - 1)} \right) \left(\frac{1}{n_1} + \frac{1}{n_2} \right)}$$

At last we are able to produce the formula for the two sample independent t:

$$t = \frac{\bar{X}_1 - \bar{X}_2}{\sqrt{\left(\dfrac{\sum X_1^2 - \dfrac{(\sum X_1)^2}{n_1} + \sum X_2^2 - \dfrac{(\sum X_2)^2}{n_2}}{(n_1 - 1) + (n_2 - 1)} \right) \left(\dfrac{1}{n_1} + \dfrac{1}{n_2} \right)}}$$

This is unfortunately rather a large formula to calculate but I hope you can see how and why it was required by the above logic. Also on many occasions we can use computer programs to aid us in our calculations. As demonstrated below, t can be calculated without too much difficulty with just a calculator. But the point here is that, while the formula looks very different from the z formula, it is still an estimate of z being a 'score' $(\bar{X}_1 - \bar{X}_2)$ minus a mean $(\mu_{\bar{X}_1 - \bar{X}_2} = 0)$ divided by a standard deviation $(s_{\bar{X}_1 - \bar{X}_2})$.

It is important to recall that we are using the assumption that the two samples come from populations with equal variances (and hence equal standard deviations). If this is not the case it is inappropriate to average our standard deviations for estimation. Only if the larger sample variance is more than three times the other would we usually decide not to perform the test.

As the samples are unrelated, the degrees of freedom of the independent t test is the sum of the degrees of freedom of each sample: $(n_1 - 1) + (n_2 - 1)$.

A worked example

A new sleeping pill was being tested on a number of volunteers. It was predicted that it would have a differential effect on men and women. There were six men and eight women who agreed to take part in the experiment. Over a two week period they took either a placebo (a pill that had no effect) or the sleeping pill. Participants were not aware of which pill they were taking each night. The number of extra hours slept during the seven 'pill nights' compared to the seven 'placebo nights' was calculated. The men slept 4, 6, 5, 4, 5 and 6 extra hours and the women slept 3, 8, 7, 6, 7, 6, 7 and 6 extra hours. Is the prediction supported?

We must find the values to fit into the t formula:

$$t = \frac{\bar{X}_1 - \bar{X}_2}{\sqrt{\left(\dfrac{\sum X_1^2 - \dfrac{(\sum X_1)^2}{n_1} + \sum X_2^2 - \dfrac{(\sum X_2)^2}{n_2}}{(n_1 - 1) + (n_2 - 1)}\right)\left(\dfrac{1}{n_1} + \dfrac{1}{n_2}\right)}}$$

I shall label the men as Sample 1 and the women as Sample 2.

Sample 1		Sample 2	
X_1	X_1^2	X_2	X_2^2
4	16	3	9
6	36	8	64
5	25	7	49
4	16	6	36
5	25	7	49
6	36	6	36
		7	49
		6	36
$n_1 = 6$		$n_2 = 8$	
$\sum X_1 = 30$	$\sum X_1^2 = 154$	$\sum X_2 = 50$	$\sum X_2^2 = 328$
$\bar{X}_1 = 5.0$		$\bar{X}_2 = 6.25$	
$(\sum X_1)^2 = 900$		$(\sum X_2)^2 = 2500$	

Inserting the figures into the t formula we get:

$$t = \frac{5.00 - 6.25}{\sqrt{\left(\dfrac{154 - \dfrac{900}{6} + 328 - \dfrac{2500}{8}}{(6-1)+(8-1)}\right)\left(\dfrac{1}{6} + \dfrac{1}{8}\right)}}$$

$$= \frac{-1.25}{\sqrt{\left(\dfrac{154 - 150 + 328 - 312.5}{5 + 7}\right)\left(\dfrac{1}{6} + \dfrac{1}{8}\right)}}$$

$$t = \frac{-1.25}{\sqrt{1.625 \times 0.292}} = \frac{-1.25}{\sqrt{0.474}} = \frac{-1.25}{0.688} = -1.82$$

The degrees of freedom, $df = (n_1 - 1) + (n_2 - 1) = (6 - 1) + (8 - 1) = 12$.

The minus sign simply indicates that Sample 2 (women) has the larger scores. As we are testing a two-tailed test we simply treat it as +1.82. From the tables of the t distribution $t = 2.179$, $df = 12$, $p = 0.05$ (from Table A.2 in the Appendix). As our calculated t value of 1.82 is not greater than the table value of 2.18 we cannot reject the null hypothesis: we have not found a significant difference in the extra sleep between men and women at the 5 per cent level of significance.

It is an interesting result however. Notice that the difference in means is 1.25 in favour of the women. The difference in means we would expect by chance is 0.688 (the bottom part of the t calculation). Even though this is not significant at $p = 0.05$ the actual probability is 0.0945, which is still quite small. There might actually be a genuine effect here 'bubbling under' but not quite strong enough to pick up in these data. If we had more participants or had made a one-tailed prediction we might have achieved significance. The reasons why this might be are explained in the next chapter.

Confidence intervals

We can work out confidence intervals for the differences in the mean values when we are comparing two samples. Recall from Chapter 6 that:

CI = Difference in means ± (critical t value × standard error of the difference in means)

For the example of the related t test given in this chapter, we calculate the 95 per cent confidence interval as follows:

$$95\%CI = (5.25 - 3.75) \pm (2.365 \times 0.567)$$

$$95\%CI = 1.50 \pm 1.341$$

$$95\%CI = (0.159, 2.841)$$

The critical t value (2.365) is found in the tables for $p = 0.05$ for a two-tailed test with $df = 7$. The standard error calculation (0.567) is the denominator in the formula for the calculated t value. Notice that the interval does not include the zero so we can confidently conclude that the difference between the sample means is not zero but a positive value.

For the example of the independent t test the 95 per cent confidence interval is calculcated thus:

$$95\%CI = (5 - 6.25) \pm (2.179 \times 0.688)$$

$$95\%CI = -1.25 \pm 1.499$$

$$95\%CI = (-2.749, 0.249)$$

The critical value of t of 2.179 is found from the tables at $p = 0.05$ for a two-tailed test, $df = 12$. Again, the standard error value (0.688) is taken from the t calculation. Notice that in this example the confidence interval includes the zero value. In this case we are not confident that the 'true' difference in the means is different from zero. Just as the t value did not reach significance so the confidence interval, whilst mostly below zero, still contains zero within it. Both analyses are telling us that we do not have enough evidence from these data to claim a difference in the sample means.

Details on how to undertake the two sample t test using the SPSS computer statistical package can be found in Chapter 7 of Hinton $et\ al.$ (2004).

Chapter 9

Significance, error and power

Type I and Type II errors

Hypothesis testing is like digging for treasure on a treasure island. The significance level sets the probability that we have actually found treasure rather than made a mistake. We are very conservative here (that is why we only accept a 5 in 100 chance of making a mistake). We do not wander about picking up any old piece of rusting metal we chance upon and claim that we have found treasure. Our fellow treasure hunters would soon get fed up with us. We want to be sure that when we claim to have found treasure then we are correct. In hypothesis testing we do not want to make a Type I error: that is, claim that we have found a significant difference between the population distributions when there is not one. We do not want to claim that we have found treasure when we have not. That is why we set the significance level at a small probability level.

In the one-tailed prediction illustrated in Figure 9.1 we are saying that if the 'score' falls beyond the significance level then it belongs to a different distribution to the known distribution, the unknown distribution. You can see in this example, where the unknown distribution really is different to the known distribution, that a score beyond the significance level is more likely to come from the unknown distribution than the known distribution as more

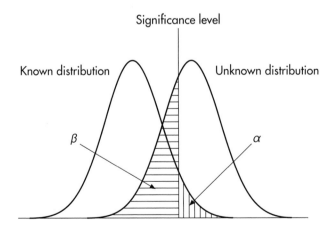

FIGURE 9.1 The risk of a Type I and Type II error

of it is beyond the significance level. However, there is still a small risk that such a score comes from the known distribution. The area labelled α is the size of this risk, the risk of a Type I error, which is the amount of the known distribution the 'wrong' side of the significance level. We specify the size of this risk by setting the significance level. By setting a significance level at $p = 0.05$ we are saying that only 5 per cent of the known distribution lies beyond it.

If the score falls below the significance level we accept the null hypothesis that the score comes from the known distribution. Looking again at Figure 9.1 we can see that 95 per cent of the known distribution lies below the significance level. Also there is more of the known distribution below the significance level than the unknown distribution, so the chances are that if a score lies this side of the significance level it comes from the known distribution and we are correct in accepting the null hypothesis.

We must be clear in understanding what 'accepting the null hypothesis' entails. All acceptance means is that we have not found a significant difference *in our experiment*. In fact some authors (Cohen, 1988, p. 16., see also Wilkinson and the Task Force on Statistical Inference, 1999) have argued that it is wrong to say that we accept the null hypothesis, rather we should always say 'we have failed to reject the null hypothesis' as this is a more accurate account of the situation – we have not found enough evidence to allow us to reject the null hypothesis. We have certainly not demonstrated that the null hypothesis is true. We can claim that we do not have the evidence to say it is not true, and there is a subtle difference between the statements. Again, if we dig for treasure on a desert island and do not find it, it does not mean that it is not there somewhere. When we 'accept the null hypothesis' we are only saying that we have not found a big enough difference for us to reject the possibility that the difference arose by chance. The probability of the difference arising by chance is too large for us to claim a genuine difference in the distributions. If we do not find treasure there are two possible reasons: one, there is no treasure there or, two, there is treasure but we have not found it. Similarly, if we do not find a significant difference when testing an hypothesis it could be that there really is no difference in the distributions or that there is a difference and we have missed it. In the former case all is well, we have not found a difference when there was not one to find. In the latter case we have committed a <u>Type II error</u>. We have not found a difference in the distributions by our test when there was a genuine difference to be found.

If a score falls below the significance level then we accept the null hypothesis that the score comes from the known distribution. However, there is a risk that the score comes from the unknown distribution (as part of the unknown distribution lies below the significance level). The risk of making a Type II error is the amount of the unknown distribution below the significance level. This is the area labelled β in Figure 9.1. Note that the risk of a Type II error, β, may well be larger than α. Researchers do not want to make claims that turn out to be false so are happier to make Type II errors than Type I errors. We would prefer to miss out on the treasure occasionally rather than make a false claim. Most scientists publish their significant results and these results are scrutinised by others so it is deemed better to err on the side of caution rather than make a potentially embarrassing claim. It is tempting to think that all we need do to avoid a mistake is to set a very small value for α, say, 0.01 or 0.001. However, this would be an error as statistical testing is not just about keeping the risk of a Type I error low but also about the balance between the risk of Type I and Type II errors. As we shall see below (in the discussion of power) ignoring the risk of a Type II error could mean that our study, involving all the time and effort to carry it out, is simply not powerful enough to find the effects we are looking for – so we are wasting our time and effort.

Essentially we want a significance level that separates the known distribution from the unknown distribution. If we could find a position along the scale where all the known distribution fell to one side of the significance level and all the unknown distribution fell to the other side, then we would not make a Type I or Type II error as the significance level would separate the distributions perfectly. But, because of the overlap of the two distributions, some of the known distribution (α) falls the 'wrong' side of the significance level as does some of the unknown distribution (β). If a score falls below the significance level we 'accept the null hypothesis' as most of the known distribution ($1 - \alpha$) lies below it, with only β of the unknown distribution. If a score falls beyond the significance level we reject the null hypothesis as only α of the known distribution lies beyond it along with $1 - \beta$ of the unknown distribution. Although we risk these two types of error, we want the probability to favour the correct judgement.

Statistical power

For a moment let us assume that there really is treasure hidden on the desert island. With a good map and proper digging equipment there is an excellent chance of finding it. This is the analogy for a well-designed study, properly carried out. Yet without a map and only a child's bucket and spade the chances of finding the treasure are slim. Similarly with the statistical analyses of our data. Some are very likely to find a difference in the two distributions whereas others may be unlikely to find it *even though it is really there*. The tests differ in their power. The power of a statistical test refers to its ability to find a difference in distributions when there really is one. In this case the unknown distribution is genuinely different to that of the known distribution. What are our chances of finding it? A score that actually comes from the unknown distribution will only be claimed to have come from the unknown distribution when that score is beyond the significance level. So we will correctly assign scores that belong to the part of the unknown distribution beyond the significance level. This is the whole of the unknown distribution excluding β. We call this area the power of the test.

The power of a test $= 1 - \beta$

The power tells us the probability of finding the unknown distribution when it is really there. The more of the unknown distribution that lies beyond the significance level, the smaller β becomes and the larger $1 - \beta$. A more powerful statistical test is more likely to find a significant result than a less powerful test. Employing the treasure hunting analogy, a more powerful test is more likely to find the treasure when it is really there: it is the mechanical digger compared to the child's bucket and spade.

There is a problem that sometimes gets overlooked in statistical analysis. We do not want to use a test that is low in power as it is not likely to find a genuine difference in distributions. We may have constructed an excellent experiment only to fail to find a significant result due to the low power of our statistical test. Interestingly, 'power' became an increasingly important topic in statistical analysis in the latter part of the twentieth century, primarily due to the work of Jacob Cohen (e.g. Cohen, 1988), who has argued that much research has been carried out without a consideration of power in the design stage to the detriment of the research process. As a result of Cohen's work more researchers consider 'power' in the early stages of their research planning.

The power of a test

When undertaking research we want to have a good chance of finding an effect if there really is one to be found. In treasure hunting terms it would be helpful to know we are starting out with a mechanical excavator. Yet there are many occasions when researchers set out with the statistical equivalent of buckets and spades. Clearly we want a powerful test but how can we achieve it?

The first thing to decide is what is the level of power we want? Crudely, just as we want α to be very small we also want $1 - \beta$ to be very large – the more powerful the test the better. But just like our consideration of α, we need to get the balance right. We want high power but not to the detriment of all other considerations. Cohen (1988) suggests that a power of 0.80 is a suitable value for a test of high power. As a result a power of 0.80 has become something of the conventional value for $1 - \beta$, just as 0.05 is the conventional value for α.

The problem is how do we design a study with the required power as many studies published in the journals have been shown to have much lower power than 0.80? The answer is that power is related to three factors that we can control: the size of α, the size of the effect we are looking for and, third, the size of the samples we select.

The choice of α level

The simplest way to increase the power of a test is to increase the size of α. We usually set the significance level at $p = 0.05$, that is $\alpha = 0.05$, but if we increase the level to say $p = 0.10$ or $p = 0.20$ then it has the effect of shifting more of the unknown distribution beyond the significance level. As α gets bigger β gets smaller and hence $1 - \beta$ gets bigger. However, while this reduces the risk of a Type II error it increases the chances of a Type I error. A significance level of $p = 0.10$ means that we will claim an effect erroneously ten times in a hundred rather than five in a hundred. And we don't want to do this for the reasons stated earlier: researchers would prefer to miss an effect than falsely claim one that could affect their reputation. Type I and Type II errors are inextricably linked, a reduction in one increases the other. Yet we can consider whether we really want to set a significance value as low as 0.01 or even 0.001. As Cohen (1988) points out, if we end up with such low power that the ratio of β to α is in the hundreds, then this implies we are stating that a Type II error is hundreds of times worse than a Type I error. If we don't really believe this, we may be happy to set our α value to a higher value (e.g. 0.05) and have a more powerful test.

However, there is a way of reducing β without increasing α: be more specific in our prediction. A one-tailed test is more powerful than a two-tailed test. In the latter case we have to consider both tails of the distribution and we hedge our bets as to the position of the unknown distribution. For an overall significance level of 0.05 we must set the cut-off point at each tail at $p = 0.025$. It is like performing two one-tailed tests at the same time, one on each tail. If the unknown distribution really is higher than the known distribution we will only find it if it is beyond the $p = 0.025$ significance level. With a one-tailed test, we can focus on only one tail and at that tail α is twice the size (0.05) than for a two-tailed test. Shifting from a two-tailed to a one-tailed test increases $1 - \beta$. (We should note that this does make our one-tailed prediction more powerful but we now have *no power* in detecting the effect if the result goes the 'wrong way'.)

Effect size

A crucial factor affecting 'power' is the size of the effect we are looking for. If we look at Figure 9.1 we can see that the amount of overlap between the two distributions is the cause of our difficulty in setting a significance level with a low α and a high β. When there is a lot of overlap the risk of a Type II error, missing a genuine difference, increases. If the overlap between the distributions can be reduced, then β is reduced and we also reduce the chance of a Type II error and increase power. If there was no overlap between the distributions we would have no difficulty setting our significance level as we could position it between the two distributions. Sadly we will always have overlapping distributions but we can look at specifying how much overlap we have and designing studies to maximise their power.

Overlapping population distributions

The amount of overlap between two distributions depends on two factors: the difference between the population means and the size of the standard deviations. If the means are far apart then the overlap is less than when they are close together. Also if the standard deviations are small then the overlap is less than when they are large. (Recall that we always assume that the two distributions have the same standard deviation.) We can sum up the overlap by defining the effect size d (from Cohen, 1988). This is a standardised measure of the difference between the means in terms of standard deviation units. Using the label μ_1 as the mean of the known distribution and μ_2 as the mean of the unknown distribution, and σ as their standard deviation, we can express the effect size, when predicting the one-tailed hypothesis that the unknown distribution will have the larger mean, as follows:

$$\text{Effect size, } d = \frac{\mu_2 - \mu_1}{\sigma}$$

For example, with $\mu_1 = 100$, $\mu_2 = 110$, and $\sigma = 15$, then the effect size $d = 0.67$. Just like the z score d is a standardised measure and does not depend on the measuring units we are using.

We need to know the size of the effect we are investigating in order to work out the power of our test *at the design stage* (a priori). You might think: how do I know the size of the effect before I have done the study? One source of information is past studies. If we were examining the speed of recognising different types of words we can look at the literature on the topic to see what other people have found in related studies. We can use these studies to get an estimate of the size of the effect we are looking for. If there is little background literature – you are studying a new area – then a pilot study might be worth carrying out to 'get a feel' for the type of results you might get.

Cohen (1988) makes the distinction between 'small' ($d = 0.2$), 'medium' ($d = 0.5$) and 'large' effects ($d = 0.8$) as helpful guide to evaluating the size of a predicted difference. He suggests that, rather than trying to work out a specific effect size by estimating means and standard deviations we can consider whether we expect a small, medium or large effect. He argues that, for new areas of research, effects are often small, partly because we may not have developed sophisticated measuring devices or experimental control leading to relatively large standard deviations. So, if we believe that the effect we are looking for is small then we can reasonably assume an effect size of 0.2. Cohen suggests that medium effects are 'visible to the naked eye' (Cohen, 1988, p. 26), meaning that we are aware of a difference such as that between experienced machine operators and novices as it is pretty clear to see but we want to examine it in detail. In cases like this we can assume a medium effect size of 0.5. Finally, there are the large effects which are blatantly obvious, or 'grossly perceptible' as Cohen (1988, p. 27) puts it, and uses as his example the height difference between 13 and 18 year old girls. If we believe that the effect we are looking for is large Cohen recommends that we select an effect size of 0.8.

In our example we do not have to estimate the effect size as I have stated the population means and standard deviations which we would not normally have. It is interesting to note that in Cohen's terms we are predicting a medium-to-large effect as d lies between 0.5 and 0.8.

Influencing effect size

You might be tempted to argue that you cannot change the effect size at all – surely a small effect is a small effect. However, if we consider for a moment what we actually mean by effect size then we can see how to influence it. A large effect size indicates only a small overlap between distributions whereas a small effect size indicates a large overlap of the distributions. What we need to do, therefore, to increase the power of a test, and increase the effect size, is to increase the difference between the means of the distributions or reduce their standard deviations.

The one major way to decrease the overlap between distributions is to *design your studies well*. It is very important to consider what a good design entails – essentially it is one that minimises error or random variability in the study and maximises the accuracy of measurement of the variables under study.

The more you reduce random variability in the study (by proper controls in the design and procedure) the greater will be the size of the effect. Imagine we are examining face recognition. We might study it in a natural setting such as an airport. However, we might choose to use computer displays with accurate timing and keypad responses in a quiet laboratory with no distractions in order to reduce the random variability in the study.

The effect of the sensitivity of the measuring device can crucially affect the power of a test. If we are investigating happiness then we might decide to use a more complex questionnaire than simply asking people if they are happy or not. Similarly, if we are testing a subtle effect such as speed of reading different passages of text then we may wish to use a more accurate time than a stopwatch. The reason for this is that the error in starting and stopping the stopwatch might be a second or two which could swamp an effect of only a few hundred milliseconds. If we can increase the accuracy of the measured times then we are more likely to find the effect (if there is one.)

Sample size

When we are studying samples to represent populations we use sampling distributions to represent our known and unknown distributions. The standard deviation of a sampling distribution, the standard error of the mean, decreases as the sample size increases. This is because the standard error is based on both the population standard deviation and the sample size:

$$\sigma_{\bar{X}} = \frac{\sigma}{\sqrt{n}}$$

With a small sample size, such as 10, the standard error is:

$$\sigma_{\bar{X}} = \frac{\sigma}{\sqrt{10}} = \frac{\sigma}{3.16} = 0.32\sigma$$

The standard error here is just under one third of the population standard deviation. With a larger sample of, say, 50, the standard error becomes:

$$\sigma_{\bar{X}} = \frac{\sigma}{\sqrt{50}} = \frac{\sigma}{7.07} = 0.14\sigma$$

This is just under a seventh of the population standard deviation. By increasing the sample size from 10 to 50 we have reduced the standard error by over a half (from a third to a seventh of the population figure). Increasing the sample size has reduced the spread of the distribution.

An increase in sample size has the effect of reducing the overlap between the distributions by reducing their standard deviations. As a result of this, more of a genuinely different unknown distribution ends up beyond the significance level (and there is an increase in power). Compare the distributions in Figure 9.2 with those of Figure 9.1. This shows the effect of

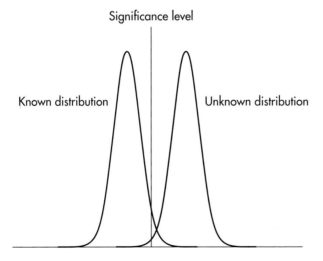

FIGURE 9.2 The effect of increasing the sample size on the overlap of the distributions

reducing the standard error by half as a result of an increase in sample size. The overlap is considerably reduced.

We can illustrate the effect of sample size on statistical power by the following example. Assume that the known population is a normal distribution with a mean of 100 and a standard deviation of 15. We will also assume that the unknown population is genuinely different with a mean of 110. In this case the population is not unknown any more so we would not need to perform any statistics as we know all we need to know – but this is for illustration only!

First we shall examine the situation when a sample of 10 is used. The sampling distributions of the two populations will have means of 100 and 110 but their standard deviations will be the standard error: $\sigma_{\bar{X}} = \dfrac{\sigma}{\sqrt{n}} = \dfrac{15}{\sqrt{10}} = 4.74$. The $p = 0.05$ significance level cuts off the last 5 per cent of the known distribution. As the distribution is normally distributed we can use the z tables (Table A.1 in the Appendix) to find which z cuts off 0.05 of the distribution. This gives a value of $z = 1.65$. Remember than z is expressed in standard deviation units, so the significance level is 1.65 standard deviations above the mean of 100. The standard deviation, the standard error, of the known distribution is 4.74, so the significance level is therefore $1.65 \times 4.74 = 7.82$ above the mean of the known distribution, so is located at 107.82 on the scale.

We now perform a similar process in reverse on the unknown distribution to work out β and then $1 - \beta$. The significance level at 107.82 positions it 2.18 below the mean of the unknown distribution (110) on the scale. We convert this to standard deviation units to find z. As we assume the standard deviations of the two distributions are the same, the standard error of the unknown distribution is also 4.74, and the significance level is $\dfrac{2.18}{4.74} = 0.46$ standard deviations below the mean. When we look up this figure in the z tables we find that $p = 0.32$. There is 0.32 of the unknown distribution below the significance level, so $\beta = 0.32$ and the power of the test is $1 - \beta = 0.68$. There is 68 per cent of the unknown distribution above the significance level. So using a sample size of 10 gives a power of 0.68.

We can do the same calculations for a sample size of 50. In this case the standard error is $\sigma_{\bar{X}} = \dfrac{\sigma}{\sqrt{n}} = \dfrac{15}{\sqrt{50}} = 2.12$. The significance level is $1.65 \times 2.12 = 3.50$ above the mean of the known distribution, at 103.50. This is 6.50 below the mean of the unknown distribution, which gives a

z of $\dfrac{6.50}{2.12} = 3.07$. From the standard normal tables this gives $p = 0.0011$, so $\beta = 0.0011$ and the power of the test $(1 - \beta)$ is 0.9989. With a sample size of 50 we now have 99.89 per cent of the unknown distribution above the significance level. So changing the sample size from 10 to 50 has increased the power from 0.68 to 0.9989.

Choosing a sample size for a statistical test

An important decision for a researcher is deciding the appropriate number of participants for a study. This is where the work of Cohen (1988) is particularly helpful. As noted above, power is related to significance level, effect size and sample size. We can turn this relationship around and see that sample size is a function of significance level, power and effect size.

A researcher was investigating different visual displays for monitoring equipment for hospitals. Two different types of display were to be compared in the laboratory to see which one led to the fewest errors in reading the display. The researcher wanted to know how many participants to use. The researcher decided on a 0.05 level of significance for a two-tailed test. The level of power required was chosen as 0.8 and it was assumed that the effect size would be medium so 0.5 was specified as the effect size. A t test was to be carried out on the error data.

Can we carry out a calculation like the one in the above section to find the answer to our question? The answer is both yes and no. Yes, we can carry out a calculation to find the number of participants and no, it is not the same as the above section as that was worked out using population data which we do not have here. When we are comparing two samples we use the t distribution as the appropriate distribution for our analysis. However, there is a complication as the t distribution we usually employ for a t test calculation is based on samples drawn from the same distribution, i.e. when the samples come from the same population. This is the t distribution assuming *no effect*. Yet in our power analysis we are proposing an effect. So we have to use a special t distribution for our power analysis called a noncentral t distribution. In order to do this we need to calculate the noncentrality parameter δ which is quite easy as it is a function of d (the effect size) and the sample sizes ($\delta = \mathrm{d} \times \sqrt{\dfrac{n_1 \times n_2}{n_1 + n_2}}$, where n_1 and n_2 are the sizes of the samples. With the noncentrality parameter (δ), the significance level (α) and the degrees of freedom (df) the power values can be calculated and, by a little reorganisation of the calculations, the sample size can be produced for a specific level of power.

Unfortunately, power analysis is not something to do by hand as we need to use distribution tables for the noncentral distribution. Cohen (1988) provided sets of useful tables that can be used to find the appropriate values. However, there are a number of easy-to-use software packages that can work out the power calculation and required sample sizes. A number of these are available free (for noncomercial use) e.g. GPOWER[6] which is very easy to use. The required values for the significance level, the effect size and the power are input and the output gives the required sample sizes. Using such a software package we can find that for an unrelated two-tailed test, using the 0.05 level of significance, examining a medium effect (d = 0.5) and seeking a power of 0.8 we need 128 participants in total or 64 in each sample.

Quite often we will find that in order to achieve the power required the sample sizes will be very large. If we had been examining a small effect (d = 0.2) in the above example we would have needed 788 participants in total or 394 in each sample. If we decide that it is not feasible to use groups of this size we can undertake a compromise power analysis. Rather than seek a sample size for a specific power (e.g. 0.8) we decide on the balance of risk we are willing to accept between a Type I and a Type II error: the ratio of β to α: where $q = \beta/\alpha$. If we decide that q = 3 is the balance of risk we can work with and we can afford to test 100 participants in each group then we can work out the power for this compromise. In this case the power is 0.5, so would be a test of medium power. We might be content with this compromise solution.

Finally, I have focused on the power calculations for a two sample t test. However, we can work out both an effect size and a noncentral distribution for a range of other statistics included in this book. So we can work out the power (or the sample size for a specific power) for the different tests we shall be considering. Fortunately, the software packages allow us to examine the power of different tests by including a menu where we simply select the statistical test we wish to perform. In the table below the 'conventional' effect size values for small, medium and large effects (from Cohen, 1988) are shown for a number of key statistical tests.

Test	Effect size	Small effect	Medium effect	Large effect
t test	d	0.2	0.5	0.8
Correlation	r	0.1	0.3	0.5
ANOVA	f	0.1	0.25	0.4
Multiple correlation and regression	f^2	0.02	0.15	0.35
Chi-square	w	0.1	0.3	0.5

Conclusion

Hypothesis testing involves making a decision concerning whether two distributions are the same or different. To make this decision we use a decision criterion, the significance level. Due to the overlap of the distributions the significance level cannot separate them completely when they are genuinely different to each other. As a result we end up with α of the known distribution and β of the unknown distribution the 'wrong' side of it. To limit the risk of Type I errors we set our significance level so that $\alpha = 0.05$, giving us a 5 in 100 chance, or smaller, of falsely rejecting the null hypothesis. We don't want to make Type I errors (and sometimes we are even more conservative, setting the significance level at $p = 0.01$, reducing the risk to 0.01).

This leaves β, the risk of making a Type II error. We do not have the same control over β as we do with α, as the distribution is unknown. Yet we do not want to use a test that is low in power, $1 - \beta$, as it reduces our chances of finding a real effect when it is there. Unfortunately, researchers do too often use tests of low power. To increase the power of our test we can do three things: design better studies, choose one-tailed tests, look for big effects, and increase the number of subjects.

When trying to decide whether the power of a test is adequate there are a couple of useful points to consider. Select the largest sample size you can *sensibly* test. If you have limited resources, time or access to subjects these restrictions may have priority. Then check the power of your test. If the power of your test is too low then you may be wasting your time continuing. However, consider the balance of risk of Type I and Type II errors. You may wish to continue with the research as you have a reasonable compromise of α and β. If you find a significant effect then you do not need any more subjects. If the test yields no significant differences yet is unexpected, or approaches significance, then repeat the test when you can test more subjects. It is worth increasing sample size to increase both the power of the test and your confidence in the findings. The new subjects may confirm the previous results or produce a significant difference. One of the major ways of deciding whether a finding is worthwhile or not is to replicate (repeat) it. If a difference continues to be significant then other researchers are more likely to accept its validity.

To recap for a moment: all we are doing is trying to decide if a 'score' comes from one distribution or another. The overlap in distributions, when the distributions are different, makes it difficult to avoid the risk of error in setting our decision criterion, the significance level. We set the risk of a Type I error (α) by choosing the significance level. Yet we should not ignore β, the risk of a Type II error, as it is no fun trying to dig up treasure with a plastic bucket and spade. Increasing the power of a test reduces β and gives us a better chance of finding treasure when it really is there.

Chapter 10

Introduction to the analysis of variance

THE *t* TEST IS LIMITED in two ways. First, it allows a comparison of only two samples at a time, such as old men versus young men on a particular task. In many cases we want to compare a number of samples, not just two, such as young men, middle-aged men and old men on the same task, and the *t* test cannot do this. Second, the *t* test examines the effect of only one independent variable, such as *age* or *teaching method*, at a time whereas we may want to compare them in combination. The analysis of variance is similar to the *t* test but is without these restrictions. It is for this reason that the analysis of variance (or ANOVA as it is known) is a very popular statistical technique in a range of research fields.

Factors and conditions

In the following chapters I shall be referring to independent variables as factors as that is the term used in the analysis of variance, so *age*, *hair colour* and *type of school attended* are all examples of factors. The conditions are the categories of the independent variable we choose to study. These are also referred to by other terms such as groups, levels or treatments, but I shall use conditions throughout. If we were investigating the independent variable of age we might select the conditions: 20 year olds, 40 year olds and 60 year olds. These age groups are the three conditions of the factor under study. We could, of course, choose different conditions for the variable *age* if we wish.

The problem of many conditions and the *t* test

Consider the situation where you want to compare more than two conditions. Rather than comparing children in a small school with children in a large school, you might want to compare a range of schools of different sizes (that we could label A, B, C, etc.). Similarly, you might want to compare three different teaching methods (A, B and C) on a group of children. The problem is to find a way to analyse the findings statistically. One solution would be to perform a number of t tests, comparing each different pair of conditions: A and B, B and C, C and A, when there are three conditions. But we do not do this for the following reasons.

We have to perform three tests instead of one. If we had four conditions we would have to undertake six different tests and if there were ten conditions the number of tests would be forty-five! We really need one single test that allows us to deal with more than two conditions simultaneously, in fact a test that we do once and not have to do forty-five times.

The second and more important reason why we do not do lots of t tests is that the more t tests we perform on the data the more likely we are to make a Type I error (accept a result as significant when it occurred by chance). With one test, with $\alpha = 0.05$, we have a probability of 0.05 of making a Type I error. This means we have a probability of $1 - \alpha$ or 0.95 of *not* making a Type 1 error. If we perform two tests, each at the 0.05 level of significance, the probability of not making a Type I error becomes $0.95 \times 0.95 = 0.90$. The probability of making a Type I error in the tests is $1 - 0.90 = 0.10$. Already the probability of making at least one Type I error has doubled. With ten tests the probability of at least one Type I error rises to 0.40, or a 40 per cent chance.

If we want the *overall* significance level of a number of tests to be 0.05, then we have to set the significance level of each of the individual tests at a much more conservative level. If, for example, we undertake five tests then the significance level for each individual test has to be set at $p = 0.01$ for the overall risk of a Type I error to be 0.05 (as $1 - 0.99 \times 0.99 \times 0.99 \times 0.99 \times 0.99 = 0.05$).

The alternative is to devise a single test which has the same effect as the multiple comparisons but with an overall significance level set at $p = 0.05$. It is this alternative test that we consider now.

Why do scores vary in an experiment?

If we look at a set of data we find that not all the scores are identical. Why is there this variability in the data? The answer to this question holds the key to the analysis of variance as a means of hypothesis testing. Let us take an example to demonstrate this. We want to know the effect of the frequency of a word in the language on anagram solution times. We select a number of conditions, such as Common Words, Less Frequent Words, and Rare Words. We might use a computer-based store of words in the language (accessible over the Internet, which gives the frequency of a word in a vast body of text) to select words appropriate to our conditions. In choosing words we make sure they differ in frequency but not in word length or other possible confounding factors. We then record the time it takes participants to solve a set of anagrams in each of the three conditions.

The null hypothesis predicts that the scores in all three conditions come from the same distribution. If there are differences between the mean solution times for the three conditions can we reject the null hypothesis and claim a genuine difference between the distributions of solution times according to word frequency? Unfortunately not, because even when the null hypothesis is true we will still find that we do not get equal means in the various conditions. What we need to find out is what causes the variation in the scores and how we can detect when the variation has arisen because of the manipulation of the factor, *word frequency*, and not for other reasons, such as the chance variation we would expect even when the null hypothesis is true.

Random variation in an experiment

It is unlikely that the participants in the same condition will produce exactly the same time for solving the anagrams. These are scores from a distribution and some participants will be fast and others slow rather than every one producing the population mean. The result is a sample of scores from a population and even if we select our sample randomly from the population there will be unsystematic or random errors that can lead to differences in the scores, and differences between the sample mean and the population mean. Even when the null hypothesis is true we would still expect the scores in the conditions to vary by random error and the means of the conditions to vary for the same reason.

When the scores come from different subjects one major category of random error is that of individual differences: participants will differ on their anagram solving ability, crossword puzzle experience and so forth. We can see from this why we need to select randomly from the population. If we select in a biased way, such as choosing only good crossword puzzlers, then their times would be systematically distorted from the population mean making them a poor estimate of it and we would not be able to generalise from our result to the wider population.

As well as individual differences, there will be a collection of other random errors, due to the difficulty of setting up equivalent conditions for the participants. Someone might drop a pencil on the floor, another might remember a word from the crossword in that morning's newspaper and a third might be distracted by a noise. These could influence the anagram solution times. Thus we would expect scores to differ in an experiment due to a range of random errors regardless of whether the null hypothesis is true or not.

Systematic variation in the scores

If the null hypothesis is true and there are no differences in the populations of solution times for the different conditions of word frequency then any differences we find between condition means should be due to random error only. However, when the null hypothesis is false, the scores between conditions might be drawn from different populations (unlike the scores within a condition) and when this is the case we should find systematic differences between the conditions. We have deliberately chosen the anagrams so that they differ on word frequency between the conditions. If Common Word anagrams really are easier to solve than Less Frequent Word anagrams then we would expect this difference in population means to be reflected in our scores. If word frequency does affect solution times then we should expect systematic differences in the scores between conditions (known as a treatment effect). This is what we are looking for, evidence that there are genuine differences in the population means of the anagram solution times between the conditions.

Random errors and systematic differences

Scores in an experiment will vary due to random errors and systematic differences. If we have selected our subjects appropriately we would expect random errors to occur anywhere in the data rather than focused in any one condition. However, if there is a genuine effect of the independent variable and it does affect the scores then we would expect systematic differences between the scores in the different conditions. The random errors will provide a certain level of variability in the data both within and between the conditions, a sort of 'background noise' in the results. If the null hypothesis is false and there really are differences between the conditions we would expect this to appear as a systematic difference in the scores from the different conditions, over and above the 'background noise'.

Look at the three examples of results to this experiment in the table below.

	(a)			(b)			(c)		
	CW	LFW	RW	CW	LFW	RW	CW	LFW	RW
	17	16	19	18	18	40	20	30	40
	16	18	25	21	18	44	19	30	41
	22	21	19	16	20	38	21	31	39
	16	18	25	21	18	42	20	29	41
	23	24	18	18	23	37	21	29	40
	20	23	20	20	23	39	19	31	39
Mean	19	20	21	19	20	40	20	30	40

(The initials CW, LFW and RW in the table stand for Common Words, Less Frequent Words and Rare Words respectively. The scores are in minutes.)

What can we say about the causes of the variability of the scores in (a), (b) and (c)? The key thing is to decide whether there are systematic differences in the scores between the conditions. In example (a) there are differences between the condition means but only of 1. This is actually quite small compared to the 'background noise' of the random variability: there are both high and low scores in all three conditions. A set of results like this could quite easily occur when the null hypothesis is true and there are no genuine differences between the populations from which the samples are drawn. Example (b) looks more indicative of an underlying difference, but only between the Rare Words and the other conditions. All the high scores are in the Rare Word condition and a mean of 40 differs by at least 10 from the other condition means and looks larger than the variability in the data that could arise from random variability alone. In this example, there appears to be a difference in the underlying population distribution for Rare Words compared to the other two but not between Common Words and Less Frequent Words. Finally, in example (c) we have large differences between all three means that seem to dominate any random variability, indicating that the three conditions have drawn samples from different distributions.

What we need to do now is to produce a statistic that formally analyses the variability of the scores in an experiment, in an equivalent manner to my informal 'eyeballing' of the above examples and allows us to decide when the variability of the scores between conditions indicates genuine differences between populations (such as in examples (b) and (c)) and when it indicates only the random variation that we would expect by chance, when the null hypothesis is true (example (a)).

Calculating the variability of scores

We need to express the variability of the scores statistically. Up to now we have used the standard deviation to do this for a sample of scores: $\sqrt{\dfrac{\sum(X - \bar{X})^2}{n - 1}}$. Now we are interested in comparing different sources of variability, to find whether there are systematic differences between conditions as well as random variability in the data, rather than seeking a standard difference from the mean. For this reason, and because we don't want to have to keep working out square roots, it is much easier for us to use variance, the square of the standard deviation:

$$\text{Sample variance, } s^2 = \frac{\sum(X - \bar{X})^2}{n - 1}$$

At the heart of the variance calculation is the sums of squares: $\sum(X - \bar{X}^2)$. This measures the variability of the scores from the mean of the sample. When the scores vary wildly from the mean the sums of squares is large and when they cluster round the mean the sums of squares is small. This is what we want for our analysis of variability.

The sums of squares is also affected by the number of scores in the sample. The more scores we have the larger the sums of squares, even though the variability of the scores is no greater, as each extra score (unless exactly the same as the mean) will add to it. Consider the two samples, Sample 1 with scores 1, 1, 2, 3, 3 and Sample 2 with scores 1, 2, 3. Their variability looks about the same, with scores deviating from the mean by no more than 1. We can see from the table below that because there are more scores in Sample 1 the sums of squares is much larger.

Sample 1		
X	$X - \bar{X}$	$(X - \bar{X})^2$
1	−1	1
1	−1	1
2	0	0
3	1	1
3	1	1

Sums of squares = $\Sigma(X - \bar{X}^2)$
= 4

Sample 2		
X	$X - \bar{X}$	$(X - \bar{X})^2$
1	−1	1
2	0	0
3	1	1

Sums of squares = $\Sigma(X - \bar{X}^2)$
= 2

In order to take account of this we need to divide the sums of squares by the degrees of freedom, $df = n - 1$, to produce an 'average' variability of a score in the sample. (Recall from Chapter 5 that we use the degrees of freedom when dealing with samples as this produces a better estimate of the population parameter we are interested in.) There are five scores in Sample 1 so $n = 5$ and $df = n - 1 = 5 - 1 = 4$. This produces a variance of 1. In Sample 2 $n = 3$ and $df = 2$. This also produces a variance of 1. This matches our intuitive view that there is the same variability in these two samples.

We are interested in the variability produced by different factors in our data: random error and systematic differences and we can use the variance formula to find it.

The process of analysing variability

The useful thing about sums of squares is that we can calculate it for different portions of the data. We can work out the total sums of squares, taking into account every single score irrespective of condition. Using the data below, the overall mean is 10, taking into account all 18 scores, and the total sums of squares is 328.

	Condition 1	Condition 2	Condition 3
	5	11	14
	6	10	15
	7	9	17
	5	11	13
	3	9	17
	4	10	14
Mean	5	10	15

We can also work out the sums of squares for the scores within a single condition. The scores in Condition 1 have a mean of 5 and a sums of squares of the six scores is 10, for Condition 2 the sums of squares is 4 and for Condition 3 it is 14. If we add these up it will provide us with a measure of the variability of the scores within the conditions. The within conditions sums of squares is therefore 28 (the sum: $10 + 4 + 14$). The scores also vary between the conditions. If we take just the three condition means 5, 10 and 15 they have a mean of 10 and a sums of squares of 50. These are not scores but means and each mean is composed of 6 scores so we multiply the figure of 50 by 6 to get the variability of the scores (rather than the means) between the conditions. The between conditions sums of squares is 300. If we use the label SS_{total} for the total sums of squares and $SS_{with.conds}$ and $SS_{bet.conds}$ for the within and between conditions sums of squares respectively, we can see that:

$$SS_{total} = SS_{with.conds} + SS_{bet.conds}$$
$$328 = 28 + 300$$

We can also separate the degrees of freedom in the same way. There are 18 scores in the experiment so the total degrees of freedom, $df_{total} = 18 - 1 = 17$. There are 6 scores in each condition giving $6 - 1 = 5$ degrees of freedom within each condition. Adding up the degrees of freedom within the three conditions we produce the within conditions degrees of freedom, $df_{with.conds}$, of 15. There are 3 conditions so there are $3 - 1 = 2$ between conditions degrees of freedom, $df_{bet.conds}$. We also see that:

$$df_{total} = df_{with.conds} + df_{bet.conds}$$
$$17 = 15 + 2$$

As we can partition both the sums of squares and the degrees of freedom into components we can also work out the variance within and between the conditions.

The variance ratio

What we want to do is to work out how much variability in the experiment is due to our manipulation, that is, the systematic differences between the conditions. The between conditions variance will tell us the 'average' variability between the conditions. This will arise from systematic differences between the conditions (if there are any) plus random errors (that will occur anywhere). This is not enough on its own to detect a difference in populations because this variance could be large for more than one reason; the systematic differences might be large or the random errors might be large, or both. What we need to do now is estimate the size of the variability due to the random errors.

Within a condition the scores will only vary due to random errors but not systematic differences (as the subjects within a condition will be performing in the same circumstances – we are not manipulating the independent variable within a condition). Assuming that random errors affect all scores equally (otherwise they would not be random) we can take the variance within the conditions as an estimate of the variance due to random errors, the error variance.[7]

Now if we compare the variance between conditions with the variance within conditions we will have a statistic for uncovering systematic differences between our conditions if there are any. We call this statistic, F, the variance ratio:

$$\text{Variance ratio } (F) = \frac{\text{Between conditions variance}}{\text{Error variance}}$$

This can also be expressed as follows:

$$\text{Variance ratio } (F) = \frac{\text{Systematic differences} + \text{Error variance}}{\text{Error variance}}$$

Note that the only difference between the top and the bottom of our equation is the systematic differences between the conditions, the error variance affecting the top and bottom equally. If there really are systematic differences between the conditions this should show up by a large value of F.

Alternatively, if the null hypothesis is true, and there are no differences between the distributions that the samples are drawn from, then we would expect to find no systematic differences between the conditions. Thus, when the null hypothesis is true, we would expect:

$$F = \frac{0 + \text{Error variance}}{\text{Error variance}} = \frac{\text{Error variance}}{\text{Error variance}} = 1$$

When the null hypothesis is true we expect F to equal 1 as the top and bottom of the equation are the same. When the null hypothesis is false we expect to find systematic differences between conditions and F to be greater than 1, with large systematic differences producing a large value of F.

The F distribution

Clearly, we need to know how large our calculated value of F must be for it to be significant at the level of significance chosen. What we need is the sampling distribution of F when the null hypothesis is true. If we select samples from the same distribution for our experimental conditions and calculated F, what values of F would we get?

First, the F values would cluster around 1 as there are no systematic differences between the conditions and the two variances making up the equation are likely to be equal. Second, F will never be less than zero as it is a ratio of numbers that have been squared and squares are never negative. This also means that we are only interested in one tail of the F distribution, the upper end: how much bigger than 1 the F value must be in order to reject the null hypothesis.

Like the t distribution F is also an estimate. We are using the variances of samples to estimate population values. Again, like t, the accuracy of this estimation will depend on the degrees of freedom of the estimate. Unlike t, however, the F statistic depends on two variances, the between conditions variance and the error variance, and so will be influenced by the degrees of freedom of both. This means that there is a different F distribution for each combination of the two degrees of freedom. Fortunately, the F distributions are known and the critical values for significance have been calculated for each combination (Table A.3 of the Appendix). As a result we can compare our calculated value of F with the appropriate table value to decide whether there are significant differences between the conditions or not.

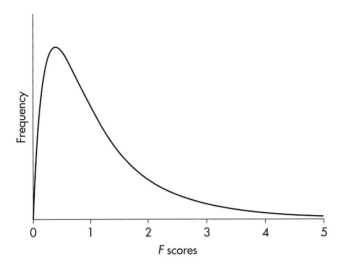

FIGURE 10.1 An example of an F distribution (degrees of freedom = 4,8)

In order to use the *F* distribution for comparison we have to make a number of assumptions: the samples for our conditions come from normally distributed populations, the samples come from distributions with equal variance, and the samples are randomly selected. These are very much the same assumptions that underlie the *t* test. When we perform the analysis of variance we must make these assumptions too, otherwise it may be inappropriate to compare our calculated value of *F* with those in the tables.

It is not surprising that I have been saying 'like *t*' throughout this section, for there is a simple relationship between *F* and *t* in the case where we can compare them (with two conditions): $F = t^2$. There is a demonstration of this in the next chapter. Figure 10.1 gives an example of an *F* distribution. It may look a little strange but imagine that all the scores in a *t* distribution (such as in Figure 6.2) were squared. All the negative values would become positive and it would turn into an *F* distribution like Figure 10.1. Another point to note about the fact that *F* is made up of squared numbers is that we no longer have the distinction between one-tailed and two-tailed tests. The squared values mean that any differences between the condition means will add to the size of *F*. Our prediction for *F* is simply that there are significant systematic differences between the conditions somewhere. A large value of *F* could mean that all the conditions differ significantly from each other or it could mean that only one differs from the others. It often needs further investigation to pin down the meaning of a significant *F* value.

Conclusion

By studying the variability in the data we have produced a statistic, the variance ratio F, that analyses the variance due to various factors in the data. The variance between the conditions contains the systematic differences between the conditions that we are seeking out. It also comprises the random errors that we expect with any data that we collect. Fortunately, we can estimate this error variance by looking at the data that is not affected by the systematic differences between conditions, the within conditions variance. When we examine the ratio of these two variances we have a statistic that provides an estimate of the systematic differences between conditions. If the calculated value of F is greater than the critical value of the F distribution at the chosen level of significance (say $p = 0.05$ or $p = 0.01$) then we can reject the null hypothesis and conclude that there are significant differences between at least some of the conditions.

By performing an analysis of variance we no longer have the problem of increasing the risk of Type I errors, as all conditions are compared in the one test, examined at a chosen level of significance. In the following chapters we shall see how the analysis of variance can be used to analyse data from a variety of different experimental designs.

Chapter 11

One factor independent measures ANOVA

THE ONE FACTOR independent measures ANOVA is similar to the independent *t* test but allows us to compare more than two conditions. It analyses data from an independent measures design, that is, employing different subjects in each condition. If we wanted to compare only two groups, such as 5 year old children to 7 year old children on a reading test then we could use either the *t* test or the ANOVA. We would get the same outcome regardless of which test we used. However, if we wanted to compare more groups, say, 5, 6 and 7 year olds then we would undertake the analysis of variance. (This form of ANOVA is also called the completely randomised design ANOVA.)

Analysing variability in the independent measures ANOVA

In the previous chapter we saw that the variability of the scores between the conditions arose from systematic differences between conditions plus random errors. In the independent measures design there are different subjects providing the scores for the different conditions, so part of the between conditions variance will be due to individual differences between the subjects. This is a random error as we are not systematically varying subjects across the conditions. The other random errors can be termed experimental error as we will always get some random errors in any experiment despite our attempts to provide equivalent conditions for the subjects. The between conditions variance can be seen as arising from three sources: systematic differences between the conditions, individual differences and experimental error.

If we look at the variability of the scores within the conditions we see that there are no systematic differences (if we have carried out the experiment properly) but there are still different subjects within a condition so we do expect variability due to individual differences. Again, as always, we expect other random errors that once again we can term experimental error as we expect it to occur at random anywhere in the experiment. The within conditions variance thus comprises two components: individual differences and experimental error. Therefore the within conditions variance provides us with the 'error variance' we need as it is influenced by the same variability as the between conditions variance apart from the systematic differences between conditions. Comparing the between conditions variance with the within conditions variance will provide us with a variance ratio that we can compute and compare with the distribution of F in the search for an effect of our independent variable on the dependent variable.

We want to produce an F that is the following ratio:

$$F = \frac{\text{Systematic differences} + \text{Error variance}}{\text{Error variance}}$$

We can achieve this with the following:

$$F = \frac{\text{Between conditions variance}}{\text{Within conditions variance}}$$

This is because these variances only differ in the systematic differences between the conditions:

$$F = \frac{\text{Systematic differences} + \text{Individual differences} + \text{Experimental Error}}{\text{Individual differences} + \text{Experimental Error}}$$

To calculate F we must work out the between and within conditions variance.

The ANOVA summary table

The calculation of F requires us to build up the various components of the analysis of variance: the sums of squares, the degrees of freedom, the variances etc. In order to do this correctly and to display the results of the calculation clearly we produce an ANOVA summary table.

The summary table lists the sources of the variation in the scores as rows in the table. In the one factor independent measures ANOVA we are concerned with the variance between conditions and within conditions. We also need the total variability in the data in order to calculate the various sums of squares required. The columns provide the intermediate stages in the production of the variances needed for the variance ratio along with the final calculation of F and whether it is significant or not. We need the sums of squares and degrees of freedom to calculate variance. In the terminology of the analysis of variance we refer to variance as mean square (MS). It is simply an alternative label for the same thing. It can be considered more descriptive in this context because dividing the sums of squares by the degrees of freedom produces an 'average' of the 'squares'.

The significance or otherwise of the calculated value of F can be indicated in the table in two ways. One, the specific probability of the F score of this size arising from the null hypothesis can be given: for example, $p = 0.0145$. In this case the reader can observe whether the probability is larger or smaller than a chosen significance level, such as $p = 0.05$. Alternatively, the probability can be given in relation to the significance level, such as $p < 0.05$ to indicate that the F value is significant at the $p = 0.05$ level of significance and $p > 0.05$ to indicate that it is not significant at the 0.05 significance level. I will use the latter convention.

For the one factor independent measures ANOVA the summary table is laid out in the following manner:

THE ANOVA SUMMARY TABLE

Source of variation	Degrees of freedom	Sums of squares	Mean square	Variance ratio (F)	Probability
Between conditions	$df_{bet.conds}$	$SS_{bet.conds}$	$MS_{bet.conds}$	F	p
Within conditions	df_{error}	SS_{error}	MS_{error}		
Total	df_{total}	SS_{total}			

Notice that we only fill in the cells in the table we need for the variance ratio calculation. For example, we do not need the total variance as this is not required in the calculation of F. Below are listed the formulae for the calculation.

Degrees of freedom:

$$df_{total} = N - 1 \qquad \text{where } N \text{ is the total number of scores.}$$

$$df_{bet.conds} = k - 1 \qquad \text{where } k \text{ is the number of conditions.}$$

$$df_{error} = df_{total} - df_{bet.conds}$$

Sums of squares:

$$SS_{total} = \sum X^2 - \frac{(\sum X)^2}{N}$$

where $\sum X^2$ is the sum of the squared scores and $(\sum X)^2$ is the square of the sum of the scores.[8]

$$SS_{bet.conds} = \frac{\sum T^2}{n} - \frac{(\sum X)^2}{N}$$

where T refers to a total of the scores in a condition. $\sum T^2$ is the sum of the squared totals of the conditions and n is the number of scores in each condition.

$$SS_{error} = SS_{total} - SS_{bet.conds}$$

Mean square:

$$MS_{bet.conds} = \frac{SS_{bet.conds}}{df_{bet.conds}}$$

$$MS_{error} = \frac{SS_{error}}{df_{error}}$$

Variance ratio:

$$F = \frac{MS_{bet.conds}}{Ms_{error}}$$

We must always include the two degrees of freedom with our F value. We write it thus:

$$F(df_{bet.conds}, df_{error}) = \text{calculated value}$$

We compare the calculated value with the critical value in the F distribution tables at our chosen level of significance. When we look up the table value (Table A.3 in the Appendix) we use $df_{bet.conds}$ as our first degrees of freedom (the columns in the table) and df_{error} as our second degrees of freedom (the rows in the table). Our calculated value of F is only significant if it is equal to or larger than the table value.

A worked example

A researcher was interested in the effects of hints on anagram solution. The time it took a participant to solve five eight-letter anagrams was measured. The same five anagrams were used in three conditions: First Letter (where the first letter of the word was given), Last Letter (where the last letter was given) and No Letter (where no help was given). Thirty participants were chosen and ten were randomly allocated to each condition. The number of minutes it took to solve the five anagrams was recorded. These results are shown below. Is there an effect of *type of hint* (the independent variable) on solution times (the dependent variable)?

	First Letter Condition 1 X_1	Last Letter Condition 2 X_2	No Letter Condition 3 X_3
	15	21	28
	20	25	30
	14	29	32
	13	18	28
	18	26	26
	16	22	30
	13	26	25
	12	24	36
	18	28	20
	11	21	25
Mean	$\bar{X}_1 = 15.00$	$\bar{X}_2 = 24.00$	$\bar{X}_3 = 28.00$
Total	$T_1 = 150$	$T_2 = 240$	$T_3 = 280$
Squared total	$T_1^2 = 22500$	$T_2^2 = 57600$	$T_3^2 = 78400$

Sum of the scores (overall total): $\sum X = 670$
Square of the sum of the scores: $(\sum X)^2 = 448900$
Sum of the squared scores: $\sum X^2 = 16210$

Number of conditions: $k = 3$
Number of scores per condition: $n = 10$
Total number of scores: $N = 30$

Degrees of freedom:

$$df_{total} = N - 1 = 30 - 1 = 29$$
$$df_{bet.conds} = k - 1 = 3 - 1 = 2$$
$$df_{error} = df_{total} - df_{bet.conds} = 29 - 2 = 27$$

Sums of squares:

$$SS_{total} = \sum X^2 - \frac{(\sum X)^2}{N} = 16210 - \frac{448900}{30}$$
$$= 16210 - 149363.33 = 1246.67$$

$$SS_{bet.conds} = \frac{\sum T^2}{n} - \frac{(\sum X)^2}{N} = \frac{22500 + 57600 + 78400}{10} - \frac{448900}{30}$$
$$= 15850 - 14963.33 = 886.67$$

$$SS_{error} = SS_{total} - SS_{bet.conds} = 1246.67 - 886.67 = 360.00$$

Mean square:

$$MS_{bet.conds} = \frac{SS_{bet.conds}}{df_{bet.conds}} = \frac{886.67}{2} = 443.33$$

$$MS_{error} = \frac{SS_{error}}{df_{error}} = \frac{360.00}{27} = 13.33$$

Variance ratio (F):

$$F = \frac{MS_{bet.conds}}{MS_{error}} = \frac{443.33}{13.33} = 33.26$$

From the tables of the F distribution (Table A.3 in the Appendix) we find that $F(2,27) = 3.35$, at $p = 0.05$. As our value of 33.26 is greater than the table value we can reject the null hypothesis and claim that anagram solution times are affected by the type of hint given. Note that the result is highly significant, so we can adopt an even more conservative significance level. From the tables $F(2,27) = 5.49$, at $p = 0.01$, so our finding is still significant at $p < 0.01$.

The fact that we have found a significant effect does not tell us which conditions are significantly different although we can infer this by looking at the means. We will be able to be more specific in the following chapter. Also the F test has found significant differences between the conditions but it does not give the cause. We hope the experiment is so well controlled that it can only be due to *type of hint* but if the researcher introduced any inadvertent confounding factor this could also have produced the systematic differences picked up by the analysis of variance.

THE ANOVA SUMMARY TABLE

Source of variation	Degrees of freedom	Sums of squares	Mean square	Variance ratio (F)	Probability
Between conditions	2	886.67	443.33	33.26	$p < 0.01$
Within conditions	27	360.00	13.33		
Total	29	1246.67			

The above table clearly summarises the analysis. It also allows us to check our calculations: do the degrees of freedom and the sums of squares add up to the correct totals? You must never get a negative sums of squares as a sum of squares has to be positive. If you do, check the calculations, there is definitely an error.

Rejecting the null hypothesis

When we reject the null hypothesis in an ANOVA, as we have done in the example above, we are only concluding that there are systematic differences between the conditions but not where they lie. In the case of three conditions there are four alternative hypotheses to the null hypothesis:

1   All three conditions are significantly different, their samples come from different population distributions.
2   Condition 1 is significantly different to conditions 2 and 3 but conditions 2 and 3 are not significantly different. The sample in condition 1 comes from a different distribution to the samples of conditions 2 and 3.

3   Condition 2 is significantly different to conditions 1 and 3 but conditions 1 and 3 are not significantly different. The sample in condition 2 comes from a different distribution to the samples of conditions 1 and 3.

4   Condition 3 is significantly different to conditions 1 and 2 but conditions 1 and 2 are not significantly different. The sample in condition 3 comes from a different distribution to the samples of conditions 1 and 2.

With more conditions the number of alternative hypothesis increases. A significant F value simply indicates that the null hypothesis is very unlikely and hence we can reject it. We need to perform further tests to decide which one of the alternative hypotheses to accept.

Unequal sample sizes

Researchers often organise the samples in the independent measures ANOVA so that there are equal numbers of subjects in each condition. It is not necessary but makes the calculation slightly easier. Yet the test, like the independent t test, allows for different sample sizes. The formulae given above are for equal sample sizes. However, the only change we need to make for unequal sample sizes is to the first term in the $SS_{bet.conds}$ formula. We replace $SS_{bet.conds} = \dfrac{\sum T^2}{n} - \dfrac{(\sum X)^2}{N}$ with $SS_{bet.conds} = \sum \left(\dfrac{T^2}{n} \right) - \dfrac{(\sum X)^2}{N}$.

We have a different n for each sample and we divide the squared total of each condition by its sample size *before* we add them up. A worked example is shown below.

Unequal sample sizes usually occur when you have planned for equal numbers in each condition but for some reason a subject is unable to provide a score. In the anagram example we might find a person who simply cannot solve an anagram no matter how much time allowed. One solution is to replace the participant with another. However, the change to the formula is so small that unequal sample sizes are not really a problem (as long as the equal population variance assumption is still met).

A worked example

As an example of the calculation of unequal sample sizes I shall take the data we used to calculate the independent t test in Chapter 8. This compared the effects of a sleeping pill on 6 men and 8 women. The scores for the men

(Condition 1) were 4, 6, 5, 4, 5 and 6 extra hours slept and for the women (Condition 2) were 3, 8, 7, 6, 7, 6, 7 and 6 extra hours.

Sum of the scores (overall total): $\sum X = 80$
Square of the sum of the scores: $(\sum X)^2 = 6400$
Sum of the squared scores: $\sum X^2 = 482$

Number of conditions: $k = 2$
Number of scores per condition: $n_1 = 6$, $n_2 = 8$
Total of the scores in condition 1, $T_1 = 30$ and the squared total, $T_1^2 = 900$
Total of the scores in condition 2, $T_2 = 50$ and the squared total, $T_2^2 = 2500$
Total number of scores: $N = 14$

Degrees of freedom:

$$df_{total} = N - 1 = 14 - 1 = 13$$

$$df_{bet.conds} = k - 1 = 2 - 1 = 1$$

$$df_{error} = df_{total} - df_{bet.conds} = 13 - 1 = 12$$

Sums of squares:

$$SS_{total} = \sum X^2 - \frac{(\sum X)^2}{N} = 482 - \frac{6400}{14}$$

$$= 482 - 457.14 = 24.86$$

$$SS_{bet.conds} = \sum \left(\frac{T^2}{n}\right) - \frac{(\sum X)^2}{N} = \left(\frac{900}{6} + \frac{2500}{8}\right) - \frac{6400}{14}$$

$$= 462.5 - 457.14 = 5.36$$

where $\sum \left(\frac{T^2}{n}\right) = \left(\frac{T_1^2}{n_1} + \frac{T_2^2}{n_2}\right)$ as there are two conditions.

$$SS_{error} = SS_{total} - SS_{bet.conds} = 24.86 - 5.36 = 19.50$$

Mean square:

$$MS_{bet.conds} = \frac{SS_{bet.conds}}{df_{bet.conds}} = \frac{5.36}{1} = 5.36$$

$$MS_{error} = \frac{SS_{error}}{df_{error}} = \frac{19.50}{12} = 1.625$$

Variance ratio (F):

$$F = \frac{MS_{bet.conds}}{MS_{error}} = \frac{5.36}{1.625} = 3.30$$

THE ANOVA SUMMARY TABLE

Source of variation	Degrees of freedom	Sums of squares	Mean square	Variance ratio (F)	Probability
Between conditions	1	5.36	5.36	3.30	$p > 0.05$
Within conditions	12	19.50	1.625		
Total	13	24.86			

From the F distribution tables (Table A.3 in the Appendix) we find $F(1,12)$ = 4.75 at $p = 0.05$. As the calculated value of 3.30 is less than the table value we cannot reject the null hypothesis at this level of significance.

The relationship of F to t

The example in the section above allows us to compare an ANOVA with an independent t test on the same two samples. If you look back to the t calculations you can see the similarity in the calculations; for example note the SS_{error} of 1.625 in the bottom of the t calculation. If we explored further we could see how the two formulae are related. The calculated F of 3.30 is indeed the square of the calculated t of 1.82.[9] Similarly, the table values of F and t are also related in the same way and so we have the same outcome whichever of the tests we perform on the data.

Details on calculating the one factor independent measures ANOVA using the SPSS computer statistical package can be found in Chapter 10 of Hinton *et al.* (2004).

Multiple comparisons

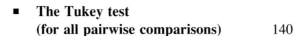

W HEN WE COMPARE more than two groups in an ANOVA a signifi-cant F value does not indicate where the effect lies, simply that there is an effect between the conditions somewhere. A researcher compared four groups of children (6, 8, 10 and 12 year olds) on a test of social skills. She found a significant F value and concluded that the scores from the four conditions were not drawn from the same distribution. But this conclusion does not really provide the researcher with the information about which ages show the significant differences. Let us assume that the means were respectively 10, 12, 18 and 23 on the test (out of 50). Given that there is a significance variance ratio it seems likely that the scores of the 6 year olds differ significantly from those of the 12 year olds as this comparison provides the largest difference in means. Is the difference between the 6 and 8 year olds or 8 year olds and 10 year olds significant? And what about the smallest difference, between the 6 and 8 year olds? The data needs to be inspected further to find the source of the significant F value.

The way we answer these questions is to perform post hoc tests. The name comes from the Latin, meaning 'after this'. The first stage in the analysis is to find a significant F value in the ANOVA. Only then do we perform a post hoc test. These tests are called multiple comparison tests as they allow us to undertake various comparisons between the conditions. In the example above we want to compare each of the four groups with each of the others to show where the significant differences lie.

The problem with multiple comparisons is that the more comparisons we make using the same data the greater the risk of making at least one Type I error. We saw in Chapter 10 that this was the same problem we had with undertaking multiple t tests: when we start undertaking multiple tests on the data we increase the risk of finding differences by chance. The solution is to find a post hoc test that takes account of this increased risk and controls for it.

There are a range of multiple comparison tests. Some of these ignore the problem completely. The Least Significant Difference test takes no account of the number of comparisons being made and the increased risk of a Type I error is simply accepted. Other tests such as the Newman–Keuls and the Duncan tests take account of the number of comparisons being made and compute different values accordingly. At the more conservative end of the scale the Tukey and Scheffé tests allow all comparisons to be made as the test corrects for the increased risk of Type I errors by reducing the significance level of the individual comparisons. The simplest and most conservative method is to apply a Bonferroni correction to the significance level. For example, if a one factor independent measures ANOVA had shown a significant F value then follow-up t tests on each of the 6 pairs of conditions could be undertaken with a Bonferroni correction to the significance level for these tests. The Bonferroni correction requires us to divide the significance level by the number of tests, so in this case we would compare each test against the 0.05/6 level of significance ($p = 0.0083$) rather than the 0.05 significance level. This does influence the power of the test (see Chapter 9) and can be viewed as overly conservative due to the reduction in power.

I am going to describe the Tukey and the Scheffé tests, both conservative tests, for the following reasons. Usually, after we have found a significant varaince ratio in the ANOVA, we want to compare all the conditions to find the interesting (significant) differences, such as in the social skills test example above. The Tukey and Scheffé tests allow us to do this without worrying unduly about the risks of Type I errors. Second, they are easy to carry out, particularly the Tukey test. The fact that they set high critical values for significance need not lead us to miss out on potentially significant findings because we have set too rigorous a criterion for significance. We might not accept some differences as significant when using these tests when we would with some other tests but this does not have to be a problem if we remember to use our judgment as researchers. If there is a difference which does not quite reach significance using these tests yet we have reason to believe that it is an important difference then, as in other cases of this kind, we should trust our judgement and follow it up: replicate the experiment, run more subjects, use a more sensitive design, essentially adopt measures to improve the power of our test. If it is a genuine difference it will eventually show, even with a Tukey test. Statistics are only tools to help us. They do not replace experimenter skill and intelligence. I happen to like a conservative test as it gives me confidence in the results of the analysis. But I do not let it disturb my interest in the comparisons that 'bubble under' (do not quite reach significance). I check these out in subsequent experiments.

The reason for presenting both the Tukey and the Scheffé tests is that the Tukey test is more sensitive for pairwise comparisons, comparing two conditions at a time, than the Scheffé test, in that it is more likely to accept a difference as significant. The Scheffé test, however, is more sensitive than the Tukey test for complex comparisons, combining conditions and comparing the composite condition with others, such as comparing the 8 year olds with the combination of the 10 and 12 year olds on the social skills test.

The Tukey test (for all pairwise comparisons)

The Tukey HSD (honestly significant difference) test allows us to compare each pair of conditions to see if their difference is significant. What the Tukey test does is to look at the random variation that exists between any pair of means. This is the standard error of the difference between pairs of means. If we then compare a specific difference between two means with this standard error we have a statistic for telling us how big the difference between the mean is compared to the random variation between means. We call this statistic q:

$$q = \frac{\text{the difference between any two means}}{\text{the standard error of the difference between any two means}}$$

We already have a measure of the error variance that we can take from the ANOVA, MS_{error}. The standard deviation is the square root of the variance: $\sqrt{MS_{error}}$ and so the standard error of the differences in means is $\frac{\sqrt{MS_{error}}}{\sqrt{n}}$, where n is the number of subjects in each condition. Hence:

$$q = \frac{\overline{X}_i - \overline{X}_j}{\sqrt{\dfrac{MS_{error}}{n}}}$$

where $\overline{X}_i$ and $\overline{X}_j$ are any two means (the i and j standing for 1, 2, 3, etc. or whichever means we choose to compare).

Notice the similarity of q to t. This is not by chance; the logic of the two statistics is the same. With a t test we use a different standard error for every pair of means:

$$t = \frac{\text{the difference between two means}}{\text{the standard error of the difference between the two means}}$$

With q, however, we are using a 'general purpose' standard error that can be used for any pair of means. Like t we can find the distribution of q

under the null hypothesis. Using this distribution we can decide whether a specific difference in means is significant by observing whether the calculated q exceeds the table value of q for the level of significance chosen. The Tukey test overcomes the problem of the increased risk of Type I errors that occurs with multiple t tests by setting an overall level of significance. This means that the risk of a Type 1 error has a probability of, say, 0.05 when we compare every pair of means. Thus the Tukey test allows *all* pairwise comparisons so we can work out q for each pair of means knowing that the risk of a Type I error will not exceed 0.05. In the social skills test example we can make six pairwise comparisons as we have four conditions. If we had five age groups: 6, 8, 10, 12 and 14 year olds, as long as we achieved a significant F in the ANOVA, the Tukey test would allow us to make every one of the 24 pairwise comparisons between condition means.

Rather than working out a q every time we compare a pair of means we can rearrange the formula as follows:

$$\bar{X}_i - \bar{X}_j = q\sqrt{\frac{MS_{error}}{n}}$$

If we no longer calculate q but use the critical value (for significance) of q from the table in the formula we can write:

An honestly significant difference between means, HSD $= q\sqrt{\dfrac{MS_{error}}{n}}$

All we need to do is look up q at the chosen significance level, work out Tukey's HSD and use HSD to compare any or all of the differences in means. If a difference in means is greater than HSD then that difference is significant (honestly!).

The statistic q is called the Studentized range statistic (after a famous statistician who wrote under the pseudonym of Student. You also see t referred to as Student's t for the same reason). We find the appropriate value of q in the table (Table A.4 in the Appendix) by deciding on the level of significance we require (usually either 0.05 or 0.01), and then looking up the critical value of q in the table using df_{error}, the degrees of freedom of the error variance in the ANOVA and k, the number of conditions in the experiment.

(Normally, with equal numbers of subjects in each condition the Tukey HSD test is easy to undertake but with different sample sizes we cannot put a single n in the equation for HSD as there are different ns: n_1, n_2, etc. To deal with this we can be cautious and simply take the smallest sample size as n. A more sophisticated way of producing a single ('average') n is by the following formula:

$$n = \frac{k}{\left(\dfrac{1}{n_1} + \dfrac{1}{n_2} + \ldots + \dfrac{1}{n_k}\right)}$$

where n_1 to n_k are the sample sizes. However, we should be wary of using the test with any but relatively small differences in sample sizes as the basic assumptions of the test may be violated.)

A worked example

The anagram example of the previous chapter provides a good example as we found a significant effect of *type of hint* on anagram solution times. The significant F value allows us to undertake post hoc tests, and see which differences in means are significant. The means are shown in the table below.

	First Letter $\overline{X}_1$	Last Letter $\overline{X}_2$	No Letter $\overline{X}_3$
Mean	15	24	28

Taking each pair of means we can work out the difference between them:

Difference of means	$\overline{X}_2$	$\overline{X}_3$
$\overline{X}_1$	−9	−13
$\overline{X}_2$		−4

The differences in the table are calculated by subtracting the column mean from the row mean. The fact that our differences are negative is a result of the way we have subtracted the means. This indicates $\overline{X}_1$ is faster than $\overline{X}_2$ by

9 minutes, etc. For the moment we are only concerned about the difference in the size of the means not whether the difference is positive or negative at this point. For the Tukey test we treat all the differences as positive.

From the ANOVA summary table we have $df_{error} = 27$ and $MS_{error} = 13.33$. The number of conditions, k, is 3, and the number of participants in each condition, $n = 10$. Selecting a significance level of $p = 0.05$, we can work out HSD. From the tables (Table A.4 in the Appendix) at $p = 0.05$, for $k = 3$ and $df_{error} = 27$, we find a value of q of 3.51. (As $df = 27$ is not in the table we take the figure midway between that for $df = 24$ and $df = 30$ for our value for $df = 27$.)

$$\text{HSD} = q\sqrt{\frac{MS_{error}}{n}} = 3.51 \times \sqrt{\frac{13.33}{10}} = 3.51 \times 1.15 = 4.04$$

The differences between the First Letter and No Letter conditions (13) and the First Letter and Last Letter conditions (9) are highly significant at $p = 0.05$ as they both exceed HSD. The difference between the Last Letter and No Letter conditions (4) is not significant at $p = 0.05$ but further investigations might find an effect here as the difference does approach significance but does not reach it. Now we know where the significant differences lie we check to see which way the differences occur (which condition produces the faster times) for our conclusion.

We can conclude that the First Letter condition results in significantly faster solution times than both the Last Letter and No Letter conditions. The Last Letter times are not significantly faster than the No Letter condition (although there appears be a non-significant tendency for the Last Letter times to be faster).

We can very easily work out confidence intervals for our comparisons, as we know the difference in means, we have the appropriate critical value and we also have a standard error (see Chapter 6 for an introduction to confidence intervals). So we can write the confidence interval as follows:

$$95\%\text{CI} = \overline{X}_i - \overline{X}_j \pm q\sqrt{\frac{MS_{error}}{n}}$$

where $\overline{X}_i$ and $\overline{X}_j$ are the two means we are comparing, q is the critical value (and we found that above) and $\sqrt{\frac{MS_{error}}{n}}$ is the standard error of the comparison (which we also found out above). Furthermore, $q\sqrt{\frac{MS_{error}}{n}} = \text{HSD}$, so:

$$95\%CI = \overline{X}_i - \overline{X}_j \pm HSD$$
$$95\%CI = \overline{X}_i - \overline{X}_j \pm 4.04$$

And now we can produce the confidence intervals for our three comparisons:

For $\overline{X}_1 - \overline{X}_2$, 95%CI = -9 ± 4.04, producing 95%CI = $(-13.04, -4.96)$
For $\overline{X}_1 - \overline{X}_3$, 95%CI = -13 ± 4.04, producing 95%CI = $(-17.04, -8.96)$
For $\overline{X}_2 - \overline{X}_3$, 95%CI = -4 ± 4.04, producing 95%CI = $(-8.04, +0.04)$

It is interesting to note that for the first two comparisons the differences are consistent across the confidence interval and even in the 'worst case' are still quite large (4.96 and 8.96 seconds difference). However, the third confidence interval includes zero so, even though the 'best case' gives us a difference of 8.04 seconds, the difference might still be zero. Even though the zero is near the end of the interval we cannot confidently exclude the possibility. The confidence intervals are expressing the findings in a different way to the significance test but the same implication arises: we can be confident that only the first two differences imply genuine population differences.

The Scheffé test (for complex comparisons)

Out of the 'between conditions sums of squares' the Scheffé test calculates the part of it relevant to the comparison being made. From the sums of squares of the comparison we can then go on to produce a mean square and then an F value for the comparison. We can test this against the F distribution to see if the comparison is significant. To correct for the increase in the risk of a Type I error that could arise with multiple comparisons we adjust the size of the table value of F according to the Scheffé correction. The calculated value of F for the comparison has to be larger than the corrected table value before we can claim a significant difference between the conditions being compared.

The Scheffé test is most useful for complex post hoc comparisons. In the example of the social skills experiment cited at the beginning of this chapter we shall assume that the researcher was interested in the difference between the children under 10 years old and the 10 year old group. Here we have a complex comparison, as two groups are being combined (the 6 and 8 year olds) to compare with the 10 year olds with one group being left out of the comparison (the 12 year olds) altogether.

The Scheffé test calculates a sums of squares for the comparison of interest by the following formula:

$$SS_{comp} = \frac{(\sum cT)^2}{n \sum c^2}$$

where the Ts are the totals of the scores in the conditions (T_1 is the total of the scores in condition 1, etc.), n is the number of subjects in each condition, and the cs are the <u>coefficients</u> of the conditions (c_1 is the coefficient of condition 1, etc.).

The choice of coefficients allows us to select the conditions we are interested in, in the correct combination, and exclude the conditions we do not wish to be included in the comparison. Essentially they 'weight' the contribution of the condition to the comparison. The conditions on one side of the comparison are given positive coefficients and the ones of the other side given negative coefficients. In order to properly balance the comparison the coefficients must sum to zero, $\sum c = 0$. In an experiment with three conditions where the comparison to be made is between condition 1 on one side with a combination of conditions 2 and 3 on the other then the coefficients could be $c_1 = +1$, $c_2 = -0.5$, $c_3 = -0.5$. Notice that the sum of the coefficients equal zero: $c_1 + c_2 + c_3 = 1 - 0.5 - 0.5 = 0$. Conditions 2 and 3 are equally weighted on their side of the comparison, as each is given the same coefficient of -0.5. The two sides of the comparison are equally weighted with $+1$ on one side and -1 on the other. (The actual numbers we choose for the coefficients can be anything as long as the above restrictions are met, so we could have chosen $+2, -1, -1$ for the coefficients or $+10, -5, -5$. We usually choose the ones that make the calculations easiest.)

The choice of coefficients results in a sums of squares for the comparison only. This comparison is always between two new conditions that are combinations of the experimental conditions. In the above paragraph the two new conditions are: condition 1 from the original experiment as the first new condition and a combination of conditions 2 and 3 as the second new condition. As there are always two conditions in the comparison the degrees of freedom for the comparison is always 1.

Hence the mean square for the comparison is:

$$MS_{comp} = \frac{SS_{comp}}{df_{comp}} = \frac{SS_{comp}}{1} = SS_{comp}$$

The calculated variance ratio for the comparison uses the error mean square from the original ANOVA, so the F value for the comparison is:

$$F = \frac{MS_{comp}}{MS_{error}}$$

At this point we must select the correct table value to compare our calculated F with. This depends on whether the comparison is <u>planned</u> prior to the calculation of the ANOVA or whether it was <u>unplanned</u>; that is, a post hoc comparison made after the significant ANOVA F value had been found.

A planned comparison

With a planned comparison we are saying that, prior to knowing whether the ANOVA F value was significant or not, we were interested in this comparison in particular. In this case we are not concerned with the increased risk of Type I errors with multiple comparisons as this is the only comparison of interest. Hence we can look up the table value using the degrees of freedom contributing to the comparison F value: df_{comp} and df_{error} at the chosen level of significance.

Unplanned comparisons

Unplanned comparisons are more usual in the use of the Scheffé test as post hoc tests are used to seek out the interesting results after a significant ANOVA. We may have certain comparisons in mind prior to the experiment but the data can lead us to follow up the most interesting, and unexpected, lines of research. As we wish to make any comparison *post hoc* we need to correct for the increased risk of a Type I error. The Scheffé test does this by creating a new, larger table value F'. Only if the calculated value exceeds F' can we say the comparison is significant. We calculate F' by the following formula: $F' = (k - 1)F$, where k is the number of conditions in the original experiment and F is the table value used in the original ANOVA, found using degrees of freedom $k - 1$ and $k(n - 1)$. The calculation of F' allows us to undertake any post hoc comparison without worrying about increasing the risk of a Type I error.

A worked example

At the beginning of this chapter I briefly mentioned a social skills study looking at four different age groups of children. The researcher was looking for an effect of age on the social skills test. The analysis produced the following summary table for the one factor independent measures ANOVA, with a highly significant F value:

THE ANOVA SUMMARY TABLE

Source of variation	Degrees of freedom	Sums of squares	Mean square	Variance ratio (F)	Probability
Between conditions	3	838.00	279.33	12.415	$p < 0.01$
Within conditions	28	630.00	22.50		
Total	31	1468.00			

In this experiment there were eight children in each condition. The totals of the scores of the four conditions are shown below:

Condition 1 6 year olds	Condition 2 8 year olds	Condition 3 10 year olds	Condition 4 12 year olds
T_1 80	T_2 96	T_3 144	T_4 184

The researcher decided post hoc that she wanted to know whether there was a significant difference between the 10 year olds and the younger children, combining the 6 and 8 year olds. To produce this comparison she chose the coefficients $c_1 = +1$, $c_2 = +1$, $c_3 = -2$ and $c_4 = 0$. These coefficients exclude condition 4 and combine conditions 1 and 2, which are then balanced on the other side of the comparison to condition 3.

The sums of squares of the comparison is calculated from the formula:

$$SS_{comp} = \frac{(c_1T_1 + c_2T_2 + c_3T_3 + c_4T_4)^2}{n(c_1^2 + c_2^2 + c_3^2 + c_4^2)}$$

$$SS_{comp} = \frac{((+1 \times 80) + (+1 \times 96) + (-2 \times 144) + (0 \times 184))^2}{8((+1)^2 + (+1)^2 + (-2)^2 + (0)^2)}$$

$$= \frac{-112^2}{8 \times 6} = \frac{12544}{48} = 261.33$$

As the degrees of freedom of the comparison is 1,

$$MS_{comp} = \frac{SS_{comp}}{df_{comp}} = \frac{261.33}{1} = 261.33$$

Using the error variance from the ANOVA,

$$F = \frac{MS_{comp}}{MS_{error}} = \frac{261.33}{22.50} = 11.61$$

We now calculate F':

$$F' = (k - 1)F(k - 1, k(n - 1)) = (4 - 1)F(4 - 1, 4(8 - 1))$$

$$= 3F(3, 28)$$

From the tables $F(3,28) = 2.95$, $p = 0.05$, so

$$F' = 3 \times 2.95 = 8.85$$

As the calculated value of F is greater than F' we can conclude that there is a significant difference in the performance of the 10 year olds compared to the combination of the 6 and 8 year olds on the social skills test, with the 10 year olds scoring significantly higher than the younger children.

One factor repeated measures ANOVA

$\mathbf{T}$HE INDEPENDENT MEASURES ANOVA assumes that the scores in each condition are unrelated and the subjects have contributed a score to only one of them. However, there are many cases when we want to use the same subjects in all conditions. This is particularly useful as it matches subjects with themselves across the conditions. An experiment on memory, comparing retention of different types of words might use the same participants in each condition (as long as the carry-over effects of practice or fatigue are controlled for). The analysis of variance that deals with this form of data is called a repeated measures design and, as we see below, the calculations are a little different to the independent measures design but the general logic of the ANOVA remains the same.

Deriving the *F* value

A research programme was set up to develop user-friendly computer equipment for those people with physical disabilities. Three new designs of computer keyboard for people with difficulties in hand and finger movement were developed and prototypes created. The research task was to decide which of these prototypes is the most successful. Four potential users of the new equipment agreed to take part in a test of the new keyboards. Each participant was asked to use the keyboard to input a piece of text and the number of errors was recorded. Three equally difficult pieces of text were used so that a participant did not improve performance by practice on the same piece of text. The choice of text and the order in which the keyboards were tested by each participant was controlled for, to account for possible confounding variables. The results of the experiment are shown below.

Participant	Keyboard 1	Keyboard 2	Keyboard 3
1	5	6	10
2	1	2	3
3	0	4	5
4	2	4	6

Notice that there is quite a bit of subject variability, with Participant 1 making the most mistakes and Participant 2 the least. Yet the repeated measures design matches the subjects with themselves across the conditions so that, even though they differ markedly from each other, the question is whether they follow a similar pattern across the conditions, i.e. is one condition the worst for all despite their differences in general accuracy?

If we performed an independent measures ANOVA on these data it would not be informative as it assumes that there is subject variability both between and within the conditions. We can see this by considering the way we calculate F for the independent measures design:

$$F = \frac{\text{Between conditions variance}}{\text{Within conditions variance}}$$

$$F = \frac{\text{Systematic differences} + \text{Individual differences} + \text{Experimental error}}{\text{Individual differences} + \text{Experimental error}}$$

Now as there are no individual differences between the conditions in the repeated measures design (as the subjects are the same) the same formula with repeated measures would produce:

$$F = \frac{\text{Between conditions variance}}{\text{Within conditions variance}}$$

$$= \frac{\text{Systematic differences} + \text{Experimental error}}{\text{Individual differences} + \text{Experimental error}}$$

This is not a very useful measure of the systematic differences between conditions as F is no longer sensitive to only this one factor but to the individual differences which are now only in the bottom of the equation. A large value of F could mean a large treatment effect but it could mean small individual differences. A small value of F might not mean a lack of systematic differences but simply large individual differences swamping the effect. If we can get rid of the individual differences from the within conditions variance (the bottom part of the formula) we will end up with an excellent formula for a repeated measures design as it will be highly sensitive to systematic differences between conditions.

$$F = \frac{\text{Systematic differences} + \text{Experimental error}}{\text{Experimental error}}$$

To produce this we need to find a way of removing the individual differences from the within conditions variance so that we can calculate the appropriate F value.

$$F = \frac{\text{Between conditions variance}}{\text{Within conditions variance} - \text{Individual differences}}$$

Removing the individual differences

When we look at the keyboard data we can see that, despite the individual differences in the participants, there is a general pattern across the participants with Keyboard 1 producing the lowest errors, Keyboard 2 more errors and Keyboard 3 the most. So despite the different level of performance the pattern across the conditions is similar for each of the participants. It is the strength of this pattern, the systematic differences between the conditions, we wish to measure.

The key to extracting the subject differences lies in the sums of squares. So far (see Chapter 10) we have only calculated sums of squares for the conditions: between conditions and within conditions. The table below shows the means of the conditions so that we can calculate these sums of squares.

Participant	Keyboard 1	Keyboard 2	Keyboard 3	Participant mean
1	5	6	10	7
2	1	2	3	2
3	0	4	5	3
4	2	4	6	4
Condition mean	2	4	6	Overall mean = 4

The sums of squares within each condition is as follows:

Keyboard 1 $(5 - 2)^2 + (1 - 2)^2 + (0 - 2)^2 + (2 - 2)^2 = 14$
Keyboard 2 $(6 - 4)^2 + (2 - 4)^2 + (4 - 4)^2 + (4 - 4)^2 = 8$
Keyboard 3 $(10 - 6)^2 + (3 - 6)^2 + (5 - 6)^2 + (6 - 6)^2 = 26$

The within conditions sums of squares = $14 + 8 + 26 = 48$.

The sums of squares between the condition means $= (2 - 4)^2 + (4 - 4)^2 + (6 - 4)^2 = 8$. As there are four participants per condition the between conditions sums of squares $= 4 \times 8 = 32$.

In the above calculations of sums of squares we have focused on the conditions, which are the <u>columns</u> in the above table, and we have calculated the within columns variation and the between columns variation in the scores. The same logic can be applied to the <u>rows</u>, where the sums of squares can be calculated within and between the rows. Notice that the rows are the subjects. Within the rows the variability is not due to differences in subjects as within a row it is always the same subject. However, the variation between the rows is the <u>variation between the subjects</u>. This is a measure of the individual differences between the participants, exactly what we are trying to find.

The sums of squares within each subject is as follows:

Subject 1 $(5 - 7)^2 + (6 - 7)^2 + (10 - 7)^2 = 14$
Subject 2 $(1 - 2)^2 + (2 - 2)^2 + (3 - 2)^2 \ = \ 2$
Subject 3 $(0 - 3)^2 + (4 - 3)^2 + (5 - 3)^2 \ = \ 14$
Subject 4 $(2 - 4)^2 + (4 - 4)^2 + (6 - 4)^2 \ = \ 8$

The within subjects sums of squares $= 14 + 2 + 14 + 8 = 38$.

The sums of squares between the subject means $= (7 - 4)^2 + (2 - 4)^2 + (3 - 4)^2 + (4 - 4)^2 = 14$. As there are three conditions per subject the between subjects sums of squares $= 3 \times 14 = 42$.

Notice that however we work out the sums of squares the total is always 80. We are not interested in the within subjects sums of squares for the ANOVA but we now have a measure of the individual differences (the between subjects sums of squares of 42). We can now remove the individual differences from the within conditions sums of squares. The residual, our error sums of squares, is $48 - 42 = 6$.

As we are able to take out the between subjects variability from the within conditions variability we no longer use the within conditions variance in our calculation of F but employ the new, smaller, error term. Thus, in the repeated measures design we have more chance of finding a significant effect as we have removed the individual differences completely from the calculation.[10]

The ANOVA summary table

The summary table for a repeated measures ANOVA has two extra rows compared to the independent measures ANOVA because we have to separate the within conditions sums of squares into the between subjects sums of squares and the error sums of squares.

THE ANOVA SUMMARY TABLE

Source of variation	Degrees of freedom	Sums of squares	Mean square	Variance ratio (F)	Probability
Between conditions	$df_{bet.conds}$	$SS_{bet.conds}$	$MS_{bet.conds}$	F	p
Within conditions	$df_{with.conds}$	$SS_{with.conds}$			
Between subjects	$df_{bet.subjs}$	$SS_{bet.subjs}$			
Error	df_{error}	SS_{error}	MS_{error}		
Total	df_{total}	SS_{total}			

Below are listed the formulae for the calculations.

Degrees of freedom:

$df_{total} = N - 1$ where N is the total number of scores

$df_{bet.conds} = k - 1$ where k is the number of conditions

$df_{with.conds} = df_{total} - df_{bet.conds}$

$df_{bet.subjs} = n - 1$ where n is the number of subjects per condition

$df_{error} = (n - 1)(k - 1)$

Sums of squares:

$$SS_{total} = \sum X^2 - \frac{(\sum X)^2}{N}$$ where $\sum X^2$ is the sum of the squared scores and $(\sum X)^2$ is the square of the sum of the scores[8]

$$SS_{bet.conds} = \frac{\sum T_c^2}{n} - \frac{(\sum X)^2}{N}$$

where T_c refers to a total of the scores in a condition, e.g. T_{c_1} is the total of the scores in condition 1. $\sum T_c^2$ is the sum of the squared totals of the conditions

(Notice that we use T_c for the condition totals and not just T. This is to distinguish them from the subject totals T_s.)

$$SS_{with.subjs} = SS_{total} - SS_{bet.conds}$$

$$SS_{bet.subjs} = \frac{\sum T_s^2}{n} - \frac{(\sum X)^2}{N}$$

where T_s refers to a total of the scores for a subject, e.g. T_{s_1} is the total of the scores for subject 1. $\sum T_s^2$ is the sum of the squared totals of the subjects

$$SS_{error} = SS_{with.conds} - SS_{bet.subjs}$$

Mean square:

$$MS_{bet.conds} = \frac{SS_{bet.conds}}{df_{bet.conds}}$$

$$MS_{error} = \frac{SS_{error}}{df_{error}}$$

Variance ratio:

$$F = \frac{MS_{bet.conds}}{MS_{error}}$$

The degrees of freedom accompanying F are the between conditions and error degrees of freedom.

$$F(df_{bet.conds}, df_{error}) = \text{calculated value}$$

We compare the calculated value with the critical value in the F distribution tables at our chosen level of significance (Table A.3 in the Appendix).

When we look up the table value we use $df_{bet.conds}$ as our first degrees of freedom (the columns in the table) and df_{error} as our second degrees of freedom (the rows in the table). Our calculated value of F is only significant if it is equal to or larger than the table value.

A worked example

The keyboard example provides us with some illustrative data for calculating the repeated measures ANOVA. First we calculate the totals for the formulae.

Participant	Keyboard 1	Keyboard 2	Keyboard 3	Participant totals
1	5	6	10	$T_{s_1} = 21$
2	1	2	3	$T_{s_2} = 6$
3	0	4	5	$T_{s_3} = 9$
4	2	4	6	$T_{s_4} = 12$
Condition totals	$T_{c_1} = 8$	$T_{c_2} = 16$	$T_{c_3} = 24$	Overall total $\sum X = 48$

We also need:

The number of subjects per condition, $n = 4$
The number of conditions, $k = 3$
The total number of scores, $N = 12$
The overall total squared, $(\sum X)^2 = 2304$
The sums of the squared scores, $\sum X^2 = 5^2 + 1^2 + \ldots + 5^2 + 6^2$
$$= 272$$

We next calculate the degrees of freedom:

$df_{total} = N - 1 = 12 - 1 = 11$
$df_{bet.conds} = k - 1 = 3 - 1 = 2$
$df_{with.conds} = df_{total} - df_{bet.conds} = 11 - 2 = 9$
$df_{bet.subjs} = n - 1 = 4 - 1 = 3$
$df_{error} = (n - 1)(k - 1) = 3 \times 2 = 6$

Sums of squares:

$$SS_{total} = \sum X^2 - \frac{(\sum X)^2}{N} = 272 - \frac{2304}{12} = 272 - 192 = 80$$

$$SS_{bet.conds} = \frac{\sum T_c^2}{n} - \frac{(\sum X)^2}{N} = \frac{8^2 + 16^2 + 24^2}{4} - \frac{2304}{12}$$

$$= 224 - 192 = 32$$

$$SS_{with.conds} = SS_{total} - SS_{bet.conds} = 80 - 32 = 48$$

$$SS_{bet.subjs} = \frac{\sum T_s^2}{n} - \frac{(\sum X)^2}{N}$$

$$= \frac{21^2 + 6^2 + 9^2 + 12^2}{3} - \frac{2304}{12}$$

$$= 234 - 192 = 42$$

$$SS_{error} = SS_{with.conds} - SS_{bet.subjs} = 48 - 42 = 6$$

Note that most of the variability of the scores within the conditions occurs due to individual differences. Our error sums of squares is consequently a lot smaller than the within conditions sums of squares.

We can now work out the appropriate mean squares and variance ratio:

$$MS_{bet.conds} = \frac{SS_{bet.conds}}{df_{bet.conds}} = \frac{32}{2} = 2$$

$$MS_{error} = \frac{SS_{error}}{df_{error}} = \frac{6}{6} = 1$$

$$F = \frac{MS_{bet.conds}}{MS_{error}} = \frac{16}{1} = 16$$

We therefore have the following summary table:

THE ANOVA SUMMARY TABLE

Source of variation	Degrees of freedom	Sums of squares	Mean square	Variance ratio (F)	Probability
Between conditions	2	32	16	16	$p < 0.01$
Within conditions	9	48			
Between subjects	3	42			
Error	6	6	1		
Total	11 (Between + within)	80			

From the F distribution table, Table A.3 in the Appendix, $F(2,6) = 10.92$ at $p = 0.01$. As our calculated value of F is greater than the table value we can reject the null hypothesis at $p = 0.01$. We can conclude that there is a significant difference between the keyboards on the number of errors made.

(This particular example was deliberately chosen so that the calculations are very simple with whole numbers throughout. This is not typical of the numbers we would normally obtain but shows the working of the repeated measures ANOVA very clearly. For interest we can consider what would have happened if these data had come from 12 different people rather than the same four in each condition. We would have had to perform an independent measures ANOVA and used the within conditions mean square as our error variance. We can see from the above table that this value would have been 48 divided by 9, which equals 5.33. This would have resulted in an F value of 3 (16/5.33) which would not have been significant, as the critical value of $F(2,9) = 4.26$ at $p = 0.05$. The effect of different keyboards would have been lost in all the subject variability.)

Multiple comparisons

We can perform post hoc tests on a repeated measures design ANOVA to find the source of the significant differences. The only difference from the independent measures design is choosing the appropriate error term in the

comparison. Whilst not universally agreed on, it is reasonable to use the MS_{error} and df_{error}, as calculated in the ANOVA, in the Tukey calculation of HSD and not the within conditions variance.

For the keyboard example, our means are: $\overline{X}_1 = 2$, $\overline{X}_2 = 4$, $\overline{X}_3 = 6$. We have $MS_{error} = 1$, $df_{error} = 6$, $n = 4$, $k = 3$. In the tables of the Studentized range statistic $q = 4.34$ for 3 conditions and 6 error degrees of freedom at $p = 0.05$, so:

$$\text{HSD} = q\sqrt{\frac{MS_{error}}{n}} = 4.34\sqrt{\frac{1}{4}} = 4.34 \times 0.5 = 2.17$$

The difference of 4 between means of Keyboards 1 and 3 is significant at $p = 0.05$ as it is larger than 2.17. The other differences in means are not significant. The size of the difference in means of 2 between Keyboards 1 and 2, and also between Keyboards 2 and 3, might reach significance if more participants were tested so it is worth exploring these non-significant differences further.

We can look at this information in a slightly different way by calculating confidence intervals. Quite simply, the 95% confdence interval of a mean difference is $95\%\text{CI} = \overline{X}_i - \overline{X}_j \pm \text{HSD}$, where $\overline{X}_i$ and $\overline{X}_j$ are any two means (the i and j standing for 1, 2, 3 etc. or which ever means we choose to compare). So,

For $\overline{X}_1 - \overline{X}_2$, $95\%\text{CI} = -2 \pm 2.17$, producing $95\%\text{CI} = (-4.17, +0.17)$
For $\overline{X}_1 - \overline{X}_3$, $95\%\text{CI} = -4 \pm 2.17$, producing $95\%\text{CI} = (-6.17, -1.83)$
For $\overline{X}_2 - \overline{X}_3$, $95\%\text{CI} = -2 \pm 2.17$, producing $95\%\text{CI} = (-4.17, +0.17)$

Notice that the confidence intervals for $\overline{X}_1 - \overline{X}_2$ and $\overline{X}_2 - \overline{X}_3$ contain zero so this shows why we cannot claim a genuine difference in means for these conditions for the population. However, the zero value is close to one end of the confidence interval, plus, with so few participants (as our example is for illustration purposes), we have low power in our test. A more powerful test with larger sample sizes might show a larger effect.

Details on calculating the one factor repeated measures ANOVA using the SPSS computer statistical package can be found in Chapter 10 of Hinton *et al.* (2004).

Chapter 14

The interaction
of factors in the
analysis of variance

QUITE OFTEN RESEARCHERS wish to study the effects of more than one independent variable in their research rather than just a single factor, such as observing the effects of *age* and *experience* on motorway driving performance. Fortunately, the analysis of variance can be applied to more than a single independent variable. In fact we could consider any number of independent variables in an analysis, the problem being to explain the complexity of the results. However, as we shall see, the two factor analysis of variance offers advantages over studying the two independent variables separately, particularly as the two factor design allows us to examine the effect of the interaction of the two variables on the scores. In this chapter we shall see the importance of an interaction in data analysis. This will be explained via the use of the following example.

It has been suggested to the city Education Committee that one school in the city (Old School) has gained a reputation for discouraging girls from studying the sciences. A researcher is commissioned to investigate the matter. The researcher chooses another school in the city (New School) that matches Old School on the range of subjects pupils can choose to study (and also matches Old School on a number of other appropriate factors, such as size, standards, ages taught, ratio of boys to girls, etc. to control for confounding factors). In this city the maximum choice for pupils occurs at the age of fifteen and this is also when the pupils study the widest range of subjects. The researcher randomly selects 20 fifteen year old boys and 20 fifteen year old girls from each school and finds out how many science subjects they have chosen to study. In this experiment there are two independent variables, *school* and *gender*, and the dependent variable measured is *number of science subjects chosen*.

The researcher is not particularly interested in the separate effects of the independent variables, but a combination of the two: is the difference between the boys and girls, in terms of the number of science subjects chosen, significantly greater for Old School than for New School? A two factor analysis of variance can be performed on the data to answer this question.

The two factor analysis of variance provides us with not one but three variance ratios. The first two of these concern the main effects of the two factors, that is, taking each factor separately and looking at its effect on the dependent variable. The <u>main effect of school</u> will tell us whether there is a significant difference in the number of science subjects chosen at Old School compared to New School (combining the boys' and girls' scores at each school). This might be of interest, as it will tell us which school is more science-oriented but it will not tell us the difference between the boys and girls. The <u>main effect of gender</u> will tell us whether there is a significant difference between the boys and girls on the number of science subjects chosen. This will combine the boys from both schools and the girls from both schools. Again this might tell us something about differences in science subjects chosen based on gender but will not tell us how they differ between the two schools.

What the two factor ANOVA also tells us is whether there is a significant <u>interaction</u> between the factors or not. A significant interaction occurs when the effect of one factor is different at the different conditions of the other factor. Thus, the effect of *school* on the choice of science subjects for the boys is different to the effect of *school* on the choice of science subjects for the girls. If we found that *school* had no effect on the boys then there would be no difference in number of science subjects chosen whichever school they went to. However, if there was an effect of *school* on the girls with the Old School girls taking fewer science subjects than the New School girls then we would find an interaction in support of the experimental hypothesis. Here the effect of *school* is different for the two conditions of *gender*. The best way to understand a significant interaction is to plot the means for the various conditions on a graph, as in Figure 14.1, where the interaction described above is shown.

It is worth noting that if we obtained the significant interaction of the form shown in Figure 14.1 we would almost certainly have a significant main effect of *school*, as overall there are more science subjects taken at New School compared to Old School, and a significant main effect of *gender*, as overall the boys took more science subjects than the girls, but these main effects are only a by-product of the interaction, not important results in their own right. It is clear from this interaction that at Old School the girls are taking fewer science subjects than the boys whereas at New School there is no such difference.

Even if we had found that the boys in New School chose more science subjects than the girls the experimental hypothesis would still be supported if the boy–girl difference was larger at Old School than at New School. The interaction would again show a significant difference between the two schools in the effect of *gender* on the science subjects chosen.

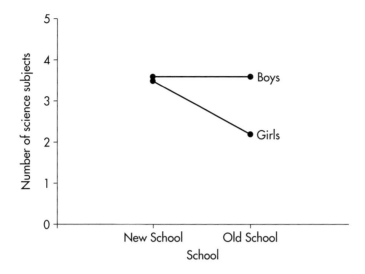

FIGURE 14.1 An interaction of school by gender

Interactions

When the effect of one factor upon another is <u>additive</u> then there is not an interaction in the results. Look at the example data from the schools study in Figure 14.2(a). There is a significant main effect of *gender* here (the girls choose significantly more science subjects than the boys) but no effect of *school* (the same number of science subjects are chosen at the two schools). It does not matter which school we take, the effect of gender is the same: changing from boy to girl adds one science subject to the mean score. In the example data of Figure 14.2(b) there is a main effect of *school*, more science subjects are chosen at New School and a main effect of *gender*, the boys take more science subjects than the girls. But despite having a different pattern of main effects to Figure 14.2(a) there is still no interaction. Going from girls to boys (at either school) simply adds a set amount (0.5) to the mean score. Similarly going from Old School to New School adds a set amount (1) to the mean score, regardless of whether we look at the boys' scores across the two school or the girls' scores. In any graph of means from a two factor experiment we can tell there is not an interaction when the lines on the graph are <u>parallel</u>, as this indicates that the effects of the factors are additive.

The examples in Figures 14.2(c) and 14.2(d) are clearly not additive as the lines on the graphs are not parallel. In these cases we will find an

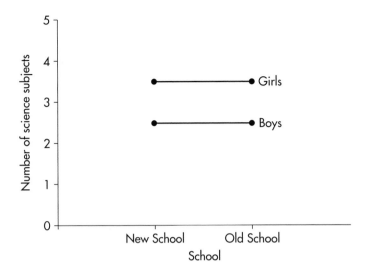

FIGURE 14.2(a) No interaction in the data

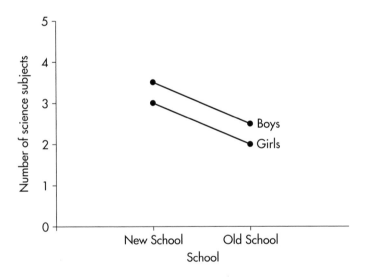

FIGURE 14.2(b) No interaction in the data again

interaction and we can decide on its significance from the two factor ANOVA. In Figure 14.2(c) there are no main effects but the interaction shows that the gender effects reverse as we move from one school to the other. At Old School the boys take one more science subject than the girls but at New School it is the girls who take one more than the boys. In Figure 14.2(d) we

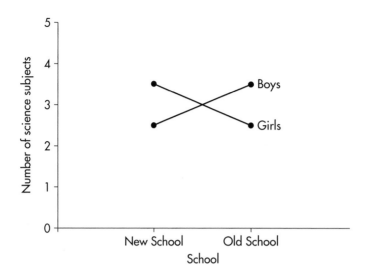

FIGURE 14.2(c) An example of an interaction

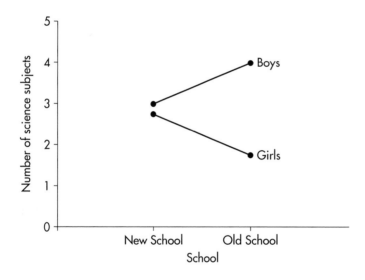

FIGURE 14.2(d) Another example of an interaction

also have an interaction as there is a wider boy–girl gap at Old School compared to New School. There will also be a main effect of *gender* as boys take more science subjects overall but not a main effect of *school* in this example.

The above examples are not exhaustive but the basic rules apply regardless of how many conditions we have for the two factors: parallel lines indicate additivity of factors and hence no interaction. When the lines are not parallel we have an interaction which indicates (if significant) a different effect of one factor at the different conditions of the other factor.

Dividing up the between conditions sums of squares

We have seen in the one factor ANOVA that it is the between conditions variability that contains the systematic differences between conditions. It is only the choice of the error term that differs when we choose repeated measures as opposed to independent measures. The same is true of the two factor ANOVA. However, in the two factor case we have systematic differences that could arise from three possible sources: the effect of the first factor (called Factor A, such as *school*), the effect of the second factor (called Factor B, such as *gender*) and the interaction of the two factors (referred to as Factor $A \times B$).

Just as we are able to partition the total sums of squares into two, the between conditions sums of squares and the within conditions sums of squares, we are also able to divide up the between conditions sums of squares into the sums of squares due to Factor A, Factor B and Factor $A \times B$. Recall that the between conditions sums of squares is:

$$SS_{bet.conds} = \frac{\sum T^2}{n} - \frac{(\sum X)^2}{N}$$

This uses the totals for the conditions in the calculation of variability of the scores between the conditions. If we used this formula for the two factor design then it would indicate a significant difference between conditions but not which factor is producing it. In our example we have four conditions each with 20 subjects ($n = 20$): Old School-Boys, Old School-Girls, New School-Boys and New School-Girls. If we consider for a moment that we are only interested in Factor A (*school*) then we combine the conditions across Factor B to produce conditions of Factor A only: we combine Old School-Boys with Old School-Girls and New School-Boys with New School-Girls to give the conditions of Factor A, Old School (A_1) and New School (A_2). We can then find a sums of squares for Factor A:

$$SS_A = \frac{\sum T_A^2}{bn} - \frac{(\sum X)^2}{N}$$

This formula uses the totals of the conditions of Factor A (in this case T_{A_1} and T_{A_2}) and bn, the number of scores in each of the conditions of Factor A, where b is the number of conditions of Factor B (in this case there are two: Boys and Girls). Combining the 20 Old School-Boys and the 20 Old School-Girls gives 40 (bn) subjects in Old School. We can then work out a mean square using the degrees of freedom for Factor A ($a - 1$, where a is the number of conditions of Factor A which, in this case, is 2).

We can do the same thing for Factor B, by combining the conditions of Factor A within the conditions of Factor A. Old School-Boys are combined with New School-Boys to produce condition B_1, Boys, and Old School-Girls and New School-Girls are combined to produce B_2, Girls. We then work out the formula for the sums of squares for Factor B:

$$SS_B = \frac{\sum T_B^2}{an} - \frac{(\sum X)^2}{N}$$

Dividing by the degrees of freedom ($b - 1$) gives us a mean square for Factor B.

The interaction sums of squares can now be worked out. We do not want to combine any conditions as we are interested in all the different conditions of Factor A and Factor B, referred to as AB conditions. In our example we have Old School-Boys (A_1B_1), Old School-Girls (A_1B_2), New School-Boys (A_2B_1) and New School-Girls (A_2B_2). We can work out the following sums of squares:

$$SS_{bet.conds} = \frac{\sum T_{AB}^2}{n} - \frac{(\sum X)^2}{N}$$

Notice that this is the same formula as the overall between conditions sums of squares. The only difference is one of labelling: the totals of conditions are referred to as T_{AB}, rather than T or T_c, as condition 1 is A_1B_1, condition 2 is A_1B_2, condition 3 is A_2B_1 and condition 4 is A_2B_2. This contains all the variability in the scores due to Factor A, Factor B and the interaction Factor $A \times B$. If we now remove from it the sums of squares from Factor A and Factor B then the remainder will provide us with the sums of squares of the interaction:

$$SS_{A \times B} = \frac{\sum T_{AB}^2}{n} - \frac{(\sum X)^2}{N} - SS_A - SS_B$$

Dividing this by the degrees of freedom of the interaction, $(a - 1)(b - 1)$, gives us the interaction mean square.

All we need to do now is to find the appropriate error variances to compare the mean squares to, in order to calculate F values for the three factors. The choice of error mean square depends on whether the factors are independent or repeated measures and the next chapter describes how this is done.

Simple main effects

If we find a significant interaction in a set of data we know that one factor is having a different effect at the different conditions of the other factor. In our schools example a significant interaction means that the effect of *school* on Boys is different to the effect of *school* on Girls. We can, if we wish, view it the other way round: the effect of *gender* is different on Old School compared to the effect of *gender* on New School. Which way round we choose to look at the interaction depends on our focus of interest. We are concerned here with the effect of *gender* as we want to know what the Boys–Girls difference is at Old School and how it compares to the Boys–Girls difference at New School.

Following the discovery of a significant interaction we may choose to look at the <u>simple main effects</u> of one factor at the conditions of the second factor. Calculating simple main effects is like performing a single factor ANOVA of one factor at each condition of the second factor. We can work out the simple main effects of *gender* on Old School and the simple main effects of *gender* on New School. For the simple main effects of *gender* on Old School we completely ignore the results of New School and work out a sums of squares between the Old School-Boys and the Old School-Girls. We then work out a mean square and an F value for this simple main effect which we compare to an appropriate table value. We can do the same for the simple main effect of gender on New School by ignoring the Old School results. If we had found the interaction as shown in Figure 14.1 we would expect a significant effect of gender at Old School (as the girls take fewer science subjects) but not a significant effect of gender at New School (where boys and girls do not differ in the number of science subjects chosen). These simple main effects would strongly support the experimental hypothesis.

The simple main effects of gender at Old School are only concerned with Old School-Boys (A_1B_1) and Old School-Girls (A_1B_2). Notice that Factor B (*gender*) varies between these two conditions but Factor A does not, it stays at A_1 (Old School), so we term this the simple main effect of B at A_1. The sums of squares of this simple main effect is calculated from the following formula:

$$SS_{B\ at\ A_1} = \frac{\sum T_{A_1B}^2}{n} - \frac{T_{A_1}^2}{bn}$$

where $\sum T_{A_1B}^2$ is sum of the squared totals of the A_1 conditions: the squared total of Old School-Boys ($T_{A_1B_1}^2$) plus the squared totals of Old School-Girls ($T_{A_1B_2}^2$), and $T_{A_1}^2$ is the squared total of all the Old School participants (Boys and Girls combined).

To find the sums of squares for the effects of B at A_2 we work out a similar formula but this time we are only concerned with New School (A_2):

$$SS_{B\ at\ A_2} = \frac{\sum T_{A_2B}^2}{n} - \frac{T_{A_2}^2}{bn}$$

If we had wanted to find the simple main effects for Factor A instead of Factor B all we would have done is use the same formula for the sums of squares but replaced the Bs with As (and the b with a) and vice versa.

Conclusion

A two factor ANOVA allows us to examine the interaction of the two factors. The way we do this is to separate the between conditions sums of squares into the components due to the main effects of each factor and the interaction. We can investigate a significant interaction further by looking at the simple main effects of one factor at the various conditions of the other factor, taken one at a time. In this way we can discover the source of the interaction.

Calculating
the two factor
ANOVA

THERE ARE TWO IMPORTANT considerations when calculating the two factor ANOVA: first, it is necessary to lay out the data correctly and second, the correct error terms must be chosen for the variance ratios. In this chapter the three different types of two factor ANOVA are dealt with: the two factor independent measures ANOVA where both the factors, A and B, are independent measures; the two factor mixed design ANOVA where Factor A is independent measures and Factor B is repeated measures, and the two factor repeated measures ANOVA where both Factor A and Factor B are repeated measures.

The two factor independent measures ANOVA

The simplest two factor ANOVA to calculate is where both factors are independent measures. Here the between conditions variance has to be separated into that arising from Factor A, Factor B and the interaction $A \times B$, as in all two factor ANOVAs. As there are individual differences in all sums of squares calculations we can use the within conditions variance as the error term for <u>all</u> three variance ratios. This makes the calculations relatively easy. We, therefore, complete the following ANOVA summary table.

THE ANOVA SUMMARY TABLE

Source of variation	Degrees of freedom	Sums of squares	Mean square	Variance ratio (F)	Probability
Factor A	df_A	SS_A	MS_A	F_A	p_A
Factor B	df_B	SS_B	MS_B	F_B	p_B
Interaction $A \times B$	$df_{A \times B}$	$SS_{A \times B}$	$MS_{A \times B}$	$F_{A \times B}$	$p_{A \times B}$
Error (Within conditions)	df_{error}	SS_{error}			
Total	df_{total}	SS_{total}			

The results table

Organising the results table is important for all ANOVAs but which factor we choose as the rows and which as the columns is not as crucial for the two factor independent measures ANOVA as for the other types of two factor ANOVA, but it is important to get the various totals of the different conditions and combination of conditions correct. The following data layout is a good example to use for clarity and organisation.[11]

THE RESULTS TABLE

Factor A	Factor B				
	Condition B_1	Condition B_2	...	Condition B_b	
Condition A_1	X_1	$X_{...}$	...	$X_{...}$	
	X_2	$X_{...}$	...	$X_{...}$	
	$\vdots$	$\vdots$	...	$\vdots$	
	X_n	$X_{...}$	...	$X_{...}$	
	$T_{A_1B_1}$	$T_{A_1B_2}$	...	$T_{A_1B_b}$	T_{A_1}
Condition A_2	$X_{...}$	$X_{...}$	...	$X_{...}$	
	$X_{...}$	$X_{...}$	...	$X_{...}$	
	$\vdots$	$\vdots$	...	$\vdots$	
	$X_{...}$	$X_{...}$	...	$X_{...}$	
	$T_{A_2B_1}$	$T_{A_2B_2}$	...	$T_{A_2B_b}$	T_{A_2}
$\vdots$	$\vdots$	$\vdots$	$\vdots$	$\vdots$	
Condition A_a	$X_{...}$	$X_{...}$		$X_{...}$	
	$X_{...}$	$X_{...}$		$X_{...}$	
	$\vdots$	$\vdots$		$\vdots$	
	$X_{...}$	$X_{...}$		X_{abn}	
	$T_{A_aB_1}$	$T_{A_aB_2}$	...	$T_{A_aB_b}$	T_{A_a}
	T_{B_1}	T_{B_2}		T_{B_b}	$\sum X$

The formulae for calculation

Degrees of freedom:

$$df_A = a - 1$$
where a is the number of condition of Factor A.

$$df_B = b - 1$$
where b is the number of conditions of Factor B.

$$df_{A \times B} = (a - 1)(b - 1)$$

$$df_{error} = ab(n - 1)$$
where n is the number of scores in an AB condition.

$$df_{total} = N - 1$$
where N is the total number of scores in the data.

Sums of squares:

$$SS_{total} = \sum X^2 - \frac{(\sum X)^2}{N}$$

$$SS_A = \frac{\sum T_A^2}{nb} - \frac{(\sum X)^2}{N}$$
where $\sum T_A^2$ is $T_{A_1}^2 + T_{A_2}^2 + \ldots + T_{A_a}^2$

$$SS_B = \frac{\sum T_B^2}{na} - \frac{(\sum X)^2}{N}$$
where $\sum T_B^2$ is $T_{B_1}^2 + T_{B_2}^2 + \ldots + T_{B_b}^2$

$$SS_{A \times B} = \frac{\sum T_{AB}^2}{n} - \frac{(\sum X)^2}{N} - SS_A - SS_B$$
where $\sum T_{AB}^2$ is $T_{A_1 B_1}^2 + T_{A_1 B_2}^2 + \ldots + T_{A_a B_b}^2$

$$SS_{error} = SS_{total} - SS_A - SS_B - SS_{A \times B}$$

(There is an alternative formula for SS_{error}:

$$SS_{error} = SS_{with.conds} = \sum X^2 - \frac{\sum T_{AB}^2}{n}$$

Both formulae should give the same answer.)

Mean square:

$$MS_A = \frac{SS_A}{df_A}$$

$$MS_B = \frac{SS_B}{df_B}$$

$$MS_{A\times B} = \frac{SS_{A\times B}}{df_{A\times B}}$$

$$MS_{error} = \frac{SS_{error}}{df_{error}}$$

Variance ratio:

$$F_A(df_A, df_{error}) = \frac{MS_A}{MS_{error}}$$

$$F_B(df_B, df_{error}) = \frac{MS_B}{MS_{error}}$$

$$F_{A\times B}(df_{A\times B}, df_{error}) = \frac{MS_{A\times B}}{MS_{error}}$$

The F values are then compared to the table values (Table A.3 in the Appendix) at the chosen level of significance.

(The above calculations are based on equal numbers of scores, n, in each of the AB conditions. It is possible to perform this analysis with unequal numbers of scores in each condition, as with the single factor independent measures ANOVA, but it will not be dealt with in this book.)

A worked example

An expanding company wanted to know how to introduce a new type of machine into the factory. Should it transfer staff working on the old machine to operate it or employ new staff who had not worked on any machine before? A researcher selected 12 staff who had experience of the old machine and 12 staff who had no such experience. Half the participants from each group were allocated to the new machine and half to the old machine. The number of errors made by the participants over a set time period was measured. These errors are shown below.

Experience on old machine	Machine	
	Old	New
Novice	4	5
	5	6
	7	5
	6	6
	8	5
	5	6
Experienced	1	8
	2	9
	2	8
	3	8
	2	7
	3	9

What are the effects of the two factors *experience on old machine* and *type of machine* on the dependent variable *number of errors*?

Both factors are independent measures as a participant took part in only one experience/machine condition. I will label *experience on old machine* as Factor A, with two conditions ($a = 2$) 'novice' (A_1) and 'experienced' (A_2), and *type of machine* as Factor B, also with two conditions ($b = 2$), 'old machine' (B_1) and 'new machine' (B_2). There are four AB conditions each with six participants ($n = 6$), giving twenty-four participants in all ($N = 24$).

Factor A	Factor B	
	B_1	B_2
A_1	4	5
	5	6
	7	5
	6	6
	8	5
	5	6
	$T_{A_1 B_1} = 35$	$T_{A_1 B_2} = 33$	$T_{A_1} = 68$
A_2	1	8
	2	9
	2	8
	3	8
	2	7
	3	9
	$T_{A_2 B_1} = 13$	$T_{A_2 B_2} = 49$	$T_{A_2} = 62$
	$T_{B_1} = 48$	$T_{B_2} = 82$	$\sum X = 130$

Degrees of freedom:

$df_A = a - 1 = 2 - 1 = 1$

$df_B = b - 1 = 2 - 1 = 1$

$df_{A \times B} = (a - 1)(b - 1) = (2 - 1)(2 - 1) = 1$

$df_{error} = ab(n - 1) = 2 \times 2 \times (6 - 1) = 20$

$df_{total} = N - 1 = 24 - 1 = 23$

Sums of squares:

$$SS_{total} = \sum X^2 - \frac{(\sum X)^2}{N} = (4^2 + 5^2 + \ldots + 7^2 + 9^2) - \frac{130^2}{24}$$
$$= 127.83$$

$$SS_A = \frac{\sum T_A^2}{nb} - \frac{(\sum X)^2}{N} = \frac{68^2 + 62^2}{6 \times 2} - \frac{130^2}{24} = 1.50$$

$$SS_B = \frac{\sum T_B^2}{na} - \frac{(\sum X)^2}{N} = \frac{48^2 + 82^2}{6 \times 2} - \frac{130^2}{24} = 48.17$$

$$SS_{A \times B} = \frac{\sum T_{AB}^2}{n} - \frac{(\sum X)^2}{N} - SS_A - SS_B$$

$$= \frac{35^2 + 33^2 + 13^2 + 49^2}{6} - \frac{130^2}{24} - 1.50 - 48.17$$

$$= 60.16$$

$$SS_{error} = SS_{total} - SS_A - SS_B - SS_{A \times B}$$

$$= 127.83 - 1.50 - 48.17 - 60.16 = 18.00$$

Mean square:

$$MS_A = \frac{SS_A}{df_A} = \frac{1.50}{1} = 1.50$$

$$MS_B = \frac{SS_B}{df_B} = \frac{48.17}{1} = 48.17$$

$$MS_{A \times B} = \frac{SS_{A \times B}}{df_{A \times B}} = \frac{60.16}{1} = 60.16$$

$$MS_{error} = \frac{SS_{error}}{df_{error}} = \frac{18.00}{20} = 0.90$$

Variance ratio:

$$F_A(1,20) = \frac{MS_A}{MS_{error}} = \frac{1.50}{0.90} = 1.67$$

$$F_B(1,20) = \frac{MS_B}{MS_{error}} = \frac{48.17}{0.90} = 53.52$$

$$F_{A \times B}(1,20) = \frac{MS_{A \times B}}{MS_{error}} = \frac{60.16}{0.90} = 66.84$$

THE ANOVA SUMMARY TABLE

Source of variation	Degrees of freedom	Sums of squares	Mean square	Variance ratio (F)	Probability
Factor A	1	1.50	1.50	1.67	$p > 0.05$
Factor B	1	48.17	48.17	53.52	$p < 0.01$
A × B	1	60.16	60.16	66.84	$p < 0.01$
Error	20	18.00	0.90		
Total	23	127.83			

From the tables of the F distribution (A.3 in the Appendix), $F(1,20)$ = 4.35 at $p = 0.05$ and $F(1,20) = 8.10$ at $p = 0.01$. We can conclude that the effect of *experience on an old machine* is not significant at $p = 0.05$ ($F(1,20) = 1.67$), the effect of *type of machine* ($F(1,20) = 53.52$) and the interaction ($F(1,20) = 66.84$) are both highly significant ($p < 0.01$).

We can examine the interaction by calculating the mean values. The table of means is shown below:

Experience on old machine	*Machine*	
	Old machine	*New machine*
Novice	5.83	5.50
Experienced	2.17	8.17

These values are plotted in Figure 15.1. The first point to note is that the lines are not parallel so we have further evidence of the interaction. Notice that the experienced workers, not surprisingly, made fewest errors on the old machine. However, they made most errors on the new machine. This looks like a case of negative transfer, where previously learnt skills can be a hindrance rather than a help. An example of this occurs when a visitor to Britain, experienced in a left-hand drive car, reaches down to change gear with the wrong hand when driving a right-hand drive car. The novice workers appear to perform with equal accuracy on both machines.

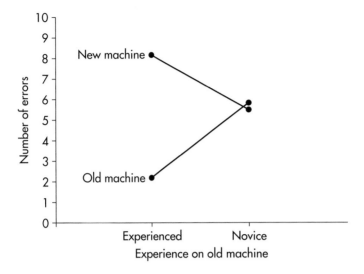

FIGURE 15.1 The interaction of experience and machine on the number of errors

In this case the interaction is quite clear. However, for illustration the simple main effects will be calculated for the effect of *type of machine* on the two levels of experience. In the two factor independent design ANOVA the error term is once again the single error term from the summary table: $MS_{error} = 0.90$, $df_{error} = 20$. This error term is used in all the simple main effects.

The simple main effect of *type of machine* on the novice operators, B at A_1:

$$SS_{B \ at \ A_1} = \frac{\sum T_{A_1 B}^2}{n} - \frac{T_{A_1}^2}{bn} = \frac{35^2 + 33^2}{6} - \frac{68^2}{2 \times 6} = 0.33$$

$df_{B \ at \ A_1} = b - 1 = 2 - 1 = 1$ (as it is the effect of B and B has 2 conditions)

$$MS_{B \ at \ A_1} = \frac{SS_{B \ at \ A_1}}{df_{B \ at \ A_1}} = \frac{0.33}{1} = 0.33$$

$$F_{B \ at \ A_1} = \frac{MS_{B \ at \ A_1}}{MS_{error}} = \frac{0.33}{0.90} = 0.37$$

with degrees of freedom $df_{B \ at \ A_1} = 1$ and $df_{error} = 20$.

From the F distribution tables we know that $F(1,20) = 4.35$ at $p = 0.05$, so we can conclude, as the calculated value of F is smaller, that we have not found an effect of *type of machine* on the novice operators.

The simple main effect of *type of machine* on the experienced operators, B at A_2:

$$SS_{B\ at\ A_2} = \frac{\sum T^2_{A_2,B}}{n} - \frac{T^2_{A_2}}{bn} = \frac{13^2 + 49^2}{6} - \frac{62^2}{2 \times 6} = 108.00$$

$df_{B\ at\ A_2} = b - 1 = 2 - 1 = 1$ (as it is the effect of B, and B has 2 conditions)

$$MS_{B\ at\ A_2} = \frac{SS_{B\ at\ A_2}}{df_{B\ at\ A_2}} = \frac{108.00}{1} = 108.00$$

$$F_{B\ at\ A_2} = \frac{MS_{B\ at\ A_2}}{MS_{error}} = \frac{108.00}{0.90} = 120.00$$

with degrees of freedom $df_{B\ at\ A_1} = 1$ and $df_{error} = 20$.

From the F distribution tables we know that $F(1,20) = 8.10$ at $p = 0.01$, so we can conclude, as the calculated value of F is considerably larger, that we have a found a highly significant effect of *type of machine* on the experienced operators.

The simple main effects usually explain the cause of an interaction but we can perform post hoc tests such as the Tukey or Scheffé tests if we wish. We need to be careful to select the appropriate comparison and the correct error term although it is particularly easy with the independent measures design as we use just the one error term.

The two factor mixed design ANOVA

The two factor mixed design ANOVA involves one independent measures factor and one repeated measures factor. This design is often used when we want to compare independent groups across a number of 'trials', such as comparing men and women on, say, alertness at different times of the day, or two groups of students on their knowledge at different points throughout the academic year.

For consistency we label the independent measures factor as Factor *A* and the repeated measures factor as Factor *B*. This is important as the error calculations are different for the two types of factor. This leads us to produce two error terms and this makes the calculations a little more complex than for the independent measures design. In the summary table below we see how the subjects' variability, *S*, needs to be considered in the calculations.

THE ANOVA SUMMARY TABLE

Source of variation	Degrees of freedom	Sums of squares	Mean square	Variance ratio (F)	Probability
Factor A	df_A	SS_A	MS_A	F_A	p_A
Error for A (S within A)	df_{errorA}	SS_{errorA}	MS_{errorA}		
Factor B	df_B	SS_B	MS_B	F_B	p_B
Factor A × B	$df_{A \times B}$	$SS_{A \times B}$	$MS_{A \times B}$	$F_{A \times B}$	$p_{A \times B}$
Error for B and A × B (B × AS)	df_{errorB}	SS_{errorB}	MS_{errorB}		
Total	df_{total}	SS_{total}			

The results table

We designate the independent measures factor (Factor *A*) as the rows and the repeated measures factor (Factor *B*) as the columns in the results table so that the results from a single subject form one row of the table. We must be careful to lay out our results consistently so that we do not analyse the results of the two factors incorrectly. Also if we use a computer program to analyse our data it could analyse the factors the wrong way round if the layout is different.[11]

THE RESULTS TABLE

Factor A		Factor B				
		Condition B_1	Condition B_2	...	Condition B_b	
Condition A_1	S_1	X_1	$X_{...}$	...	$X_{...}$	T_{S_1}
	S_2	X_2	$X_{...}$	...	$X_{...}$	T_{S_2}
	⋮	⋮	⋮	⋮	⋮	⋮
	S_n	X_n	$X_{...}$	...	$X_{...}$	T_{S_n}
		$T_{A_1 B_1}$	$T_{A_1 B_2}$	...	$T_{A_1 B_b}$	T_{A_1}
Condition A_2	S_{n+1}	$X_{...}$	$X_{...}$	...	$X_{...}$	$T_{S...}$
	S_{n+2}	$X_{...}$	$X_{...}$	...	$X_{...}$	$T_{S...}$
	⋮	⋮	⋮	⋮	⋮	⋮
	S_{2n}	$X_{...}$	$X_{...}$	...	$X_{...}$	$T_{S...}$
		$T_{A_2 B_1}$	$T_{A_2 B_2}$	...	$T_{A_2 B_b}$	T_{A_2}
⋮		⋮	⋮	⋮	⋮	⋮
Condition A_a	$S_{...}$	$X_{...}$	$X_{...}$		$X_{...}$	...
	$S_{...}$	$X_{...}$	$X_{...}$		$X_{...}$	...
	⋮	⋮	⋮		⋮	⋮
	S_{an}	$X_{...}$	$X_{...}$		X_{abn}	$T_{S_{an}}$
		$T_{A_a B_1}$	$T_{A_a B_2}$	...	$T_{A_a B_b}$	T_{A_a}
		T_{B_1}	T_{B_2}		T_{B_b}	... ΣX

The formulae for calculation

Degrees of freedom:

$$df_A = a - 1$$

where a is the number of conditions of Factor A.

$$df_{errorA} = a(n - 1)$$

where n is the number of scores in an AB condition.

$$df_B = b - 1$$ where b is the number of conditions of Factor B.

$$df_{A \times B} = (a - 1)(b - 1)$$

$$df_{errorB} = a(b - 1)(n - 1)$$

$$df_{total} = N - 1$$ where N is the total number of scores in the data.

Sums of squares:

$$SS_{total} = \sum X^2 - \frac{(\sum X)^2}{N}$$

$$SS_A = \frac{\sum T_A^2}{nb} - \frac{(\sum X)^2}{N}$$ where $\sum T_A^2$ is $T_{A_1}^2 + T_{A_2}^2 + \dots + T_{A_a}^2$

$$SS_{errorA} = \frac{\sum T_S^2}{b} - \frac{(\sum X)^2}{N} - SS_A$$ where $\sum T_S^2$ is $T_{S_1}^2 + T_{S_2}^2 + \dots + T_{S_{an}}^2$

(The sums of squares between subjects, the first two components of the error A sums of squares, comprises all the Factor A variation. If we take away the variation between the A conditions, SS_A, we are left with the variation within the A conditions as our error term.)

$$SS_B = \frac{\sum T_B^2}{na} - \frac{(\sum X)^2}{N}$$ where $\sum T_B^2$ is $T_{B_1}^2 + T_{B_2}^2 + \dots + T_{B_b}^2$

$$SS_{A \times B} = \frac{\sum T_{AB}^2}{n} - \frac{(\sum X)^2}{N} - SS_A - SS_B$$ where $\sum T_{AB}^2$ is $T_{A_1B_1}^2 + T_{A_1B_2}^2 + \dots + T_{A_aB_b}^2$

$$SS_{errorB} = \sum X^2 - \frac{\sum T_S^2}{b} - SS_B - SS_{A \times B}$$

(The variation within subjects, the first two components of the error B sums of squares, contains the B and $A \times B$ variation. Removing the between condition variation for B and $A \times B$ leaves the error sums of squares for B and $A \times B$, unaffected by individual differences.)

Mean square:

$$MS_A = \frac{SS_A}{df_A}$$

$$MS_{errorA} = \frac{SS_{errorA}}{df_{errorA}}$$

$$MS_B = \frac{SS_B}{df_B}$$

$$MS_{A \times B} = \frac{SS_{A \times B}}{df_{A \times B}}$$

$$MS_{errorB} = \frac{SS_{errorB}}{df_{errorB}}$$

Variance ratio:

$$F_A(df_A, df_{errorA}) = \frac{MS_A}{MS_{errorA}}$$

$$F_B(df_B, df_{errorB}) = \frac{MS_B}{MS_{errorB}}$$

$$F_{A \times B}(df_{A \times B}, df_{errorB}) = \frac{MS_{A \times B}}{MS_{errorB}}$$

The F values are then compared to the table values (using Table A.3 in the Appendix) at the chosen level of significance.

A worked example

A company has introduced a new machine on the factory floor and it wants to see how the workers gain skill on the machine. There is particular interest in comparing the performance of workers experienced on the old machine with that of novice operators who have not operated a machine on the factory floor before. A researcher randomly selects 6 experienced operators and 6 novices and monitors the errors they make on the new machine over a three week period to see whether there are differences between the two groups in their performance on the machine. The results are shown below.

Participants	Time		
	Week 1	Week 2	Week 3
Novices			
1	7	6	5
2	4	4	3
3	6	4	4
4	7	6	5
5	6	5	4
6	4	2	2
Experienced			
7	7	3	2
8	8	4	2
9	6	2	1
10	9	6	3
11	7	4	3
12	10	6	3

We have an independent factor *experience* which will be designated Factor A, with 'novice' as A_1 and 'experienced' as A_2. The repeated measures factor is *time*, so this is Factor B, with 'Week 1' as B_1, 'Week 2' as B_2 and 'Week 3' as B_3. We can draw up the results table as follows.

THE RESULTS TABLE

Factor A		Factor B				
		B_1	B_2	B_3		
A_1	S_1	7	6	5	$T_{S_1} = 18$	
	S_2	4	4	3	$T_{S_2} = 11$	
	S_3	6	4	4	$T_{S_3} = 14$	
	S_4	7	6	5	$T_{S_4} = 18$	
	S_5	6	5	4	$T_{S_5} = 15$	
	S_6	4	2	2	$T_{S_6} = 8$	
		$T_{A_1B_1} = 34$	$T_{A_1B_2} = 27$	$T_{A_1B_3} = 23$		$T_{A_1} = 84$
A_1	S_7	7	3	2	$T_{S_7} = 12$	
	S_8	8	4	2	$T_{S_8} = 14$	
	S_9	6	2	1	$T_{S_9} = 9$	
	S_{10}	9	6	3	$T_{S_{10}} = 18$	
	S_{11}	7	4	3	$T_{S_{11}} = 14$	
	S_{12}	10	6	3	$T_{S_{12}} = 19$	
		$T_{A_2B_1} = 47$	$T_{A_2B_2} = 25$	$T_{A_2B_3} = 14$		$T_{A_2} = 86$
		$T_{B_1} = 81$	$T_{B_2} = 52$	$T_{B_3} = 37$		$\Sigma X = 170$

Degrees of freedom:

$$df_A = a - 1 = 2 - 1 = 1$$

$$df_{errorA} = a(n - 1) = 2(6 - 1) = 10$$

$$df_B = b - 1 = 3 - 1 = 2$$

$$df_{A \times B} = (a - 1)(b - 1) = (2 - 1)(3 - 1) = 2$$

$$df_{errorB} = a(b - 1)(n - 1) = 2(3 - 1)(6 - 1) = 20$$

$$df_{total} = N - 1 = 36 - 1 = 35$$

Sums of squares:
We can make our calculations easier if we work out the following parts of the formulae first:

$$\frac{(\sum X)^2}{N} = \frac{170^2}{36} = 802.78$$

$$\frac{\sum T_A^2}{nb} = \frac{84^2 + 86^2}{6 \times 3} = 802.89$$

$$\frac{\sum T_B^2}{na} = \frac{81^2 + 52^2 + 37^2}{6 \times 2} = 886.17$$

$$\frac{\sum T_S^2}{b} = \frac{18^2 + 11^2 + \ldots + 14^2 + 19^2}{3} = 852.00$$

$$\frac{\sum T_{AB}^2}{n} = \frac{34^2 + 27^2 + 23^2 + 47^2 + 25^2 + 14^2}{6} = 907.33$$

$$\sum X^2 = 7^2 + 4^2 + \ldots + 3^2 + 3^2 = 962.00$$

Now we can work out the sums of squares:

$$SS_{total} = \sum X^2 - \frac{(\sum X)^2}{N} = 962.00 - 802.78 = 159.22$$

$$SS_A = \frac{\sum T_A^2}{nb} - \frac{(\sum X)^2}{N} = 802.89 - 802.78 = 0.11$$

$$SS_{errorA} = \frac{\sum T_S^2}{b} - \frac{(\sum X)^2}{N} - SS_A = 852.00 - 802.78 - 0.11$$
$$= 49.11$$

$$SS_B = \frac{\sum T_B^2}{na} - \frac{(\sum X)^2}{N} = 886.17 - 802.78 = 83.39$$

$$SS_{A \times B} = \frac{\sum T_{AB}^2}{n} - \frac{(\sum X)^2}{N} - SS_A - SS_B$$

$$= 907.33 - 802.78 - 0.11 - 83.39 = 21.05$$

$$SS_{errorB} = \sum X^2 - \frac{\sum T_S^2}{b} - SS_B - SS_{A \times B}$$

$$= 962.00 - 852.00 - 83.39 - 21.05 = 5.56$$

Mean square:

$$MS_A = \frac{SS_A}{df_A} = \frac{0.11}{1} = 0.11$$

$$MS_{errorA} = \frac{SS_{errorA}}{df_{errorA}} = \frac{49.11}{10} = 4.91$$

$$MS_B = \frac{SS_B}{df_B} = \frac{83.39}{2} = 41.70$$

$$MS_{A \times B} = \frac{SS_{A \times B}}{df_{A \times B}} = \frac{21.05}{2} = 10.53$$

$$MS_{errorB} = \frac{SS_{errorB}}{df_{errorB}} = \frac{5.56}{20} = 0.28$$

Variance ratio:

$$F_A(1,10) = \frac{MS_A}{MS_{errorA}} = \frac{0.11}{4.91} = 0.02$$

$$F_B(2,20) = \frac{MS_B}{MS_{errorB}} = \frac{41.70}{0.28} = 148.93$$

$$F_{A \times B}(2,20) = \frac{MS_{A \times B}}{MS_{errorB}} = \frac{10.53}{0.28} = 37.61$$

THE ANOVA SUMMARY TABLE

Source of variation	Degrees of freedom	Sums of squares	Mean square	Variance ratio (F)	Probability
Factor A	1	0.11	0.11	0.02	p > 0.05
ErrorA	10	49.11	4.91		
Factor B	2	83.39	41.70	148.93	p < 0.01
Factor A × B	2	21.05	10.53	37.61	p < 0.01
ErrorB	20	5.56	0.28		
Total	35	159.22			

In conclusion, the main effect of *experience* $(F(1,10) = 0.02)$ is not significant $(F(1,10) = 4.96$ at $p = 0.05)$, whereas the main effect of *time* $(F(2,20) = 148.93)$ and the interaction $(F(2,20) = 37.61)$ are both highly significant $(F(2,20) = 5.85$ at $p = 0.01)$.

As we have found a significant interaction we can look at the means to see the source of the interaction. The means are listed in the table below and plotted in Figure 15.2.

Experience	*Time*		
	Week 1	*Week 2*	*Week 3*
Novice	5.67	4.50	3.83
Experienced	7.83	4.17	2.33

We can see that, taken over the three weeks, the total number of errors of the two groups of operators does not differ by very much which is why there was no main effect of *experience*. All the operators made fewer errors over time, which is responsible for the highly significant effect of *time*. The highly significant interaction is interesting, as the experienced operators

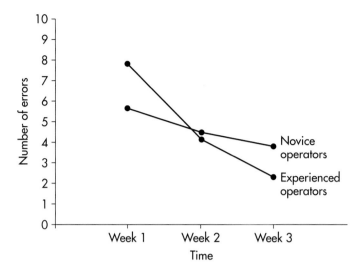

FIGURE 15.2 The interaction of time and experience on machine operator errors

began by making more errors than the novices but by Week 2 had caught them up and at Week 3 were making fewer errors. The initial difficulty for them might have been due to negative transfer (see page 179) from the old machine to the new but after a while their experience began to help them and they leapt ahead. Clearly this is speculation but it is consistent with the outcome of the analysis.

With the mixed design ANOVA, when we have a significant interaction, we are much more likely to look at the simple main effects of the independent measures factor at the various conditions of the repeated measures factor than vice versa. In our example it is more interesting to look at the effect of *experience* at Week 1 and then at Week 2, and Week 3 rather than looking at the effect of *time* on novice operators, and then on experienced operators. I shall therefore only look at the simple main effects of Factor A.[12] The simple main effects allow us to look at the effect of *experience* on the errors at one week only, ignoring the data from the other weeks. In this design we work out a different error term for each simple main effect.

The simple main effect of *experience* at Week 1:

$$SS_{A \text{ at } B_1} = \frac{\sum T_{AB_1}^2}{n} - \frac{T_{B_1}^2}{an} = \frac{34^2 + 47^2}{6} - \frac{81^2}{2 \times 6}$$

$$= 560.83 - 546.75 = 14.08$$

$$df_{A \, at \, B_1} = a - 1 = 2 - 1 = 1$$

$$MS_{A \, at \, B_1} = \frac{SS_{A \, at \, B_1}}{df_{A \, at \, B_1}} = \frac{14.08}{1} = 14.08$$

$$SS_{errorA \, at \, B_1} = \sum T^2_{AB_1S} - \frac{\sum T^2_{AB_1}}{n}$$

$$= 7^2 + 4^2 + \ldots + 7^2 + 10^2 - 560.83$$

$$= 581 - 560.83 = 20.17$$

where $\sum T^2_{AB_1S}$ is the sum of the squared scores of each subject in each A condition (novice and experienced) at B_1 (Week 1).

$$df_{errorA \, at \, B_1} = a(n - 1) = 2(6 - 1) = 10$$

$$MS_{errorA \, at \, B_1} = \frac{SS_{errorA \, at \, B_1}}{df_{errorA \, at \, B_1}} = \frac{20.17}{10} = 2.02$$

$$F_{A \, at \, B_1}(1,10) = \frac{MS_{A \, at \, B_1}}{MS_{errorA \, at \, B_1}}$$

$$= \frac{14.08}{2.02} = 6.97 \quad \text{(from Table A.3, } F(1,10) = 4.96, p = 0.05)$$

There is a significant ($p < 0.05$) simple main effect of experience at Week 1. We can conclude that the experienced operators are making significantly more errors than the novice operators in Week 1.

We replace B_1 with B_2 in the above calculations to find the simple main effect of *experience* at Week 2. $F_{A \, at \, B_2}(1,10) = 0.14$, so there is not a significant difference between the errors made by the operators in Week 2. We calculate the simple main effect of *experience* at Week 3 in the same way and $F_{A \, at \, B_3}(1,10) = 6.64$, which is significant at $p = 0.05$. In Week 3 there is a significant difference in the number of errors made between the two groups of operators, with the experienced operators making significantly fewer errors. Thus, the simple main effects have confirmed the source of the interaction observed by 'eyeballing' the graph in Figure 15.2.

The two factor repeated measures ANOVA

The advantage of having repeated measures on both the factors under study is that we can perform a two factor analysis with relatively few subjects. It also allows us to extract out the subjects' variability and consider whether the subjects are performing at similar levels.

The calculation of the two factor ANOVA is most complex when we have repeated measures on both factors. This is because we have to calculate a different error term for each of the three factors under study (A, B and $A \times B$). In this design we are able to extract the variation between subjects, so subjects (S) can be seen as a random (independent measures) factor in the analysis. To produce an error term for a factor we select the interaction of S with the factor under test. This is shown in the summary table below.

THE ANOVA SUMMARY TABLE

Source of variation	Degrees of freedom	Sums of squares	Mean square	Variance ratio (F)	Probability
Factor A	df_A	SS_A	MS_A	F_A	p_A
Factor B	df_B	SS_B	MS_B	F_B	p_B
Subjects S	df_S	SS_S	(MS_B)	(F_S)	(p_S)
Factor $A \times B$	$df_{A \times B}$	$SS_{A \times B}$	$MS_{A \times B}$	$F_{A \times B}$	$p_{A \times B}$
Error for A ($A \times S$)	df_{errorA}	SS_{errorA}	MS_{errorA}		
Error for B ($B \times S$)	df_{errorB}	SS_{errorB}	MS_{errorB}		
Error for $A \times B$ ($A \times B \times S$)	$df_{errorAB}$	$SS_{errorAB}$	$MS_{errorAB}$		
Total	df_{total}	SS_{total}			

I have include the mean square and F for the subjects in parentheses as we only need to calculate these when we are concerned that there are significant individual differences between the subjects.

The results table

In the mixed design we arranged the data so that columns in the results table refer to the repeated measures factor. We keep the same pattern when both factors are repeated by laying out the table in the format shown below, with the subjects as the rows and the conditions of Factors A and B as the columns. As both factors are repeated measures it does not matter which we choose as Factor A and Factor B as long as we are consistent throughout.[11]

THE RESULTS TABLE

	Condition A_1			...	Condition A_a			
Subjects	Condition B_1	...	Condition B_b	...	Condition B_1	...	Condition B_b	T_S
S_1	X_1		X_b		$X_{..}$		$X_{..}$	T_{S_1}
S_2	$X_{..}$		$X_{..}$		$X_{..}$		$X_{..}$	T_{S_2}
S_3	$X_{..}$		$X_{..}$		$X_{..}$		$X_{..}$	T_{S_3}
$\vdots$	$\vdots$		$\vdots$		$\vdots$		$\vdots$	$\vdots$
S_n	$X_{..}$		$X_{..}$		$X_{..}$		X_{abn}	T_{S_n}
	$T_{A_1B_1}$	...	$T_{A_1B_b}$	...	$T_{A_aB_1}$	...	$T_{A_aB_b}$	$\sum X$

We also calculate two additional tables to aid the calculations: the AS matrix and the BS matrix. We work out the former by adding up the scores across B, and the latter by adding up the scores across A. For subject 1, $T_{A_1S_1}$ is the total of the scores in condition A_1 summed across B, so it is the sum of subject 1's scores in conditions A_1B_1 to A_1B_b. Similarly, $T_{B_1S_1}$ is the sum of subject 1's scores in conditions A_1B_1 to A_aB_1.

AS Matrix

Subject	A_1S	...	A_aS
S_1	$T_{A_1S_1}$	...	$T_{A_aS_1}$
S_2	$T_{A_1S_2}$	...	$T_{A_aS_2}$
S_3	$T_{A_1S_3}$	...	$T_{A_aS_3}$
$\vdots$	$\vdots$	$\vdots$	$\vdots$
S_n	$T_{A_1S_n}$	...	$T_{A_aS_n}$
	T_{A_1}	...	T_{A_a}

BS Matrix

Subject	B_1S	...	B_bS
S_1	$T_{B_1S_1}$	...	$T_{B_bS_1}$
S_2	$T_{B_1S_2}$	...	$T_{B_bS_2}$
S_3	$T_{B_1S_3}$	...	$T_{B_bS_3}$
$\vdots$	$\vdots$	$\vdots$	$\vdots$
S_n	$T_{B_1S_n}$	...	$T_{B_bS_n}$
	T_{B_1}	...	T_{B_b}

The formulae for the calculation

Degrees of freedom:

$df_A = a - 1$ where a is the number of conditions of Factor A.

$df_B = b - 1$ where b is the number of conditions of Factor B.

$df_S = n - 1$ where n is the number of subjects.

$df_{A \times B} = (a - 1)(b - 1)$

$df_{errorA} = (a - 1)(n - 1)$

$df_{errorB} = (b - 1)(n - 1)$

$df_{errorAB} = (a - 1)(b - 1)(n - 1)$

$df_{total} = N - 1$ where N is the total number of scores in the data.

Sums of squares:

$$SS_{total} = \sum X^2 - \frac{(\sum X)^2}{N}$$

$$SS_A = \frac{\sum T_A^2}{nb} - \frac{(\sum X)^2}{N}$$ where $\sum T_A^2$ is $T_{A_1}^2 + T_{A_2}^2 + ... + T_{A_a}^2$

$$SS_B = \frac{\sum T_B^2}{na} - \frac{(\sum X)^2}{N}$$

where $\sum T_B^2$ is $T_{B_1}^2 + T_{B_2}^2 + \ldots + T_{B_b}^2$

$$SS_S = \frac{\sum T_S^2}{ab} - \frac{(\sum X)^2}{N}$$

where $\sum T_S^2$ is $T_{S_1}^2 + T_{S_2}^2 + \ldots + T_{S_n}^2$

$$SS_{A\times B} = \frac{\sum T_{AB}^2}{n} - \frac{(\sum X)^2}{N} - SS_A - SS_B$$

where $\sum T_{AB}^2$ is $T_{A_1B_1}^2 + T_{A_1B_2}^2 + \ldots + T_{A_aB_b}^2$

$$SS_{errorA} = \frac{\sum T_{AS}^2}{b} - \frac{(\sum X)^2}{N} - SS_A - SS_S$$

where $\sum T_{AS}^2$ is $T_{A_1S_1}^2 + \ldots + T_{A_aS_n}^2 + \ldots + T_{A_aS_1}^2 \ldots + T_{A_aS_n}^2$

$$SS_{errorB} = \frac{\sum T_{BS}^2}{a} - \frac{(\sum X)^2}{N} - SS_B - SS_S$$

where $\sum T_{BS}^2$ is $T_{B_1S_1}^2 + \ldots + T_{B_1S_n}^2 + \ldots + T_{B_bS_1}^2 \ldots + T_{B_bS_n}^2$

$$SS_{errorAB} = SS_{total} - SS_A - SS_B - SS_S - SS_{A\times B} - SS_{errorA} - SS_{errorB}$$

Mean square:

$$MS_A = \frac{SS_A}{df_A}$$

$$MS_B = \frac{SS_B}{df_B}$$

$$MS_S = \frac{SS_S}{df_S}$$

$$MS_{A\times B} = \frac{SS_{A\times B}}{df_{A\times B}}$$

$$MS_{errorA} = \frac{SS_{errorA}}{df_{errorA}}$$

$$MS_{errorB} = \frac{SS_{errorB}}{df_{errorB}}$$

$$MS_{errorAB} = \frac{SS_{errorAB}}{df_{errorAB}}$$

Variance ratio:

$$F_A(df_A, df_{errorA}) = \frac{MS_A}{MS_{errorA}}$$

$$F_B(df_B, df_{errorB}) = \frac{MS_B}{MS_{errorB}}$$

$$F_S(df_S, df_{errorAB}) = \frac{MS_S}{MS_{errorAB}}$$

$$F_{A\times B}(df_{A\times B}, df_{errorAB}) = \frac{MS_{A\times B}}{MS_{errorAB}}$$

The F values are then compared to the table values at the chosen level of significance.

A worked example

In a factory a machine produces two kinds of product, one that requires the operator to follow a complex set of instructions and one that is very simple to make. There are two shifts in the factory, a day shift and a night shift. The factory manager wants the factory to make the products with the minimum of errors. A researcher decides to study the effect of *shift* (day versus night) and *product* (complex versus simple to make) on the errors made by the operators. All operators work both shifts on a rotation system. Six operators are randomly selected and their error performance is measured during a day shift and a night shift. Appropriate balancing is undertaken so that carry-over effects from one shift to another are controlled for by testing three operators on the day shift first and three on the night shift first. The number of errors made during a shift are shown in the table below.

Operator	Complex product		Simple product	
	Day shift	Night shift	Day shift	Night shift
1	5	9	3	2
2	5	8	2	4
3	7	7	4	5
4	6	10	5	4
5	4	8	3	3
6	6	9	5	6

There are repeated measures on both factors so the repeated measures ANOVA can be used to test the effect of the independent variables on performance. Due to the way I have laid out the conditions above, I shall label *product* as Factor A, with 'complex product' as A_1 and 'simple product' as A_2, and *shift* as Factor B, with 'day shift' as B_1 and 'night shift' as B_2. There are two conditions of Factor A ($a = 2$), two of Factor B ($b = 2$), six participants ($n = 6$) and twenty-four scores in total ($N = 24$).

First we produce the results table:

Participants	Condition A_1		Condition A_2		
	Condition B_1	Condition B_2	Condition B_1	Condition B_2	T_S
S_1	5	9	3	2	$T_{S_1} = 19$
S_2	5	8	2	4	$T_{S_2} = 19$
S_3	7	7	4	5	$T_{S_3} = 23$
S_4	6	10	5	4	$T_{S_4} = 25$
S_5	4	8	3	3	$T_{S_5} = 18$
S_6	6	9	5	6	$T_{S_6} = 26$
	$T_{A_1B_1} = 33$	$T_{A_1B_2} = 51$	$T_{A_2B_1} = 22$	$T_{A_2B_2} = 24$	$\Sigma X = 130$

The *AS* and *BS* matrices can be created from the results table.

AS Matrix		
Participant	A_1S	A_2S
S_1	14	5
S_2	13	6
S_3	14	9
S_4	16	9
S_5	12	6
S_6	15	11
	$T_{A_1} = 84$	$T_{A_2} = 46$

BS Matrix		
Participant	B_1S	B_2S
S_1	8	11
S_2	7	12
S_3	11	12
S_4	11	14
S_5	7	11
S_6	11	15
	$T_{B_1} = 55$	$T_{B_2} = 75$

We can now calculate the F values:

Degrees of freedom:

$$df_A = a - 1 = 2 - 1 = 1$$
$$df_B = b - 1 = 2 - 1 = 1$$
$$df_S = n - 1 = 6 - 1 = 5$$
$$df_{A \times B} = (a - 1)(b - 1) = (2 - 1)(2 - 1) = 1$$
$$df_{errorA} = (a - 1)(n - 1) = (2 - 1)(6 - 1) = 5$$
$$df_{errorB} = (b - 1)(n - 1) = (2 - 1)(6 - 1) = 5$$
$$df_{errorAB} = (a - 1)(b - 1)(n - 1) = (2 - 1)(2 - 1)(6 - 1) = 5$$
$$df_{total} = N - 1 = 24 - 1 = 23$$

Sums of squares:

We can make the calculations easier if we work out the components of the formulae first:

$$\frac{(\sum X)^2}{N} = \frac{130^2}{24} = 704.17$$

$$\frac{\sum T_A^2}{nb} = \frac{84^2 + 46^2}{6 \times 2} = 764.33$$

$$\frac{\sum T_B^2}{na} = \frac{55^2 + 75^2}{6 \times 2} = 720.83$$

$$\frac{\sum T_S^2}{ab} = \frac{19^2 + 19^2 + 23^2 + 25^2 + 18^2 + 26^2}{2 \times 2} = 719.00$$

$$\frac{\sum T_{AB}^2}{n} = \frac{33^2 + 51^2 + 22^2 + 24^2}{6} = 791.67$$

$$\frac{\sum T_{AS}^2}{b} = \frac{14^2 + 13^2 + 14^2 + \dots + 9^2 + 6^2 + 11^2}{2} = 783.00$$

$$\frac{\sum T_{BS}^2}{a} = \frac{8^2 + 7^2 + 11^2 + \dots + 14^2 + 11^2 + 15^2}{2} = 738.00$$

$$\sum X^2 = 820.00$$

We can now work out the sums of squares:

$$SS_{total} = \sum X^2 - \frac{(\sum X)^2}{N} = 820.00 - 704.17 = 115.83$$

$$SS_A = \frac{\sum T_A^2}{nb} - \frac{(\sum X)^2}{N} = 764.33 - 704.17 = 60.16$$

$$SS_B = \frac{\sum T_B^2}{na} - \frac{(\sum X)^2}{N} = 720.83 - 704.17 = 16.66$$

$$SS_S = \frac{\sum T_S^2}{ab} - \frac{(\sum X)^2}{N} = 719.00 - 704.17 = 14.83$$

$$SS_{A\times B} = \frac{\sum T_{AB}^2}{n} - \frac{(\sum X)^2}{N} - SS_A - SS_B$$

$$= 791.67 - 704.17 - 60.16 - 16.66 = 10.68$$

$$SS_{errorA} = \frac{\sum T_{AS}^2}{b} - \frac{(\sum X)^2}{N} - SS_A - SS_S$$

$$= 783.00 - 704.17 - 60.16 - 14.83$$

$$= 3.84$$

$$SS_{errorB} = \frac{\sum T_{BS}^2}{a} - \frac{(\sum X)^2}{N} - SS_B - SS_S$$

$$= 738.00 - 704.17 - 16.66 - 14.83$$

$$= 2.34$$

$$SS_{errorAB} = SS_{total} - SS_A - SS_B - SS_S - SS_{A \times B} - SS_{errorA} - SS_{errorB}$$

$$= 820.00 - 60.16 - 16.66 - 14.83 - 10.68 - 3.84 - 2.34$$

$$= 7.32$$

Mean square:

$$MS_A = \frac{SS_A}{df_A} = \frac{60.16}{1} = 60.16$$

$$MS_B = \frac{SS_B}{df_B} = \frac{16.66}{1} = 16.66$$

$$MS_S = \frac{SS_S}{df_S} = \frac{14.83}{5} = 2.97$$

$$MS_{A \times B} = \frac{SS_{A \times B}}{df_{A \times B}} = \frac{10.68}{1} = 10.68$$

$$MS_{errorA} = \frac{SS_{errorA}}{df_{errorA}} = \frac{3.84}{5} = 0.77$$

$$MS_{errorB} = \frac{SS_{errorB}}{df_{errorB}} = \frac{2.34}{5} = 0.47$$

$$MS_{errorAB} = \frac{SS_{errorAB}}{df_{errorAB}} = \frac{7.32}{5} = 1.46$$

Variance ratio:

$$F_A(1,5) = \frac{MS_A}{MS_{errorA}} = \frac{60.16}{0.77} = 78.13$$

$$F_B(1,5) = \frac{MS_B}{MS_{errorB}} = \frac{16.66}{0.47} = 35.45$$

$$F_S(5,5) = \frac{MS_S}{MS_{errorAB}} = \frac{2.97}{1.46} = 2.03$$

$$F_{A \times B}(1,5) = \frac{MS_{A \times B}}{MS_{errorAB}} = \frac{10.68}{1.46} = 7.32$$

THE ANOVA SUMMARY TABLE

Source of variation	Degrees of freedom	Sums of squares	Mean square	Variance ratio (F)	Probability
Factor A	1	60.16	60.16	78.13	$p < 0.01$
Factor B	1	16.66	16.66	35.45	$p < 0.01$
Subjects S	5	14.83	2.97	2.03	$p > 0.05$
Factor $A \times B$	1	10.68	10.68	7.32	$p < 0.05$
ErrorA	5	3.84	0.77		
ErrorB	5	2.34	0.47		
ErrorAB	5	7.32	1.46		
Total	23	115.83			

In conclusion there is a highly significant effect of Factor A (*product*) with $F(1,5) = 78.13$, and of Factor B (*shift*) with $F(1,5) = 35.45$ (compared to a table value of $F(1,5) = 16.26$, $p = 0.01$). The interaction of *product* and *shift* ($F(1,5) = 7.32$) is significant at the $p = 0.05$ level of significance

($F(1,5) = 6.61$, $p = 0.05$). The effect of *subjects* ($F(5,5) = 2.03$) is not significant ($F(5,5) = 5.05$, $p = 0.05$) which indicates no significant differences between the participants in their level of performance.

    The mean number of errors in each condition is shown in the table below.

Complex product		Simple product	
Day shift	Night shift	Day shift	Night shift
5.50	8.50	3.67	4.00

These means are plotted in Figure 15.3 to help us interpret the interaction. More errors are made on the complex product than the simple product (producing the effect of *product*) and more errors are made on the night shift (producing the effect of *shift*). However, from Figure 15.3 we can see that the difference in the errors between the day and night shifts is much greater on the complex product. More errors are made at night relative to the day for the complex product in comparison to day–night difference for the simple product.

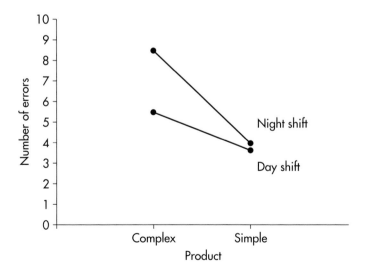

FIGURE 15.3 The interaction of product and shift on machine operator errors

We can perform the simple main effects of shift on the two products separately to confirm the above interpretation of the significant interaction. There is a different error term of each simple main effect but the same formula is used with the As and Bs adjusted accordingly, whichever of the two factors we choose.[13] First, the simple main effect of *shift* (Factor B) on the complex product (A_1).

$$SS_{B \ at \ A_1} = \frac{\sum T_{A_1B}^2}{n} - \frac{T_{A_1}^2}{bn} = \frac{33^2 + 51^2}{6} - \frac{84^2}{2 \times 6} = 615 - 588 = 27$$

$$df_{B \ at \ A_1} = b - 1 = 2 - 1 = 1$$

$$MS_{B \ at \ A_1} = \frac{SS_{B \ at \ A_1}}{df_{B \ at \ A_1}} = \frac{27.00}{1} = 27.00$$

$$SS_{errorB \ at \ A_1} = \sum T_{A_1BS}^2 - \frac{\sum T_{A_1B}^2}{n} - \frac{\sum T_{A_1S}^2}{b} + \frac{T_{A_1}^2}{bn}$$

where $\sum T_{A_1BS}^2 = 5^2 + 5^2 + 7^2 + \ldots + 10^2 + 8^2 + 9^2 = 626$

$$\frac{\sum T_{A_1B}^2}{n} = 615 \text{ (from above)}$$

$$\frac{\sum T_{A_1S}^2}{b} = \frac{14^2 + 13^2 + 14^2 + 16^2 + 12^2 + 15^2}{2} = 593$$

$$\frac{T_{A_1}^2}{bn} = 588 \text{ (from above)}$$

$$SS_{errorB \ at \ A_1} = 628 - 615 - 593 + 588 = 6$$

$$df_{errorB \ at \ A_1} = (b - 1)(n - 1) = (2 - 1)(6 - 1) = 5$$

$$MS_{errorB \ at \ A_1} = \frac{SS_{errorB \ at \ A_1}}{df_{errorB \ at \ A_1}} = \frac{6}{5} = 1.20$$

$$F_{errorB \ at \ A_1}(1,5) = \frac{MS_{B \ at \ A_1}}{MS_{errorB \ at \ A_1}} = \frac{27.00}{1.20} = 22.50$$

We can conclude that there is a highly significant effect ($p < 0.01$) of *shift* on the errors made on the complex product. Observing the means we see that there is a significant increase in errors during the night shift compared to the day shift.

We can perform the simple main effect of *shift* (Factor B) on the simple product (A_2) in the same way by replacing A_1 in the formulae with A_2. We find that $F_{B \ at \ A_2}(1,5) = 0.47$, so we have not found a significant difference between the number of errors made on the simple product between the two shifts ($p > 0.05$).

A non-significant interaction

In the examples chosen for the three types of two factor ANOVA there has always been a significant interaction. This has been done to illustrate what an interaction entails and also how we can examine the simple main effects to explore the source of the interaction. There will be many cases when the interaction will not be significant, because the effect of the factors is either additive or non-significant. In these cases we can examine the main effects in more detail if we wish by post hoc tests, such as the Tukey or Scheffé as long as we select the appropriate error term for the analysis. In the Tukey for example we would use the mean square error of a significant factor if we wanted to consider the differences in means for the conditions of that factor.

Details on how to calculate the different types of two factor ANOVAs using the SPSS computer statistical package can be found in Chapter 11 of Hinton *et al.* (2004).

Chapter 16

An introduction to nonparametric analysis

CONSIDER THE FOLLOWING SITUATION. A researcher is interested in investigating a number of possible differences in behaviour between boys and girls in the classroom. One of the hypotheses the researcher wants to test is that girls are more attentive in class than boys. Whilst the researcher has access to a class of children that are suitable for testing it is not possible to video the classroom and analyse the recordings. Although aware of the problems, the researcher decides that the only solution in this specific case is to rely on the teacher's opinion. The teacher is asked to rate each of the children in the class in terms of their attentiveness on a scale of 0–100. The teacher is not, for obvious reasons, informed of the hypothesis of the test until after completing the task. In a class of ten children the following results are produced:

Child	Teacher's rating
Susan	67
Linda	55
John	26
Mary	70
Peter	36
Ian	57
Trevor	32
Andrew	65
Helen	59
Christine	24

I have plotted the results on the 0–100 scale below and indicated the teacher's rating of each child by their initial. It does look here as though there are more of the girls at the high end of the attentiveness scale and more of the boys at the lower end. And if these data were of the sort we have been considering up to now we could compare these results on a *t* test.

0	10	20	30	40	50	60	70	80	90	100

Girls			C			L H		S M			
Boys		J	T P		I		A				

The problem is that, in this case, we are making an assumption about the data which may not be valid. The problem has to do with using any form of rating scale. On the basis of the numbers there appears to be a small difference between Christine and John and a large difference between Mary and Linda. Also the difference between Christine and John, of 2, is the same as the difference between Andrew and Susan. The assumption that we are making is that the teacher is using the rating scale as an interval scale, where the numbers progress in equal intervals along the scale, with the difference between consecutive numbers always the same. (See Chapter 2 on different types of numbers.)

Why cannot we assume that the teacher is using the rating scale as an interval scale? There are two reasons. First, the teacher is not a clock or a thermometer or a tape measure. These are all measuring devices that have been deliberately designed to measure in equal intervals. Human beings may not be able to judge differences in the same formal way as other devices. Second, we cannot check the teacher in the same way as we can calibrate a clock to check that it is working properly.

In reality the teacher might see Christine and John as more similar than Andrew and Susan. Also the difference between Peter and Linda could be seen as the same as the difference between John and Trevor, even though the gap between Peter and Linda is numerically greater. It is quite possible that an interval scale is not being used. An interval scale is like a tape measure made out of rigid material, the intervals are always the same. Now consider a tape measure made out of an elastic material. The teacher's 'tape measure' (the rating scale) might be stretched at certain points and squashed at others, providing quite a different scale. The teacher's rating scale could in reality look like the scale below.

0	10	20	30	40	50	60	70	80	90	100

Girls		C				LH	S	M			
Boys	J		T P			I	A				

When we have doubts about whether a scale is interval or not we should assume that it is not, otherwise we risk producing erroneous conclusions in our data analysis. Unfortunately, this produces another problem. All the statistical tests that we have examined so far in the book (z, t test, ANOVA) assume that the dependent variable has been measured on an interval scale. In fact they require it, in order that means, standard deviations and other statistics can be properly calculated. Without an interval scale these calculations are meaningless.

We can see the problem of calculating statistics in the above example. To the teacher the difference between Andrew and Susan is larger than the difference between Christine and John as the 'tape measure' is stretched more between 60 and 70 than between 20 and 30. Even though both differences are written as 2 the Andrew–Susan difference is a larger '2' than the Christine–John '2'. Calculating a mean, or a standard deviation, is clearly inappropriate as the numbers do not reflect the underlying scale being used.

We can refer to two kinds of data here: that which comes from an interval scale and we can perform statistics on, and that which comes from an ordinal scale. Interval data is usually obtained from experiments where the dependent variable is measured on a formal measuring device, such as reaction times, weight loss, certain test scores and so forth. We can perform parametric tests on these data, such as t tests or an ANOVA. Parametric tests require interval data. The other important feature of parametric tests is that they make parametric assumptions, assumptions concerning characteristics of the underlying populations that the samples come from. These include the assumptions that populations are normally distributed and that samples come from distributions with equal variance. All the tests attempt to estimate unknown population parameters by using the sample statistics and these parameters are constrained by the assumptions. If we believe that the assumptions of the parametric tests are not met then it is inappropriate to use them as they may not test the hypothesis properly. When we are concerned that our data is not interval or that the parametric assumptions might not be valid we employ a nonparametric test instead, one that does not make the interval assumption about the scale of measurement nor any assumptions about the underlying distributions.

How can we analyse data nonparametrically? The first point to note, for the reasons cited above, is that we cannot use the actual numbers in our analysis. We cannot perform calculations on the raw data or make assumptions about the underlying population distributions. What we can assume about the numbers produced in a rating scale, such as the one the teacher used, is that these numbers allow us to rank order the data. Whilst we are unable to decide what the difference between ratings of 24 and 26 means to the teacher, what we can say is that the teacher rates the person who scored 26 as more attentive than the one who is rated at 24. Ratings are therefore ordinal data, they place the subjects into a specific order. We can look at the teacher's ratings of the children and say, from the numbers, that Mary is rated as the most attentive and Christine the least. Indeed we are able to rank order the participants on the basis of the ratings. In the table below I have ranked the children from least attentive (rank 1) to most attentive (rank 10).

Child	Teacher's rating	Rank
Susan	67	9
Linda	55	5
John	26	2
Mary	70	10
Peter	36	4
Ian	57	6
Trevor	32	3
Andrew	65	8
Helen	59	7
Christine	24	1

We can be confident that the information we have extracted from the data, the ranks, is valid as long as the data is ordinal. In analysing the ranks we will not be making any assumptions about intervals or underlying distributions. Essentially, all nonparametric analyses compare the ranks obtained in the different conditions of the independent variable. We can compare the ranks of the girls to those of the boys. If the girls receive all the high ranks and the boys the low ones then this can be used in support of the experimental hypothesis. How and when we can decide that one set of ranks is significantly different from another set of ranks lies at the heart of the various nonparametric tests. In many cases statisticians have developed nonparametric tests that can be undertaken instead of a particular parametric test when its assumptions are not met. The following table gives the nonparametric equivalents of the most popular parametric tests.

Number of samples	Parametric test	Nonparametric test
Two (independent)	Independent t test	Mann–Whitney U test
Two (related)	Related t test	Wilcoxon signed-ranks test
Two or more (independent measures)	One factor independent measures ANOVA	Kruskal–Wallis test
Two or more (repeated measures)	One factor repeated measures ANOVA	Friedman test

Calculating ranks

When working out ranks it is usual in statistical analysis to give the lowest score a rank of 1 and work up through the scores, giving the highest score the top rank. In a number of tests it does not matter whether the data are ranked from the top down or from the bottom up but when it does matter the bottom up ranking is required. It is therefore a good idea to get into the habit of ranking in this way.

It often occurs that more than one subject achieves the same score in a test. In this case it is sensible to give these subjects the same rank. The way to do this is to find out how many subjects have the same raw score. We will refer to this number as s, so if three subjects scored the same score then $s = 3$. The rank we are about to allocate is labelled r. If we had ranked the first five scores before we got to the tied scores then $r = 6$. The formula for calculating the rank to give to the tied subjects is as follows:

$$\text{rank} = \frac{r + (r + 1) + \ldots + (r + s - 1)}{s}$$

With $s = 3$ and $r = 6$ then: $\text{rank} = \dfrac{6 + 7 + 8}{3} = 7$. The three subjects are all given a rank of 7.

Looking at the example it is easy to see the reason for giving out these ranks. If the numbers had been different they would have been given the ranks 6, 7 and 8. As they are the same we give then an equal share of these three ranks. The next rank to be allocated is $r + s$. In our example, the next rank to be allocated is 9.

Sometimes the rank allocated to identical values will not be a whole number. If two subjects have identical scores and the next ranking to be allocated is 6 then both subjects would be given a rank of 6.5. It is only when scores are tied in this way that we obtain ranks that are not whole numbers.

Calculations using ranks

There are a number of calculations that we can perform with ranks. These calculations can then be used in the construction of statistical tests. Calculations with ranks rather than scores are often simpler as, say, ten scores can be anything but ten ranks are always the numbers 1 to 10. With ranks we only need to know the number of scores and then we can work out a range of rank statistics. If the number of scores is n, and R refers to a rank, then:

1   The sum of all the ranks $(\sum R)$ is $\dfrac{n(n + 1)}{2}$

If we have 10 ratings ($n = 10$) and rank them then $\sum R = \dfrac{10\,(10 + 1)}{2} = 55$

2   The sum of the top n_1 ranks, where $n_1 + n_2 = n$ is $n_1 n_2 + \dfrac{n_1(n_1 + 1)}{2}$

Again, with $n = 10$, if we wish to sum the top 3 ranks then $n_1 = 3$, $n_2 = 7$. The sum of the top three ranks $= (3 \times 7) + \dfrac{3\,(3 + 1)}{2} = 27$.

3   The mean of the ranks, which is $\left(\dfrac{\sum R}{n}\right) = \dfrac{n + 1}{2}$

When $n = 10$ the mean of the ranks $= \dfrac{10 + 1}{2} = 5.5$

4   The sum of the squared ranks $(\sum R^2)$ is $\dfrac{n(n + 1)(2n + 1)}{6}$ as long as there are no tied ranks. For this reason there are some statistics that become less valid the more tied ranks there are.

When $n = 10$ the sum of the squared ranks $= \dfrac{10(10 + 1)(20 + 1)}{6} = 385$

(as long as none of the ranks are tied).

In the following chapters we will use these calculations in the nonparametric analysis of data.

Two sample nonparametric analysis

A COMPARISON BETWEEN two samples, comparing two conditions of an independent variable on a dependent variable, would normally be analysed by a *t* test if we were able to make the assumptions that the *t* test requires about the data in our samples. When we cannot make those assumptions and can only assume that the data are ordinal, we have to build a nonparametric analysis based on the rank ordering of the data. In this chapter we will consider the nonparametric equivalents of the related and independent *t* tests, namely the Mann–Whitney *U* test and the Wilcoxon signed-ranks test.

The Mann–Whitney *U* Test (for independent samples)

The teacher's ratings of pupils' attentiveness from the previous chapter provide us with a suitable example of a two sample case with independent samples. We cannot assume that the teacher's ratings are based on an interval scale, nor can we assume any underlying distributions concerning these ratings. The statistical analysis has to be based on the ranks. The rank ordering of the participants is shown below.

Pupil	Rank
Mary	10
Susan	9
Andrew	8
Helen	7
Ian	6
Linda	5
Peter	4
Trevor	3
John	2
Christine	1

The researcher's hypothesis was that the girls would be rated as more attentive. If this was the case then we would expect the girls' ranks to be higher than the boys' ranks. Alternatively, if the boys were more attentive then they should achieve the higher ranks. And if there was no difference between the groups on attentiveness then we would expect the boys and girls to be evenly spread amongst the ranks. One way of finding out whether the groups are clustered at the top or bottom of the ranks is to find out how many participants from one group have a higher rank than each member of the other group. If we look at the table below we can see that no boys are above Mary and Susan, one above Helen, two above Linda, and five above Christine. We can do this for the boys as well and this is also shown in the table.

Pupil	Rank	Boys above	Girls above
Mary	10	0	
Susan	9	0	
Andrew	8		2
Helen	7	1	
Ian	6		3
Linda	5	2	
Peter	4		4
Trevor	3		4
John	2		4
Christine	1	5	
Total		8	17

Now if all five girls had been at the top of the rankings their total would have been $5 \times 0 = 0$ (as they would have had no boys above any of them) and the boys would have scored $5 \times 5 = 25$ (as all five of them would have had five girls above them). If the boys had all been at the top then the totals would have been reversed. With the researcher's one-tailed test we are focusing on the girls' total being small, indicating their ranks are at the top. If the girls score 0 then it seems reasonable to conclude that there is a genuine difference between the girls' and boys' ratings. If the girls scored 25 then clearly they are not ranked higher than the boys. When the score is midway between the two (12 or 13) then the two groups are mixed in their ranking. Our total for the girls is 8: is this low enough to conclude that they are genuinely higher in the ranks as a group?

The analysis we are developing here is that of the Mann–Whitney U test (for two independent samples). It compares the actual ranks achieved with the 'best possible ranks', that is what the group would have scored if all its members had been at the top of the ranks.

To work out the calculations we shall label the girls as Sample 1 with a sample size of $n_1 = 5$ and the boys as Sample 2, with $n_2 = 5$. If the girls had occupied the top $n_1(5)$ ranks then they would have had a rank total of $10 + 9 + 8 + 7 + 6 = 40$, or as a formula:

$$n_1 n_2 + \frac{n_1(n_1 + 1)}{2} = 5 \times 5 + \frac{5(5 + 1)}{2} = 40$$

How close did the girls get to this? If we add up the actual ranks of the girls we find they achieved:

$$\sum R_1 = 10 + 9 + 7 + 5 + 1 = 32$$

The top ranks minus the actual ranks for Sample 1 is $40 - 32 = 8$. We refer to this figure as U_1, $U_1 = 8$.

We can also find a U for the boys. If they had occupied the top n_2 ranks then they would have had a rank total of:

$$n_1 n_2 + \frac{n_2(n_2 + 1)}{2} = 5 \times 5 + \frac{5(5 + 1)}{2} = 40$$

The boys' actual rank total is: $\sum R_2 = 8 + 6 + 4 + 3 + 2 = 23$. For the boys $U_2 = 40 - 23 = 17$.

Notice that we have arrived at the same figures of 8 and 17 as in the table above. The is because the two analyses are the same. The Mann–Whitney U statistic is the difference between the sample's actual ranks and the maximum ranks they could have got, with a small value of U indicating a group is close to the top. It is calculated using the formulae:

$$U_1 = n_1 n_2 + \frac{n_1(n_1 + 1)}{2} - \sum R_1 \qquad U_2 = n_1 n_2 + \frac{n_2(n_2 + 1)}{2} - \sum R_2$$

As a check it is worth noting that $U_1 + U_2 = n_1 n_2$.

The significance of U

To decide whether there is a significant difference between the samples we need the probability of obtaining the two values of U when there really is no difference between the populations the samples are drawn from. What range of values, and with what probabilities, would we expect for U when the null hypothesis is true?

Imagine for a moment that we had only tested two girls and two boys and we had obtained a U for the girls of 1 and a U for the boys of 3. What is the probability of getting this result by chance rather than as a result of a genuine difference in populations? We can see that there are six possible ways in which we can order two boys and two girls:

Rank	Order 1	Order 2	Order 3	Order 4	Order 5	Order 6
4	Girl	Girl	Girl	Boy	Boy	Boy
3	Girl	Boy	Boy	Girl	Girl	Boy
2	Boy	Girl	Boy	Girl	Boy	Girl
1	Boy	Boy	Girl	Boy	Girl	Girl
U(Girls)	0	1	2	2	3	4
U(Boys)	4	3	2	2	1	0

When the null hypothesis is true we would expect each of these possibilities to occur with equal probability. As there are six of them each one has a probability of 1/6 or 0.167. We can now work out the probability of getting a U value by chance. There is only one way for the girls to get a U of 0, 1, 3, or 4 so each has a probability of 0.167, but two ways of getting a U of 2, with a probability of 0.33. In hypothesis testing we are concerned with probabilities greater than or less than a certain value. In this example it is the girls' score of 1. The probability of getting 1 or less by chance is the probability of getting 1 (0.167) plus the probability of getting 0 (0.167), which equals 0.33. If we choose the $p = 0.05$ level of significance then we can say that the probability of getting 1 or less by chance is so large (0.33) that it is not significant at $p = 0.05$.

Returning to our example of 5 boys and 5 girls, we can do the same calculation of probabilities. It is more tedious to work out as there are 252 different ways of ordering these samples but the logic is the same. When the null hypothesis is true each possibility is equally likely and we are able to work out the probability of achieving a certain value. There is one way of the girls obtaining a U of 0, so this has a probability of 1/252 or 0.004, one way of obtaining a U of 1 (probability = 0.004), two ways of obtaining a U of 2 (probability 0.008) and so on, as shown in the table below.

U	Number of ways of getting this value by chance	Probability of getting this value by chance	Probability of getting this value or lower by chance	
0	1	0.004	0.004	
1	1	0.004	0.008	
2	2	0.008	0.016	
3	3	0.012	0.028	
4	5	0.020	0.048	$\Leftarrow p < 0.05$
5	7	0.028	0.076	

I stopped calculating U at 5 for two reasons. One, it is getting rather hard work and two, if we look at the last column, we have found out which values of U occur by chance with a probability less than 0.05 (our significance level). With five boys and five girls a value of U of 4 or less can be taken as significant (at $p = 0.05$) as it is occurs by chance with a probability less than the significance level.

Fortunately we do not have to work the probability tables ourselves, they have been worked out and the critical value of U is listed for the level of probability chosen (see Table A.5 in the Appendix). You will see that for small values of n_1 and n_2 no critical value is given, there is a dash instead. As we saw with two boys and two girls, it is not possible with these small sample sizes to obtain a value with a probability lower than the significance level of $p = 0.05$.

In looking up the values in the table we must decide whether we are testing a one- or two-tailed prediction. In this example we have a one-tailed prediction: we test the girls' value of $U(U_1)$ as we are not interested in the boys' value. If we specify a two-tailed test then we simply select the smaller of U_1 and U_2 to compare with the table value. When looking up the value in the table it is important to remember that we want the calculated value to be equal to or *smaller* than the table value to be significant for the reason given above.

We can now look up the table value (Table A.5) to compare with the calculated value of U for the girls. For a one-tailed test, with $n_1 = 5$ and $n_2 = 5$, the critical value of U is 4 at a significance level of $p = 0.05$. As the girls' value is larger (8) we cannot reject the null hypothesis at this level of significance. We have not found a difference in the girls and boys in the teacher's ratings of the attentiveness.

The distribution of U

When the null hypothesis is true, any variation in the ranks between the two samples will have arisen from chance factors. Clearly we want to know what differences we would expect by chance in order to make a decision about our calculated value, so we need to know the distribution of U when the null hypothesis is true. As we saw above a value of U is calculated for each sample. The possible values of U range from 0 up to $n_1 n_2$ but when the null hypothesis is true we would not expect the extreme values very often and we would expect both values of U to be similar, around $\dfrac{n_1 n_2}{2}$, the midpoint of the distribution. As we saw above it is not too difficult to work out the distributions for small values of n_1 and n_2. These values are shown in the tables. However, when the sample sizes are large (both 20 or more) then the distribution of U turns out to approximate a normal distribution with:

$$\mu = \frac{n_1 n_2}{2} \text{ and } \sigma = \sqrt{\frac{n_1 n_2 (n_1 + n_2 + 1)}{12}}$$

With these large samples, we can work out a z score for the calculated value of U and look up the probability in the standard normal tables (Table A.1), where z is calculated as follows:

$$z = \frac{U - \dfrac{n_1 n_2}{2}}{\sqrt{\dfrac{n_1 n_2 (n_1 + n_2 + 1)}{12}}}$$

We have to be a little careful in our use of U. The more tied values we have the more inaccurate the test becomes. If we do get a lot of tied values then it is worth questioning the use of the dependent variable; is it too crude a measure to differentiate between the subjects and rank order them appropriately?

Procedure for calculating the Mann–Whitney U statistic

1. Rank all the scores from lowest to highest.
2. Calculate a U value for each sample using the following formulae:

$$U_1 = n_1 n_2 + \frac{n_1(n_1 + 1)}{2} - \sum R_1 \qquad U_2 = n_1 n_2 + \frac{n_2(n_2 + 1)}{2} - \sum R_2$$

3. Compare the smaller value with the critical value in the table (Table A.5 in the Appendix). The calculated value must be equal to or smaller than the table value for significance. (In a one-tailed test, if the sample predicted to have the highest ranks does not produce the smallest of the two U values then it certainly will not be significant!)

A worked example

Two social clubs, the Hilltop Social Club and the Valley Social Club, decide to join forces and hire a coach to take them to see a Shakespearian play in the nearby city. One of the club secretaries decides to find out how much the members enjoyed the play, so on the coach home asks everyone to rate their enjoyment of the play on a 0 to 100 scale. The members of Valley Social like to see themselves as very cultured people so the club secretary predicts that they will rate their enjoyment of the play higher than the members of Hilltop. Is the secretary's prediction supported by the following data?

Hilltop Social Club	Valley Social Club
23	46
54	45
35	62
42	62
14	75
24	50
38	80
	55
	33

We are not going to make any assumptions about the data (except that it is ordinal) or about the underlying distributions of the populations, so will perform a Mann–Whitney U test.

First we rank the rating values across all conditions, taking into account ties:

Sample 1		Sample 2	
Hilltop	Rank	Valley	Rank
23	2	46	9
54	11	45	8
35	5	62	13.5
42	7	62	13.5
14	1	75	15
24	3	50	10
38	6	80	16
		55	12
		33	4
$n_1 = 7$	$\Sigma R_1 = 35$	$n_2 = 9$	$\Sigma R_2 = 101$

We work out the two values of U:

$$U_1 = n_1 n_2 + \frac{n_1(n_1 + 1)}{2} - \sum R_1 = 7 \times 9 + \frac{7(7 + 1)}{2} - 35 = 56$$

$$U_2 = n_1 n_2 + \frac{n_2(n_2 + 1)}{2} - \sum R_2 = 7 \times 9 + \frac{9(9 + 1)}{2} - 101 = 7$$

The prediction is one-tailed so the Valley value is the U we choose. As this is the smaller value the data do follow the direction predicted. To decide if this is significant we look up the critical value using n_1 and n_2. From Table A.5, $U = 9$, $n_1 = 7$, $n_2 = 9$, $p = 0.01$ for a one-tailed test. As the calculated value of 7 is lower than the table value we can conclude that the members of Valley Social Club gave significantly higher ratings of their enjoyment of the play than the members of Hilltop Social Club.

The Wilcoxon signed-ranks test (for related samples)

The nonparametric test for comparing two related samples is the Wilcoxon signed-ranks test. This will be explained by considering an example. A teacher wanted to test the effect of a new television programme designed to encourage children's interest in mathematics. A group of nine children ($n = 9$) were asked to rate their interest in mathematics on a 0 to 10 scale before and after the programme. The results are shown below.

	Interest in mathematics	
Child	Before	After
1	2	4
2	5	8
3	5	4
4	2	8
5	3	7
6	2	9
7	7	4
8	7	7
9	4	9

The Wilcoxon test often has the words <u>matched pairs</u> in its title. This is because each score is matched in one sample with a score in the second sample, in this example the children are matched with themselves. We match the pairs in order to produce a difference score. It is not unreasonable to assume that the scores of a matched pair can be compared despite any differences in the way in which the rating scale is being used between the children. If there really is a beneficial effect of the television programme (the one-tailed prediction is correct) then we would expect the interest ratings to be consistently higher after the programme than before. This consistency should show up as a set of negative differences when we subtract the rating after the programme from the rating before the programme.

A mixture of equal positive and negative differences would indicate a lack of consistency in the differences between the samples, with some children's interest going up and others' going down after the programme. This is what we would expect with the null hypothesis. So, for significance we are looking for a consistent pattern where most difference scores are of the same sign, either mostly positive or mostly negative.

The differences are shown in the table below. Notice that child 8 produces a difference score of zero. This cannot be used to support negative differences or positive differences so we reject this participant from the analysis as the data is unhelpful to our decision making. We reduce n by one to 8.

Child	Before Sample 1	After Sample 2	Sign of difference	Size of difference	Rank of difference
1	2	4	–	2	2
2	5	8	–	3	3.5
3	5	4	+	1	1
4	2	8	–	6	7
5	3	7	–	4	5
6	2	9	–	7	8
7	7	4	+	3	3.5
8	7	7		0	
9	4	9	–	5	6

The Wilcoxon test does not just compare the sign of the differences, it also compares the size of the differences. Clearly the inconsistent differences (in our example the positive ones) are more of a problem to the research hypothesis if they are large rather than if they are small, as they are harder to explain away. The Wilcoxon test considers this by ranking the size of the differences (their absolute values) by ignoring the sign of the differences and treating them all as positive for ranking purposes. The ranks are shown in column six of the above table.

The inconsistent differences, the two positive differences (+) have ranks of 1 and 3.5. Are these small enough for us to conclude that this result is very unlikely to have occurred by chance? What is the probability of getting such ranks by chance? What we do in the Wilcoxon test is to look at the sum of the inconsistent ranks, $1 + 3.5 = 4.5$, which we call T. What is the probability of getting a T as small as 4.5 when the null hypothesis is true? We are interested in T being small for significance as it indicates a high degree of consistency: when T is zero there is no inconsistency in the ranking and the higher of each pair of scores is always in the same sample.

By chance each rank could be positive (+) or negative (−), so we have two equal possibilities for each participant when the null hypothesis is true. With eight participants that gives us $2^8 = 256$ different possibilities in total. How many of these possibilities have positive rank totals as small as or smaller than 4.5? There is only one way of achieving a positive rank total of zero (every difference is negative), so the probability of getting zero by chance is 1/256 or 0.004. There is only one way of getting a positive rank total of 1 (the lowest difference is positive and the rest are negative) and one way of a positive rank total of 2 (the second lowest difference is positive and the rest are negative). We can get a positive rank total of 3 in two ways: either the third lowest rank is the only positive one or the lowest two ranks are positive and the rest negative. We can work out further values as in the table below.

T	Number of ways of getting this value by chance	Probability of getting this value by chance	Probability of getting this value or lower by chance	
0	1	0.004	0.004	
1	1	0.004	0.008	
2	1	0.004	0.012	
3	2	0.008	0.020	
4	2	0.008	0.027	
5	3	0.012	0.039	⇐ $p < 0.05$
6	3	0.012	0.051	

(Slight differences between the sums of the figures in columns 3 and 4 are due to rounding of the third decimal place.)

Notice that the probability gets larger than 0.05 with a T of 6, but the probability of obtaining a T of 5 and below is less than 0.05. In our example with a T of 4.5 we can reject the null hypothesis at the $p = 0.05$ level of significance and conclude that there is a significant increase in the ratings of mathematical interest after the programme.

Fortunately, we do not have to work out the probability values under the null hypothesis every time. Tables of these have been constructed (Table A.6 in the Appendix). Our example was a one-tailed prediction but if we had performed a two-tailed test we would have to consider both the sum of the negative ranks and the sum of the positive ranks and taken the smaller value as T. The critical value of T for significance would also have to take into account both tails of the distribution (i.e. the chances of getting a small T with positive values *or* negative values) and hence be more conservative than for the one-tailed test. We have to remember that when we look up T we need the calculated value to be equal to or *lower* than the table value for significance.

The distribution of T

For small values of n, less than 25, we have the tables of the critical values of T when the null hypothesis is true. However, the distribution of T approximates a normal distribution as n (the number of subjects) gets larger with:

$$\mu = \frac{n(n + 1)}{4} \text{ and } \sigma = \sqrt{\frac{n(n + 1)(2n + 1)}{24}}$$

Hence, when n is 25 or larger, we can test the significance of T by calculating a z score and comparing it to the standard normal distribution tables, where

$$z = \frac{T - \frac{n(n + 1)}{4}}{\sqrt{\frac{n(n + 1)(2n + 1)}{24}}}$$

We must be cautious in the use of T when we are dealing with data that includes more than a few tied ranks as it is unlikely to be appropriate to use. In this case we should examine the measure of the dependent variable and see if we can make it more sensitive, to produce more distinction between the difference scores and hence fewer tied ranks.

Procedure for calculating the Wilcoxon signed-ranks test

1   Calculate a difference score for each subject, the score in Sample 1 minus the score in Sample 2. When a subject has a zero difference score we remove the subject from the analysis and reduce the size of n by 1 in each case.

2   Rank the difference scores from lowest to highest, ignoring the sign.

3   Sum the ranks of the positive differences (ΣR_+) and sum the ranks of the negative differences (ΣR_-). The smaller of the positive and negative sums of ranks is the calculated value of T. (If a one-tailed prediction has been made the smaller of the two values should be consistent with the prediction. If it is not then it certainly is not significant.) It is worth checking that $\Sigma R_+ + \Sigma R_- = \dfrac{n(n + 1)}{2}$, as both sides of the equation add up to the sum of the ranks.

4   Compare the calculated value of T with the critical value in the table (Table A.6), using n to find the correct value, at the chosen level of significance. The calculated value of T must be equal to or smaller than the value in the table for significance.

A worked example

An interview panel of ten interviewers were asked to rate the two final candidates on a scale of 1 to 20 in terms of their suitability for a vacant post. Is one candidate rated significantly higher than the other by the interviewers?

Interviewer	Candidate 1	Candidate 2
1	14	10
2	17	7
3	12	14
4	16	6
5	14	14
6	10	4
7	17	10
8	12	4
9	6	11
10	18	6

We shall make no assumptions about the data or the population distributions except that the data is ordinal and so perform a Wilcoxon signed-ranks test to examine the hypothesis. First we work out the difference scores (Candidate 1 − Candidate 2) for each participant (interviewer). Zero differences are excluded from the analysis and the differences are ranked on their size as in the table below.

Interviewer	Candidate 1	Candidate 2	Sign of difference	Size of difference	Rank
1	14	10	+	4	2
2	17	7	+	10	7.5
3	12	14	–	2	1
4	16	6	+	10	7.5
5	14	14		0	
6	10	4	+	6	4
7	17	10	+	7	5
8	12	4	+	8	6
9	6	11	–	5	3
10	18	6	+	12	9

Interviewer 5 is rejected from the analysis as the difference score is zero, so the number of participants, n, is now 9. We next calculate the sum of ranks for the positive differences and the negative differences.

$$\sum R_+ = 2 + 7.5 + 7.5 + 4 + 5 + 6 + 9 = 41$$

$$\sum R_- = 1 + 3 = 4$$

No specific prediction is being made so it is a two-tailed test. We take the smaller value for the calculated value of T, so $T = 4$. At the $p = 0.05$ level of significance, with $n = 9$, the table value of T is 5 for a two-tailed test. As the calculated value of T is smaller than the table value we can say that the interviewers significantly favour Candidate 1 in their ratings.

One factor ANOVA for ranked data

W HEN THE DATA FOR ANALYSIS is not from an interval scale or the assumptions of the ANOVA are not met, we have to perform a nonparametric test. With a one factor design where we are analysing more than two samples we perform either the Kruskal–Wallis test, if the samples are independent, or the Friedman test, if the samples are related. These tests are the nonparametric equivalents of the one factor independent measures ANOVA and the one factor repeated measures ANOVA.

Kruskal–Wallis test (for independent measures)

The Kruskal–Wallis test performs an analysis that is very similar to an analysis of variance on the ranks. The test is performed when the assumptions of the parametric ANOVA cannot be made. An example of such data occurs in the following illustration. A researcher was interested in differences in attractiveness and the selection of candidates for jobs. As well as examining female attractiveness a number of experiments were undertaken on male attractiveness. One of the questions considered was whether different types of facial hair led to different judgements of male attractiveness by women. A female personnel officer in a large company agreed to rate photographs of men's faces on attractiveness on a 0 to 50 scale, with a high value indicating a high level of attractiveness. Out of a large pool of photographs of different men, five men with beards, five men with moustaches and five clean shaven men were randomly selected. (The photographs in the pool had been matched on age, hairstyle and tidiness.) If we examine the data below can we observe an effect of facial hair on the attractiveness judgements?

Facial hair					
Beard		Moustache		Clean shaven	
Rating	Rank	Rating	Rank	Rating	Rank
5	1	9	3	23	10
6	2	16	6	28	12
10	4	19	8	35	13
15	5	25	11	44	14
17	7	20	9	47	15
	$T_1 = 19$		$T_2 = 37$		$T_3 = 64$

As we have independent measures on the factor *facial hair* we rank all the scores in the data, irrespective of condition. These ranks are shown above. If there was no difference between the conditions we would expect the ranks to be evenly scattered across them. If there is an effect of the independent variable we would expect there to be systematic differences between the conditions, such as all the high ranks in one condition. We need to find a way of measuring the clustering of similar ranks within specific conditions.

If we had been performing an ANOVA we would work out F, where $F = \dfrac{MS_{bet.conds}}{MS_{error}}$. However, in the Kruskal–Wallis test we calculate a slightly different statistic on the ranks, called H, where

$$H = \frac{SS_{bet.conds}}{MS_{total}}$$

We use the usual formulae for working out sums of squares and mean square but as we are dealing with ranks we can work out much simpler formulae for them in our calculation of H.

We know that $SS_{total} = \sum X^2 - \dfrac{(\sum X)^2}{N}$ but as we are dealing with ranks (R) rather than scores (X), with no tied ranks we can replace some of the terms in the formulae:

$$\sum X^2 = \sum R^2 = \frac{N(N+1)(2N+1)}{6} \text{ and}$$

$$\sum X = \sum R = \frac{N(N+1)}{2}$$

From this we have that $(\sum X)^2 = (\sum R)^2 = \dfrac{N^2(N+1)^2}{4}$

Substituting these formulae for ranks into the formula for the total sums of squares we get:

$$SS_{total} = \frac{N(N+1)(N-1)}{12}$$

As the total degrees of freedom in the data is $N - 1$, then:

$$MS_{total} = \frac{N(N+1)}{12}$$

This means that <u>whatever</u> data we collect, the MS_{total} of the ranks will be a fixed value for N. We can see why H is calculated rather than F here. MS_{total} provides us with a fixed value of 'average' variance that we get with N ranks regardless of the effect of the independent variable. If we measure the between conditions variability against this fixed value we can see how much greater the variability between the conditions actually is. For example, with an N of 15 the MS_{total} will always be 20 (when there are no tied ranks).

From the usual formula for sums of squares:

$$SS_{bet.conds} = \frac{\sum T^2}{n} - \frac{(\sum X)^2}{N}$$

When we substitute the ranks formula for $(\sum X^2)$ we get:

$$SS_{bet.conds} = \frac{\sum T^2}{n} - \frac{N(N+1)^2}{4}$$

where T is the total of the ranks in a condition and $\sum T^2 = T_1^2 + T_2^2 + \ldots + T_k^2$, k being the number of conditions, and n the number of scores in each condition.

From these calculations we can work out a relatively simple formula for H:

$$H = \frac{12}{N(N+1)} \times \frac{\sum T^2}{n} - 3(N+1)$$

H is a formula which tells us how much variability there is between the conditions (the sums of squares) compared to the 'average' variance in the ranks. As MS_{total} is always fixed for N the important degrees of freedom is that between conditions, $df = df_{bet.conds} = k - 1$ as H is influenced by the number of conditions under study.

In the *facial hair* example, $N = 15$, $n = 5$, $k = 3$, $T_1 = 19$, $T_2 = 37$, $T_3 = 64$ and

$$H = \frac{12}{15(15+1)} \times \frac{19^2 + 37^2 + 64^2}{5} - 3(15+1) = 10.26, \, df = 2$$

So the variability between the ranks of the conditions (the between conditions sums of squares) is 10.26 times larger than the 'average' variance (the total mean squares) in the ranks.

Unequal sample sizes

Just like the independent measures ANOVA we can have a different number of subjects in each condition. If this is the case then the formula for H is:

$$H = \frac{12}{N(N+1)} \times \sum \frac{T^2}{n} - 3(N+1)$$

where $\sum \frac{T^2}{n} = \frac{T_1^2}{n_1} + \dots + \frac{T_k^2}{n_k}$, and n_1 to n_k are the number of subjects in conditions 1 to k.

The distribution of H

We can ask why we find H rather than F when we have ranks. There are a number of reasons. As noted above, MS_{total} is a fixed value for N. In our example, with $N = 15$, it will always be 20 regardless of the number of conditions and the variability between them. We can therefore use MS_{total} as a benchmark with which to compare the actual variability of the ranks between the conditions. If there is no variability between the conditions $SS_{bet.conds}$ will be zero as the total of ranks within each condition will be the same, and if there is lots of variability between the conditions then $SS_{bet.conds}$ will be large, as the similar ranks will cluster within specific conditions. But how large is large? This is why we compare it to MS_{total}. In our example, when we calculate them separately we find $SS_{bet.conds} = 205.2$ and $MS_{total} = 20$, so $SS_{bet.conds}$ is over 10 times larger than MS_{total}, implying that the variability between conditions is not random, and indicates an effect of *facial hair* on the judgements of attractiveness. We now need to find the distribution of H under the null hypothesis to find the value of H required for significance.

This is where we can see how useful H is as a statistic. It turns out that the distribution of H is known, as H closely approximates a distribution called the chi-square (χ^2) distribution, which is known. As long as we have at least 5 scores in each condition H is accurate to two decimal places.[14] We shall be looking at the χ^2 distribution in more detail in the next chapter but it is worth noting the following: z is a deviation from a mean divided by a standard deviation. If we square z then z^2 is a squared deviation divided by a variance. A distribution of z^2 is a χ^2 distribution. A sum of z^2s is also a χ^2 distribution, and a sum of z^2s is a sums of squares divided by a variance, which is what we have with H.

Clearly, the size of H depends on the number of conditions and so we must look up the significance of H using $df = df_{bet.conds} = k - 1$. Fortunately the χ^2 distribution has been worked out for different degrees of freedom. In our example with $df = 2$ we can look up the appropriate value of χ^2. From the tables of the χ^2 distribution, Table A.7 in the Appendix, $\chi^2 = 9.21$, $p = 0.01$, $df = 2$. As our calculated value of H is larger than the table value we can conclude that there is a significant difference (at $p = 0.01$) between the different conditions of facial hair in the judgements of attractiveness.

Tied ranks

If we have tied ranks we really should use the original formulae on the ranks for $SS_{bet.conds}$ and MS_{total}. When we use the formula for H with tied ranks the calculated value for H will tend to be smaller than it really should be and we might miss a significant difference. To compensate we may wish

to employ a correction C, where: $C = 1 - \dfrac{\Sigma t}{N^3 - N}$, and the corrected value

of $H_c = \dfrac{H}{C}$. In the formula for C, N is the total number of scores in the data
(as above) but $\Sigma t = \Sigma(t_i^3 - t_i)$, which means that for each group of tied ranks
i, t_i is their number. Consider the following ranks: 1, 2.5, 2.5, 4, 5, 7, 7, 7,
9, 10. Here there are two sets of tied ranks: 2 at 2.5 and 3 at 7, so:
$$\Sigma t = \Sigma(t_i^3 - t_i) = (2^3 - 2) + (3^3 - 3) = 6 + 24 = 30, \text{ giving}$$
$C = 1 - \dfrac{30}{10^3 - 10} = 0.97$, so our calculated value of H would be divided by
0.97 which would give us a slightly higher value for comparison with the
table value for significance.

However, it is only when the calculated value is close to significance
that this would arise and we should always pay attention to results that only
just miss significance. In most cases we can work out the value of H using
the simpler formula without worrying about tied ranks, as long as there are
not too many of them.

Procedure for calculating the Kruskal–Wallis test

1   Rank all the scores in the experiment, irrespective of condition.
2   Add up the ranks for each condition to produce a rank total for each
    condition: $T_1, \ldots, T_k$ where k is the number of conditions.
3   Calculate H using the formula: $H = \dfrac{12}{N(N + 1)} \times \Sigma \dfrac{T^2}{n} - 3(N + 1)$,

    which allows for different numbers of subjects in each condition. N is
    the total number of subjects and $n_1, \ldots, n_k$ are the number of subjects
    in the k conditions.
4   The calculated value of H must equal or exceed the table value of χ^2
    with $k - 1$ degrees of freedom at the chosen level of significance to
    reject the null hypothesis. Table A.7 in the Appendix gives the critical
    values of the χ^2 distribution.

A worked example

A group of 18 people who found it hard to relax agreed to take part in a test
of three relaxation techniques, a pill to aid restfulness, hypnosis and exercise.

After a week employing the technique the participants were asked to rate their ability to relax on a 50 point scale (ranging from 0 much worse, 25 no change, through to 50 much better than before). Six people undertook the pill methods, five hypnosis and seven exercise. Is there an effect of *relaxation method* on their ratings?

The data are shown in the table below with their ranks.

Condition 1		Condition 2		Condition 3	
Pill	*Rank*	*Hypnosis*	*Rank*	*Exercise*	*Rank*
14	2.5	29	11	44	18
10	1	38	15	30	12
18	4	27	9	40	16
22	6	25	7	28	10
14	2.5	26	8	33	13
20	5			35	14
				42	17
$n_1 = 6$	$T_1 = 21$	$n_2 = 5$	$T_2 = 50$	$n_3 = 7$	$T_3 = 100$

We now calculate H:

$$H = \frac{12}{N(N+1)} \times \sum \frac{T^2}{n} - 3(N+1)$$

$$= \frac{12}{18(18+1)}\left(\frac{21^2}{6} + \frac{50^2}{5} + \frac{100^2}{7}\right) - 3(18+1)$$

$$H = \frac{12}{342}(73.5 + 500 + 1428.57) - 57 = 13.25$$

Degrees of freedom, $df = k - 1 = 3 - 1 = 2$.

From the χ^2 tables, at $p = 0.01$, $\chi^2 = 9.21$, $df = 2$. As the calculated value of 13.25 is greater than the table value (Table A.7 in the Appendix) we can conclude that there is a significant difference (at $p = 0.01$) between the relaxation methods on the participants' ratings.

Post hoc multiple comparisons following the Kruskal–Wallis test

We can perform a post hoc multiple comparison test after a significant Kruskal–Wallis test in a similar manner to a Tukey test. From Chapter 12 we can write: Tukey's honestly significant difference = $q \times$ standard error, where q is the Studentized range statistic. We use a variation of this called the Nemenyi test to compare pairs of samples following a Kruskal–Wallis test, where, instead of comparing the sample means, we compare the sample rank totals. Futhermore the standard error (SE) is now calculated as follows:

$$SE = \sqrt{\frac{n(nk)(nk + 1)}{12}},$$ where k is the number of conditions and n the number

of scores in each condition. We look up the value of q in Table A.4 using the significance level (usually 0.05), the number of samples k and, in this case, the infinity line of the degrees of freedom (∞). If the difference between a pair of rank totals (e.g. T_1 and T_2) is greater than $q \times$ SE then the difference between the conditions is significant at the chosen significance level.

The problem with the Nemenyi test is that it requires all samples to be of the same size (n). With unequal sample sizes we can use Dunn's test with

$$SE = \sqrt{\frac{N(N + 1)}{12}\left(\frac{1}{n_i} + \frac{1}{n_j}\right)}$$

where n_i and n_j are the sample sizes of the two conditions.[15] We must compare the mean rank for our conditions rather than the rank totals (e.g. for condition 1 the mean rank will be $\frac{T_1}{n_1}$). A difference in mean ranks must be greater than $Q \times$ SE. Q is the statistic for differences in mean ranks and the values of Q are found in the table overleaf for the different values of k at the significance levels of 0.05 and 0.01.[16]

Critical values of the Q statistic		
k	p = 0.05	p = 0.01
2	1.960	2.576
3	2.394	2.936
4	2.639	3.144
5	2.807	3.291
6	2.936	3.403
7	3.038	3.494
8	3.124	3.570
9	3.196	3.635
10	3.261	3.692

In the above worked example, the mean ranks are:

$$\bar{R}_1 = \frac{T_1}{n_1} = \frac{21}{6} = 3.50, \quad \bar{R}_2 = \frac{T_2}{n_2} = \frac{50}{5} = 10.00,$$

$$\bar{R}_3 = \frac{T_3}{n_3} = \frac{100}{7} = 14.29$$

For a significance level of $p = 0.05$, with three conditions ($k = 3$), $Q = 2.394$.

For condition 1 versus condition 2: $SE = \sqrt{\frac{18(18 + 1)}{12}\left(\frac{1}{6} + \frac{1}{5}\right)} = 3.23$, so $Q \times SE = 7.73$. Hence the difference in mean ranks for conditions 1 and 2 of 6.5 is not significant at $p = 0.05$. For condition 1 versus condition 3, $SE = 2.97$ and $Q \times SE = 7.11$. The difference in mean ranks of 10.79 is significant at $p = 0.05$. Finally, for conditions 2 and 3, $SE = 3.13$, giving $Q \times SE = 7.49$. Hence their difference in mean ranks of 4.29 is not significant at $p = 0.05$.

The Friedman test (for related samples)

The Friedman test is a nonparametric test that can be performed when we cannot make the assumptions necessary for the parametric one factor repeated measures ANOVA. In this test the analysis is performed on the ranks. As

there are repeated measures the scores are ranked within each <u>subject</u> rather than across all the scores. In the example below six personnel officers were asked to rate, on a 0–10 scale, colours of business suits in terms of *professional image*. Three suit colours were chosen for the conditions: brown, black and blue.

	Suit colour						
	Brown		Black		Blue		Rank
Participant	Rating	Rank	Rating	Rank	Rating	Rank	total
1	5	1	8	2	9	3	6
2	4	1	6	3	5	2	6
3	3	1	4	2	9	3	6
4	5	2	4	1	8	3	6
5	4	1	5	2	6	3	6
6	5	2	3	1	7	3	6
		$T_1 = 8$		$T_2 = 11$		$T_3 = 17$	

If there was no difference in the samples we would expect the ranks to be evenly spread amongst the conditions. If there is an effect of the independent variable then we would expect similar ranks to cluster in specific conditions. In the above example most the Rank 1s are in the 'brown' condition, most of the Rank 2s in the 'black' condition and most of the Rank 3s in the 'blue' conditions so we would expect our statistic to indicate a significant difference between the conditions.

With the one way repeated measures ANOVA we work out F but in the Friedman test we work out χ_r^2 which is a chi-square on the ranks, where

$$\chi_r^2 = \frac{SS_{bet.conds}}{MS_{with.subjs}}$$

Notice from the above table that when we rank the data for each participant there is no variation between the subjects ($SS_{bet.subjs} = 0$) as the rank total for each subject is always the same, in our case they all add up to 6. So all the variation in the ranks is within the subjects ($SS_{total} = SS_{with.subjs}$). We can see from this the similarity of the Kruskal–Wallis and the Friedman tests.

The formula for $SS_{with.subjs}$ is:

$$SS_{with.subjs} = \sum X^2 - \frac{\sum T_S^2}{k}$$

As we are dealing with ranks, if there are no tied ranks:

$$\sum X^2 = \sum R^2 = \frac{nk(k+1)(2k+1)}{6} \text{ and } \sum T_S^2 = \frac{nk^2(k+1)^2}{4}$$

These formulae for ranks are slightly different for those shown in Chapter 16 as we are ranking within each subject, not across all the scores in the experiment. We can now replace the ANOVA formula for scores with the replacement formulae for ranks.

$$SS_{with.subjs} = \frac{nk(k+1)(2k+1)}{6} - \frac{nk(k+1)^2}{4}$$

Simplifying the formula we get:

$$SS_{with.subjs} = \frac{nk(k+1)(k-1)}{12}$$

The degrees of freedom within the subjects is $n(k-1)$, so:

$$MS_{with.subjs} = \frac{k(k+1)}{12}$$

This is a fixed value for each value of k. With three conditions, as in our example, $MS_{with.subjs}$ will always be 1.

The sums of squares between the conditions can be worked out from the following formula:

$$SS_{bet.conds} = \frac{\sum T^2}{n} - \frac{(\sum X)^2}{nk}$$

where $nk = N$ the total number of scores and $T_1, \ldots, T_k$ are the totals of the scores in each condition.

As we have ranks, assuming no ties, we can replace $\sum X$ with $\dfrac{nk(k+1)}{2}$ in the formula and T becomes the total of the ranks in a condition:

$$SS_{bet.conds} = \frac{\sum T^2}{n} - \frac{nk(k+1)^2}{4}$$

And finally,

$$\chi_r^2 = \frac{12}{nk(k+1)} \sum T^2 - 3n(k+1) \text{ with } k-1 \text{ degrees of freedom}$$

In our *business suit colour* example, $n = 6$, $k = 3$, $T_1 = 8$, $T_2 = 11$, $T_3 = 17$:

$$\chi_r^2 = \frac{12}{6 \times 3(3+1)} (8^2 + 11^2 + 17^2) - 3 \times 6(3+1) = 7, \text{ with } df = 2$$

The distribution of χ_r^2

As with the Kruskal–Wallis H statistic, χ_r^2 compares the between conditions sums of squares to a fixed value, the 'average' variance in the ranks. If the null hypothesis is true we would expect the variability between conditions to be zero. When the null hypothesis is false we would expect the between conditions variability to be large. Our definition of large in this case is taken relative to the fixed value $MS_{with.subjs}$.

Again, as with the Kruskal–Wallis H statistic, χ_r^2 approximates the χ^2 distribution, with the appropriate distribution found using the degrees of freedom between the conditions, $k-1$. However, when there are few conditions and a small number of subjects ($k = 3$ and $n < 10$ or $k = 4$ and $n < 5$) then the χ^2 distribution is not such a good fit for χ_r^2.[17] In these cases we must work out the various probabilities for χ_r^2 when the null hypothesis is true. Let us take, for example, the case where $k = 3$ and $n = 3$. For each subject there are six ways in which the ranks 1, 2, and 3 could be arranged across the three conditions, so for three subjects there are $6 \times 6 \times 6 = 216$ ways of arranging the ranks in total. The maximum value of χ_r^2 is 6. This occurs when, for every subject, the same rank is in the same condition. This can occur in six ways. This gives us a probability of 6/216 or $p = 0.028$ of obtaining a value of $\chi_r^2 = 6$ by chance. The next largest value of χ_r^2 is 4.67 and the probability of obtaining this value is larger than 0.05. Thus, with $k = 3$ and $n = 3$ only $\chi_r^2 = 6$ is significant at $p = 0.05$. The critical values of χ_r^2 for small sample sizes are shown in Table A.8 in the Appendix.

The example of the business suits is a small sample case with $k = 3$ and $n = 6$. The table value for $p < 0.05$, is 7. As the calculated value of $\chi_r^2 = 7$ is the same we can conclude that there is a significant effect (at $p = 0.05$) of business suit colour on the judgements of professional image.

We must be careful if there are a lot of tied ranks in the data as this might make the analysis inaccurate. Fortunately as we are ranking within each subject this is not likely to occur often. However, if there are more than a few tied ranks it is worth considering whether it is possible to make the dependent variable more sensitive and reduce the number of ties.

Procedure for calculating the Friedman test

1 Set out the data with the subjects as rows and the conditions as columns.
2 Rank each of the n subjects' scores separately, from lowest to highest.
3 Work out the rank total (T) for each condition: $T_1, \ldots, T_k$, where k is the number of conditions.
4 Calculate χ_r^2 using the following formula:

$$\chi_r^2 = \frac{12}{nk(k+1)} \sum T^2 - 3n(k+1) \text{ with } k - 1 \text{ degrees of freedom.}$$

5 The calculated value of χ_r^2 must be larger than or equal to the appropriate table value of χ^2 (Table A.7 in the Appendix) or larger or equal to the value of χ_r^2 in the small samples table (Table A.8).

A worked example

Ten people stay at a hotel where they eat all their meals. On one day they are asked to rate the quality of food for the three meals, breakfast, lunch and dinner, on a scale of 0 to 100 (from bad to good). Is there a difference between the three meals in their rated quality?

The results of the ratings are shown in the table below. The data is assumed only to be ordinal and no assumptions are made about the underlying distributions.

	Breakfast		Lunch		Dinner	
Participant	Rating	Rank	Rating	Rank	Rating	Rank
1	50	1	58	3	54	2
2	32	2	37	3	25	1
3	60	1	70	3	63	2
4	41	1	66	3	59	2
5	72	1	73	2	75	3
6	37	3	34	2	31	1
7	39	1	48	3	44	2
8	25	2	29	3	18	1
9	49	2	54	3	42	1
10	51	1	63	2	68	3
$n = 10$						
$k = 3$		$T_1 = 15$		$T_2 = 27$		$T_3 = 18$

The ratings are ranked for each participant as in the table above and the total of the ranks in each condition is calculated. We now calculate χ_r^2:

$$\chi_r^2 = \frac{12}{nk(k+1)} \sum T^2 - 3n(k+1)$$

$$= \frac{12}{10 \times 3 \times 4}(15^2 + 27^2 + 18^2) - 3 \times 10 \times 4$$

$$= 0.1 \times 1278 - 120 = 7.8 \quad \text{with } df = k - 1 = 3 - 1 = 2$$

From Table A.7, $p = 0.05$, $df = 2$, $\chi^2 = 5.99$. As our calculated value of χ_r^2 is larger than the table value of χ^2 we can conclude that there is a significant difference between the meals in terms of the ratings of meal quality.

Post hoc multiple comparisons following a Friedman test

We can employ a Nemenyi test, a variation of the Tukey test, to undertake pairwise comparisons of the conditions after a significant Friedman test. In this test we compute a standard error (SE) using the formula:

$$SE = \sqrt{\frac{nk(k+1)}{12}}$$

We then look up the appropriate value of the Studentized range statistic q from Table A.4 using the chosen significance level (e.g. 0.05), the number of conditions k, and the infinity row for the degrees of freedom (∞). If a difference in the rank totals of two conditions is larger than $q \times SE$ then we can claim a significant difference between the conditions.

In the above example, with $n = 10$ and $k = 3$, $SE = \sqrt{\frac{10 \times 3 \times (3+1)}{12}} =$ 3.16 and $q = 3.31$ at $p = 0.05$. From these values we work out that $q \times SE$ = 10.46. As $T_1 = 15$, $T_2 = 27$ and $T_3 = 18$ we can conclude the following. There is a significant difference between conditions 1 and 2 (as the rank total difference of 12 is greater than 10.46), but the differences between conditions 1 and 3 (rank total difference of 3) and between conditions 2 and 3 (rank total difference of 9) are not significant at $p = 0.05$.

Details on how to calculate the Kruskal–Wallis and Friedman tests using the SPSS computer statistical package can be found in Chapter 13 of Hinton *et al.* (2004).

Chapter 19

Analysing frequency data: chi-square

Nominal data, categories and frequency counts

There are many occasions when we want to examine the effects of an independent variable on the dependent variable when the data are nominal: the numbers indicate the category the subject belongs to rather than a position on an ordinal or interval scale. An experimenter interested in hair length of female students might categorise hair length into two categories: long (on or below the shoulder) and short (above the shoulder). Female students could then be sampled to see whether there is a preference for long or short hair on campus. Note that the data collected from the students is neither a score nor a rating. The researcher is collecting frequency data, that is adding up the number of participants in each category. If 100 female students were randomly sampled and 62 had long hair and 38 short hair can we conclude that there is a significant preference for long hair? The statistic examined in this chapter, chi-square (χ^2), allows us to analyse frequency data to answer such questions. We are not limited in the number of (independent) categories we choose, which makes this a very useful statistic, particularly when we are undertaking questionnaires or surveys. If we wanted to compare liberals and conservatives on, say, a proposed piece of new taxation legislation we could ask a number of liberals and conservatives whether they are for or against the legislation. Here we have four categories: liberals-for, liberals-against, conservatives-for and conservatives-against, with their respective frequency counts. If we included the category 'don't know' for each political group we would increase our categories to six.

Introduction to χ^2

The simplest way to view the χ^2 statistic is as the square of the z statistic:

$$\chi^2 = z^2 = \frac{(X - \mu)^2}{\sigma^2}$$

χ^2 is the square of the deviation of a score from its population mean divided by the population variance, where the population is normally distributed.

Just as we saw that the F statistic in its simplest case is t^2 and therefore never negative we also find that χ^2, also a squared value, is always positive. Like F we are only interested in the high values of the χ^2 distribution but it is always a two-tailed test in that a large positive z score or a large negative z score both square to a large positive χ^2.

In most cases we are testing samples rather than individual scores and this is where χ^2 turns out to be so useful in data analysis. If we select mutually independent samples from which to obtain X then it turns out that the sum of the individual χ^2s is also a χ^2:

$$\chi^2 = \sum z^2 = \sum \left(\frac{(X - \mu)^2}{\sigma^2} \right)$$

This means that we can find a χ^2 for each sample and the sum of the χ^2s will also be a χ^2. This allows us to compare samples against the sampling distribution of χ^2. However, the shape of the χ^2 distribution depends on the number of χ^2s that are summed, so we must take into account the degrees of freedom of the samples (the number of samples minus one). If we have four categories then the degrees of freedom for χ^2 is $c - 1 = 3$, where c is the number of categories.

In the hair length example there are two categories ($c = 2$). The two samples are mutually independent as a student cannot be in both categories. Imagine that we tested 100 women students ($N = 100$). If there was no preference for hair length then we would expect to find half the students with long hair (probability, $p_1 = 0.5$, where 'long hair' is Category 1) and half the students with short hair (probability, $p_2 = 0.5$, where 'short hair' is Category 2). Thus, when the null hypothesis is true we would expect Np_1 students ($100 \times 0.5 = 50$) to have long hair and Np_2 (50 as well) to have short hair. Are the figures of 62 and 38 significantly different from the 50 we would expect in each category under the null hypothesis? This is where χ^2 comes in. The following formula turns out to approximate the χ^2 distribution when the null hypothesis is true.

$$\chi^2 = \sum \left(\frac{(X - Np)^2}{Np} \right) \text{ with } c - 1 \text{ degrees of freedom}$$

where X is the observed frequency count in a category and Np is the frequency count we would expect when the null hypothesis is true.

This is not exactly a χ^2 distribution but the approximation is very good as long as we make sure that Np is at least 5, that is the expected frequency of each category under the null hypothesis must be at least 5. This formula provides us with a distribution to compare our actual values to in order to test the significance of our differences between frequency counts.

There are two categories in the hair length experiment, so we can work out a χ^2 using the new formula.

$$\chi^2 = \frac{(X_1 - Np_1)^2}{Np_1} + \frac{(X_2 - Np_2)^2}{Np_2} = \frac{(62 - 50)^2}{50} + \frac{(38 - 50)^2}{50}$$

$$= \frac{144}{50} + \frac{144}{50} = 5.76$$

with $df = c - 1 = 2 - 1 = 1$ degree of freedom.

If we look up the tables for the χ^2 distribution (Table A.7 in the Appendix) the critical value for $\chi^2 = 3.84$ with $df = 1$ and $p = 0.05$. As the calculated value is greater than the table value we can conclude that there is a significant preference for long hair by the female students on campus.

The more usual way to express the above formula for χ^2 is to rename X as the observed frequency (O) and Np as the expected frequency (E) so the χ^2 formula that we use is:

$$\chi^2 = \sum \left(\frac{(O - E)^2}{E} \right) \text{ with } df = c - 1$$

Chi-square (χ^2) as a 'goodness of fit' test

In many cases we wish to examine whether a pattern of frequencies significantly differs from an expected pattern of frequencies. Usually the expected frequencies are those found when the null hypothesis is true but they do not have to be, we can compare the observed frequencies with any pattern of expected frequencies we wish to choose. This is why the test is called a 'goodness of fit' test: we can use it to decide if a set of observed frequencies are a good fit for a particular pattern of expected frequencies.

A worked example

An experimenter set out to test whether there is a difference in colour preference for cars. One hundred participants were given four pictures of cars, identical but for the colour, and asked to state their preference. The colours presented were red, blue, black and white.

If there was no preference then we would expect each colour to be chosen equally, so we would expect the probability of each category being chosen to be 1/4 or $p = 0.25$ when the null hypothesis is true. With a total (N) of 100, we would expect each category to be chosen by Np of them, 100×0.25, which is 25. On performing the experiment, the researcher finds 48 participants choose the red car, 15 the blue, 10 the black and 27 the white. Do these observed frequencies differ significantly from the expected frequencies?

We compare the pattern of observed frequencies with that of the expected frequencies by calculating χ^2.

$$\chi^2 = \Sigma\left(\frac{(O - E)^2}{E}\right)$$

$$= \frac{(48 - 25)^2}{25} + \frac{(15 - 25)^2}{25} + \frac{(10 - 25)^2}{25} + \frac{(27 - 25)^2}{25} = 34.32$$

with $df = c - 1 = 4 - 1 = 3$.

From Table A.7, $\chi^2 = 11.34$, $df = 3$, $p = 0.01$. As our calculated value of χ^2 is greater than the table value we can reject the null hypothesis. There is a significant difference ($p < 0.01$) between the observed and expected frequencies; the four colours are not equally preferred.

Testing the 'goodness of fit' to the normal distribution

In most cases we will compare observed frequencies with those found under the null hypothesis but there is one case in particular where we might choose another set of expected frequencies. We are often making the assumption with parametric tests that the sample or samples come from normally distributed populations. There might be occasions when we actually want to check this out. This is where the χ^2 goodness of fit test can be used.

Two hundred people were tested on a complex hand–eye co-ordination test and the number of errors each participant made was measured. The scores range from 22 to 69. The sample has a mean of $\overline{X} = 46.86$ and a standard deviation of $s = 6$. Does this sample differ significantly from the normal distribution?

First we choose the categories to adopt. The more categories we choose the more sensitive the test but we end up with fewer scores in each category. With a range from 22 to 69 categories of size 5 will result in 10 categories. These are shown in the first column of the table below. The boundaries of the categories are chosen at 0.5, half the smallest possible difference between the scores. (The minimum possible difference between the scores is 1, one error.) This is done so no two categories overlap. If I had taken 25 as a category boundary then a score of 25 could go into both the 20–25 and the 25–30 category but with 25.5 as a boundary it only goes into the 20.5–25.5 category and not the 25.5–30.5. It also means that there are no gaps between the categories, they cover the whole range. The next thing to do is to allocate the 200 scores to their correct categories. These are our observed frequencies and they are shown in the second column of the table.

We now need to work out the expected frequencies. To do this we convert the category boundaries to z scores using the z formula. Unfortunately we do not have the population mean and standard deviation which we need to work out a z score so we estimate them using the sample values, $\overline{X}$ and s.

$$\text{Estimated } z = \frac{X - \overline{X}}{s} = \frac{X - 46.86}{6}$$

For the first category, scores of 20.5 and 25.5 convert to z scores of -4.39 and -3.56. We do this for all the category boundaries. These results are shown in the third column of the table.

If we look these figures up in the standard normal distribution table (Appendix A.1) we can find the probabilities associated with each score. These probabilities are shown in the fourth column. (Recall that the probability of a z score less than -4 is so small as to be taken as zero.) The difference in the probability between the category boundaries will tell us the probability of finding a score in this category when the distribution is normal. These are shown in the fifth column. (It is a little difficult finding the probability of the category surrounding the mean as one z score is positive and one negative. We simply take the difference of each from 0.5 and add the results.)

Multiplying the probability of finding a score in a category when the distribution is normal (p) by the number of participants ($N = 200$) will give us the expected frequency in each category. These are shown in the sixth column.

Category boundary	Observed frequency	z score	Probability	Diff. in prob.	Expected frequency	χ^2
20.5	1	−4.39	0.0000	0.0002	0.04	
25.5		−3.56	0.0002			
25.5	2	−3.56	0.0002	0.0030	0.60	0.1317
30.5		−2.73	0.0032			
30.5	2	−2.73	0.0032	0.0262	5.24	
35.5		−1.89	0.0294			
35.5	26	−1.89	0.0294	0.1152	23.04	0.3803
40.5		−1.06	0.1446			
40.5	55	−1.06	0.1446	0.2644	52.88	0.0850
45.5		−0.23	0.4090			
45.5	60	−0.23	0.4090	0.3201	64.02	0.2524
50.5		0.61	0.2709			
50.5	34	0.61	0.2709	0.1960	39.20	0.6898
55.5		1.44	0.0749			
55.5	16	1.44	0.0749	0.0633	12.66	
60.5		2.27	0.0116			
60.5	3	2.27	0.0116	0.0107	2.14	1.6823
65.5		3.11	0.0009			
65.5	1	3.11	0.0009	0.0009	0.18	
70.5		3.94	0.0000			

We are nearly ready to calculate χ^2, however, there are categories with expected frequencies less than 5 and we must not allow this for the test to be valid. What we can do to overcome this is to combine categories. If we combine the top three categories to make one new one and also do the same with the bottom three categories we end up with six categories all with expected frequencies greater than 5. The new category 20.5–40.5 has an observed frequency of 5 and an expected frequency of 5.88. the new category 55.5–70.5 has an observed frequency of 20 and expected frequency of 14.98. Finally,

$$\chi^2 = \sum \left(\frac{(O - E)^2}{E} \right)$$

$$= 0.1317 + 0.3803 + 0.0850 + 0.2524 + 0.6898 + 1.6823$$

$$\chi^2 = 3.2215$$

The degrees of freedom are one less than the number of categories so are $6 - 1 = 5$. However, in this case we did not know the population mean and standard deviation and used our sample to estimate them. In doing this we 'used up' a degree of freedom on each estimation, so we take our degrees of freedom as 3. From tables χ^2 is 7.82, $df = 3$, $p = 0.05$. We can conclude that as the calculated value is *less than the table value* we have *not found* a significant difference between the distribution of our scores and a normal distribution.

Chi-square (χ^2) as a test of independence

The χ^2 test of independence operates in the same way as the goodness of fit test in that it compares observed with expected frequencies, but in the test of independence we are comparing two or more patterns of frequencies to see if they are different from each other (independent or not). If we sampled conservatives and liberals on new taxation legislation then we could see if the pattern of frequencies 'for' and 'against' was different for the conservatives compared to the liberals using the χ^2 test.

A worked example

A researcher wanted to test the difference of opinion between conservatives and liberals on some new taxation legislation. In a survey, 120 people were identified as conservatives and 80 as liberals. A question on the survey asked whether the respondent agreed with the new taxation legislation ('for'), disagreed with it ('against'), or had no opinion or did not know about it ('don't know'). The results, the observed values, are shown in the table below.

Observed frequencies	For	Against	Don't know	Row totals
Conservatives	78	30	12	120
Liberals	18	50	12	80
Column totals	96	80	24	200

Notice that, with different numbers of conservatives and liberals, we would not expect the same numbers in the various categories even under the null hypothesis. As there are more conservatives than liberals the 12 conservatives in the 'don't know' category are 12/120 or 10 per cent of their group whereas the 12 liberals in the same category are 12/80 or 15 per cent of their group. Relatively more liberals gave this answer than conservatives. What we would expect, when there is no difference between the groups in their pattern of responses, is that there is the same <u>proportion</u> of each group total in each category. We can work out the expected values, when the null hypothesis is true, by the following formula.

$$\text{The expected value of a cell} = \frac{\text{row total} \times \text{column total}}{\text{overall total}}$$

A cell is a category, so we have six cells, $c = 6$. Let us take the first cell (conservatives-for) as an example. If there was no difference between the two political groups in terms of the proportion answering 'for' then the 96 people who actually responded 'for' should be divided into conservative and liberal in proportion to their relative number. Out of the 200 people the proportion of conservatives is 120/200. So, of the 96 people answering 'for' we would expect the following to be the number of conservatives if there is no difference between the groups:

$$E = \frac{96 \times 120}{200} = 57.6$$

We can do this for all the cells to produce the expected values.

Expected frequencies	For	Against	Don't know	Row totals
Conservatives	57.6	48.0	14.4	120
Liberals	38.4	32.0	9.6	80
Column totals	96	80	24	200

We now work out χ^2 using the usual formula.

$$\chi^2 = \sum\left(\frac{(O-E)^2}{E}\right) = \frac{(78-57.6)^2}{57.6} + \frac{(30-48.0)^2}{48.0} + \frac{(12-14.4)^2}{14.4} +$$

$$\frac{(18-38.4)^2}{38.4} + \frac{(50-32.0)^2}{32.0} + \frac{(12-9.6)^2}{9.6}$$

$$\chi^2 = 7.23 + 6.75 + 0.4 + 10.84 + 10.13 + 0.6 = 35.95$$

To decide whether this is significant we must compare it to the appropriate χ^2 distribution. We have to be careful here, the degrees of freedom is <u>not</u> the number of categories minus one, $c - 1$. This is because we are interested in comparing the rows (the two political groups) on pattern of results across the columns (the different opinions). This is a difference between the goodness of fit and test of independence. Here, we have 2 rows, $R = 2$, and two columns, $C = 3$. For the test of independence the degrees of freedom is:

$$df = (R - 1)(C - 1)$$

In our example $df = (2 - 1)(3 - 1) = 2$. From tables $\chi^2 = 9.21$, $df = 2$, $p = 0.01$. As our calculated value is greater than the table value we can reject the null hypothesis at the $p = 0.01$ level of significance. There is a significant difference in the patterns of responses of the conservatives and liberals to the taxation legislation.

We must make sure that the expected frequencies are 5 or larger for the χ^2 distribution to be appropriate. In this case there was not a problem. If the 'don't know' responses had been too few for an expected frequency of 5 then we could leave out the 'don't know' category and compare just the 'for' and 'against' for a valid test, or collect more data to make the frequencies larger.

The chi-square distribution

Being a squared value or a sums of squares χ^2 will always be greater than zero. However, the shape of the distribution will alter with changes in the degrees of freedom. Under the null hypothesis we would expect the sums of squares to be around zero but random variation will mean that they will not always be exactly zero when the null hypothesis is true. If we sum a number of positive values, each a little bigger than zero, the sum will gradually get larger the more numbers we add. The more degrees of freedom there are,

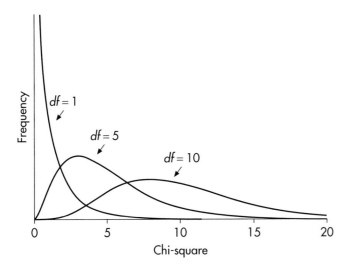

FIGURE 19.1 The chi-square distribution

then the more sums of squares we have and the larger these sums of squares become.

When $df = 1$ we expect, under the null hypothesis, most results to be close to zero with little difference between the observed and expected values (see Figure 19.1). Consider what the standard normal distribution would look like if we squared the values. Now when we increase the degrees of freedom we are adding together a set of independent χ^2s each with $df = 1$. Taking $df = 5$, for example, we have a sum of five independent χ^2s. Whilst each individual χ^2 will pile up close to zero, when added together their sum will pile up further along the scale (see Figure 19.1). As we increase the degrees of freedom the mean of the distribution moves up the scale. Whilst the distribution is very asymmetrical when the degrees of freedom are small, it becomes more symmetrical as df gets larger (see $df = 10$ in Figure 19.1). When the degrees of freedom get as large as 30 and above the distribution approximates the normal distribution. As a result of this tables of the χ^2 distribution usually only go up to $df = 30$, as beyond that we can use the tables of the normal distribution (Table A.7 in the Appendix).

The assumptions of the χ^2 test

In order that we compare our calculated value of χ^2 with the appropriate distribution we must make certain assumptions when performing a χ^2 test.

As with most distributions we must have randomly sampled from the population otherwise a biased sample will affect the resultant statistic. For χ^2 it is crucial that we have mutually independent categories. Essentially we must check that a subject could not possibly contribute to the frequency of more than one cell.

The chi-square distribution is 'continuous', meaning that there are no breaks in it, the curve is continuous. However, the values we calculate in the χ^2 test are not from a continuous scale but a discrete one. This is because observed frequencies vary in discrete units. We can observe a frequency of 10 or 11 but not 10.4 or 10.6. With degrees of freedom greater than 1 and with expected frequencies of at least 5 (and preferably 10) this is not a problem as the difference between the statistic and the true sampling distribution is so small. This is why large cell frequencies are encouraged. For example, the difference between 100 and 101 is small. It is a step of 1/100 or 1 per cent of the original frequency. However the step from 5 to 6 is 1/5 or 20 per cent, so is a large jump. Furthermore, because we are limited by the size of these steps (we cannot step in smaller units than whole numbers) any difference between observed and expected frequencies (even as small as 1) will appear large when we have small cell frequencies and χ^2 will tend to be significant (and possibly a Type I error).

To compensate for this problem when $df = 1$ we can apply the <u>Yates' correction for discontinuity</u>. This adjusts the χ^2 formula in the following manner.

$$\text{Corrected } \chi^2 = \sum \frac{(|O - E| - 0.5)^2}{E}$$

The lines either side of the $O - E$ refer to the absolute value, meaning that if the difference is negative we ignore the minus sign and treat it as positive. Thus, the χ^2 for every cell is reduced by 0.5 before it is squared. This will result in a smaller calculated value of χ^2 and will reduce the risk of a Type I error. However, the Yates' correction does tend to overcompensate for discontinuity and may result in a more conservative decision than necessary. As a simple rule, if a result is still significant with the correction or still nonsignificant without it, then we can be confident in our decision. It is only when a significant result becomes nonsignificant with the correction that a problem arises. In this case we should be cautious in making inferences from such a finding. As with any result that is 'bubbling under' (close but not quite significant) we should consider resolving the ambiguity by increasing the sample size or exploring the question further.

Details on how to calculate the chi-square statistic using the SPSS computer statistical package can be found in Chapter 14 of Hinton *et al.* (2004).

Chapter 20

Linear correlation and regression

Introduction

Do the students who spend the most time studying achieve the highest marks in examinations and do those who spend the least time studying get the lowest marks? What we are asking here is whether the variable *study time* correlates with the variable *examination performance*. If we found that this was the case then we would say that there is positive correlation between the variables, that is, as a score on one variable increases so the corresponding score on the other variable does the same. Sometimes we find a correlation between two variables where as one goes up the other goes down. This is termed a negative correlation. We are likely to find a negative correlation between smoking and health as the more a person smokes the less healthy that person tends to be.

If we find that two variables do correlate then we can use this information to predict the value of a score on one variable by using the corresponding score on the other variable. In this chapter we shall be looking at how we can produce a regression equation to allow us to do this. If we do not find a relationship between two variables we say that they are uncorrelated and a change in one cannot be used to predict a change in the other.

As an example we shall use the following data, giving the results of ten first year university students, showing how much time they spent studying (on average per week throughout the year) along with their end of year examination mark (out of 100). Do these data show a correlation?

Student	Study time	Examination mark
1	40	58
2	43	73
3	18	56
4	10	47
5	25	58
6	33	54
7	27	45
8	17	32
9	30	68
10	47	69

There appears to be a positive correlation when we look at these results by eye but a clearer way to show this is to produce a scatterplot, that is a graph of the data, where the axes are the two variables. Figure 20.1 provides a scatterplot of these results.

Note that the points are not randomly scattered about the graph (which we would expect if there was not a correlation) but generally fall within a band, indicating a correlation. (To illustrate this, imagine cutting out a piece of paper to cover up all, or most of, the points in the graph. We can do this,

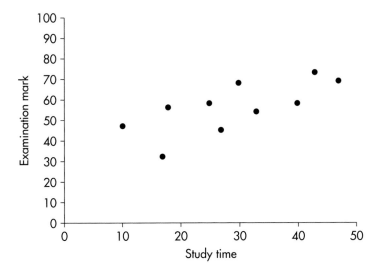

FIGURE 20.1 Scatterplot of study time by examination performance

in this case, with a fairly narrow strip of paper.) When this occurs we argue that, but for random errors, the scores would have fallen along a line, the regression line, and in our analysis we can calculate which line would 'best fit' the data. In many cases, but not all, we assume that the line of best fit is a straight line. When we make this assumption we are assuming that we have a linear correlation, and we calculate a linear regression. This is also referred to as a linear model as we are assuming that the model for the relationship between the variables is a straight line (see Chapter 23 on linear models). This is a reasonable assumption in our example as the points on the graph fall within a band that appears straight. If the pattern of points had been along a curved line there would still be a correlation but it would not be linear. In this book I am only considering linear correlation and regression.

What we need to do is to find a way to measure the strength of the correlation. If all the points lie exactly along a straight line then we have a perfect correlation. A correlation such as the one in Figure 20.1 is not perfect as the points are more widely scattered but they still fall within a fairly narrow band. This is a reasonable correlation, as we could infer that the points would lie on a straight line but for random errors. As the points become more scattered so the correlation gets weaker until we say that they are randomly scattered, and there is no correlation at all. The measurement we use to describe the degree with which the points cluster along a straight line is the Pearson correlation coefficient, r.

Pearson r correlation coefficient

In our example, as in most we examine, the two variables are measured on different interval scales. This makes it difficult to decide how well the scores on one variable correlate with the scores on the other variable. Is 30 hours per week as large a *study time* score as 60 out of 100 on *examination performance*? To overcome this problem we need to standardise the scores. We do this by finding the z scores of the scores on the two variables.[18] The standard scores find the position of a score relative to its mean in terms of its standard deviation. By calculating standard scores we can compare the relative position of each score on the distribution of the variable. Study time has a mean of 29 and a standard deviation of 11.42. We will call this variable X. Examination performance has a mean of 56 and a standard deviation of 11.80. We will call this variable Y. The z scores for each variable are shown in the table below.

Student	Study time	Study time z score	Examination mark	Examination z score	Product of the z scores
	X	z_X	Y	z_Y	$z_X z_Y$
1	40	0.96	58	0.17	0.16
2	43	1.23	73	1.44	1.77
3	18	−0.96	56	0.00	0.00
4	10	−1.66	47	−0.76	1.26
5	25	−0.35	58	0.17	−0.06
6	33	0.35	54	−0.17	−0.06
7	27	−0.18	45	−0.93	0.17
8	17	−1.05	32	−2.03	2.13
9	30	0.09	68	1.02	0.09
10	47	1.58	69	1.10	1.74

We can now see whether the score on one variable corresponds to the same position on its distribution as the score on the second variable for each participant. Looking at the table above, the z scores tend to be similar for each participant: a similar size of z score indicates a correlation and the same sign (either both positive or both negative) indicates a positive correlation. (Had the sizes been similar but the signs different we would have been looking at a negative correlation.) How can we acknowledge this similarity mathematically? One way is to multiply the z scores on the two variables for each participant. When there is a correlation the size of the z scores will be similar, so large numbers will be multiplied by large numbers and small numbers by small numbers. With a positive correlation we will mostly multiply z scores of the same sign together (either both positive or both negative) to produce products that will be mostly positive. With a negative correlation we will multiply mostly z scores with different signs and the products will be mostly negative. Thus, if we sum the products of the z scores ($\sum z_X z_Y$) we should get a large positive number when there is a positive correlation and a large negative number when there is a negative correlation. If there is no correlation at all we should get some positive products and some negative products which will tend to cancel each other out and the sum ends up around zero. If there is a perfect correlation the participants will get the same z score on both variables. Multiplying these together is like squaring the z scores of one of them. The sum of N squared z scores always equals N

(try it!) so a perfect positive correlation will result in the sum of the product of the z scores equalling N. When there is a perfect negative correlation the sum will be $-N$. In our example, $\sum z_X z_Y = 7.2$, so it is a positive correlation (above 0) but not perfect as $N = 10$ (we have 10 participants).

Finally, if we divide the sum of the products of the z scores by N we produce a statistic that equals 1 when there is a perfect positive correlation, -1 when there is a perfect negative correlation and 0 when there is no correlation at all. This statistic is called the Pearson correlation coefficient r.

$$r = \frac{\sum z_X z_Y}{N}$$

A positive correlation is shown by an r greater than zero and a negative correlation by r less than zero. The strength of the correlation is shown by how close r is to 1 (or -1 if the correlation is negative). In our example $r = 0.72$, which is a high positive correlation as it is much closer to 1 than 0. We will see whether it is significant in a moment.

The importance of r is that, as well as telling us the strength and direction of a correlation, it also provides us with a formula for predicting the scores on one variable by using the scores of the other variable. If we plotted the z scores of the two variables on a scatterplot we would find that r is the slope of the regression line (the straight line that best represents the linear relationship between the variables, the 'line of best fit'), the line we assume the z scores would fall along but for random error. If we write the formula for the line on the graph that best fits the z scores it is $z_Y = r z_X$. Thus, given any z score on one variable we can use this formula, now we know r, to predict what the z score would be on the other variable if the scores fell along a straight line. This is all very well but we are not actually interested in z scores! We need to get back to the original scores.

A convenient way to work out r

We do not need to work out z scores to find r. We can use an alternative formula that is identical to that above but involves only the original scores.

Pearson's $r = \dfrac{SP}{\sqrt{SS_X \times SS_Y}}$

SP is called the <u>sums of products</u> and gives a measures of how the scores of the two variables vary together:

$$SP = \sum(X - \bar{X})(Y - \bar{Y}) = \sum XY - \frac{(\sum X)(\sum Y)}{N}$$

SS_X is the <u>sums of squares</u> of the scores of the first variable, labelled X (in our example *study time*). This gives a measure of how these scores vary on their own:

$$SS_X = \sum(X - \bar{X})^2 = \sum X^2 - \frac{(\sum X)^2}{N}$$

SS_Y is the <u>sums of squares</u> of the scores of the second variable, labelled Y (in our example *examination performance*). This gives a measure of how these scores vary on their own:

$$SS_Y = \sum(Y - \bar{Y})^2 = \sum Y^2 - \frac{(\sum Y)^2}{N}$$

We can see that SP will be large if each X score is the same distance from its mean $\bar{X}$ as each Y score is from its mean $\bar{Y}$. If the X and Y scores do not vary together SP will be small and in the case of no correlation it will become zero. The formula $\sqrt{SS_X \times SS_Y}$ gives us a measure of individual variability of the scores in the two variables. If we can explain all the individual variability of the scores by the joint variability (SP) then $\sqrt{SS_X \times SS_Y}$ and SP will be the same size and r will be $+1$ for a positive correlation and -1 for a negative correlation.

We can use our example to show the calculation:

Participant	X	X^2	Y	Y^2	XY
1	40	1600	58	3364	2320
2	43	1849	73	5329	3139
3	18	324	56	3136	1008
4	10	100	47	2209	470
5	25	625	58	3364	1450
6	33	1089	54	2916	1782
7	27	729	45	2025	1215
8	17	289	32	1024	544
9	30	900	68	4624	2040
10	47	2209	69	4761	3243

$N = 10$ $\sum X = 290$ $\sum X^2 = 9714$ $\sum Y = 560$ $\sum Y^2 = 32752$ $\sum XY = 17211$

$$SP = \sum XY - \frac{(\sum X)(\sum Y)}{N} = 17211 - \frac{290 \times 560}{10} = 971$$

$$SS_X = \sum X^2 - \frac{(\sum X)^2}{N} = 9714 - \frac{290 \times 290}{10} = 1304$$

$$SS_Y = \sum Y^2 - \frac{(\sum Y)^2}{N} = 32752 - \frac{560 \times 560}{10} = 1392$$

$$r = \frac{SP}{\sqrt{SS_X \times SS_Y}} = \frac{971}{\sqrt{1304 \times 1392}} = 0.72$$

We now have to work out the probability of finding a value of r as large or larger than 0.72 by chance, that is when there really is no correlation between the variables. Only then can we decide if we have found a significant correlation.

The distribution of r

When there is no correlation between two variables we would expect r to be zero. However, there will be random variation around this point. We will,

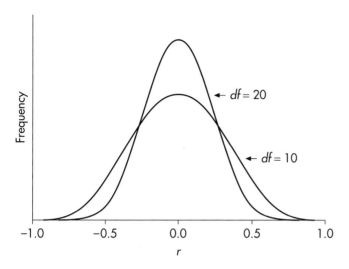

FIGURE 20.2 The distribution of Pearson's r

by chance, obtain values of r that deviate from zero but this will become less likely as we get closer to +1 or −1. We can see from this that the distribution of r under the null hypothesis will be symmetrical about a mean of 0, tailing off towards +1 and −1. The distribution will be flatter when there are fewer subjects and more bunched around the mean when there are more subjects. When there are more subjects the effect of individual subjects will have less influence on the correlation so there will be less chance of r deviating so far from zero.

It is not the actual number of subjects that is important when considering which distribution of r to compare our calculated value to, but the degrees of freedom. For r the degrees of freedom is $N - 2$ (and not $N - 1$) for the following reason. r is actually the slope of the 'best fit' regression line for the z scores. We need the information from at least two points to draw a specific straight line, so we have 'used up' two of our degrees of freedom in finding this line. (In other tests we use up only one degree of freedom on the sample mean.) The distribution of r is shown in Figure 20.2.

A prediction about a correlation can be one-tailed or two-tailed. A one-tailed test specifically states whether the correlation will be positive or negative, whereas a two-tailed prediction merely predicts a significant correlation. We need to take account of this in setting the significance level. In our example we are predicting a positive correlation, that examination performance increases as study time increases, so we have a one-tailed test. From the tables of r (Table A.9 in the Appendix), for a one-tailed test at

$p = 0.05$, with 8 degrees of freedom, $r = 0.5494$. As our calculated value of 0.72 is greater than the table value we can reject the null hypothesis and claim a significant correlation between the variables.

Linear regression

There are books that separate linear correlation from linear regression by putting them in different chapters. It can appear neater that way but we should not lose sight of the fact that correlation and regression are like the two sides of a coin. A linear correlation tells us how close the relationship between two variables is to a straight line. A linear regression is the straight line that best describes the linear relationship between the two variables. With a high correlation we are able to see (more or less) where the regression line occurs by drawing the scatterplot. It is not so obvious when the correlation is weak as the points might be scattered more widely than a narrow band. Yet even though we get a low correlation we can still ask: if there is a linear relationship between these variables what would that line be?

With a regression line we can predict what a score on one variable will be given a score of the other variable. We saw that r is the slope of the regression line for the z scores but this is not what we want. We would like to know the line of best fit for the actual scores so that we can predict a score on one variable from the other directly without having to go through the z scores.

We need a little algebra here, although it should not be too painful. The formula for a straight line relationship between two variables X and Y, is $Y = a + bX$, where 'a' and 'b' are constants (they always stay the same even though X and Y vary) and X and Y are the two variables. You can choose any numbers for a and b, then put any values of X you choose into the equation, work out Y, plot X and Y on a graph and the points will fall along a straight line every time. For example, if I choose, say $a = 2$ and $b = 3$ then $Y = 2 + 3X$ is a straight line. I can take any value of X, say 4, then find $Y = 2 + (3 \times 4) = 14$. I can do this for any value of X and if I plot X and Y on a graph the points will fall along a straight line. When $X = 0$ then $Y = a$ (in my example when $X = 0$, $Y = 2$), so a is the point where the straight line cuts the Y axis. The slope of the line is given by the constant b, which tells us how steeply the line rises or falls. It is like walking along a straight road going up or down hill. A slope of more than 1 is steep, as with every step we take along the X axis we are going up hill, along the Y axis, by at least the same amount and the line lies relatively close to the Y axis.

A slope of less than 1 is shallow, as with every step along the X axis we rise, along the Y axis, by less than that amount and the line lies closer to the X axis than the Y axis. Try making up a few straight line equations and plotting some points for each line on a graph with a horizonal X axis and a vertical Y axis.

We can employ the straight line formula in working out the regression line for the two variables under study. If there is a perfect correlation ($r = +1$ or -1) then the points on the scatterplot will all lie along a straight line. This is our regression line. More usually we do not get a perfect correlation and the regression line is less obvious. With the linear model we are assuming that the points would lie on a straight line but for the random variation. So we need to work out what is the most likely straight line for the data. Notice that a significant correlation gives us the confidence that there is a genuine linear relationship between the two variables. When the correlation is weak we can still work out a regression line but the linear relationship might not be genuine.

First we must decide which variable to predict (in our case we choose *examination performance*, variable Y) and which variable to use for prediction (*study time*, variable X). The first stage in the logic of regression analysis is to assume that the scores for variable X are correct and the reason why the Y scores do not fall along a straight line is due to random error. We are basing our analysis on the X scores. We express this in a formula in the following way:

$$Y = \text{Regression (on } X) + \text{Error}$$

$$Y = Y' + E$$

We are assuming that the actual Y scores are a combination of the ones along the straight line (Y') plus a deviation from that straight line due to error (E). What we want to know is what Y values we would get if they really did fall along a straight line and we could get rid of the error: what are the values of Y' where $Y' = Y - E$? The straight line that we are looking for is therefore:

$$Y' = a + bX$$

which is the <u>regression line of Y on X</u> without the error (E). What we now have to find are the appropriate values for a and b.

Next in the analysis we use the fact that the 'line of best fit' is the line that gives the smallest error values. We do not want a line that is nowhere

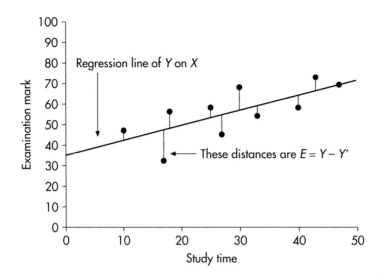

FIGURE 20.3 Finding the regression line by minimising the error values (E)

near the points on the scatterplot. The regression line should be the straight line that goes closest to the data points. We want to find the line that produces the smallest values for E, where $E = Y - Y'$. A mathematical way of putting it is to say that we want the line that 'minimises' E where E is the distance of an actual data point from the regression line. Figure 20.3 shows this for our example.

We work out the minimum values of E by a procedure called the least squares method of linear regression. We could add up the error $(Y - Y')$ for each subject to produce $\sum E = \sum(Y - Y')$ but some errors will be positive and some negative and so cancel each other out (as you can see from Figure 20.3), hiding the size of the error. To overcome this we square the errors so that they all become positive, to produce the sums of squares: $\sum E^2 = \sum(Y - Y')^2$. (Once again we can see the importance of 'sums of squares' at the heart of a statistical analysis.) Now we need to find when this sums of squares is at its smallest. We can replace Y' by $a + bX$ in the sums of squares to give a formula containing only X and Y, which are the values we know rather than Y' which we want to find out: $\sum(Y - a - bX)^2$. We now want to know what values of a and b would minimise this formula so that $\sum E^2 = \sum(Y - a - bX)^2$ is the smallest it can be. The way we do this is by employing a mathematical technique called differentiation. (There is not space to explain differentiation here, but for readers not familiar with it, all that is necessary to know for the logic of the current argument is that this

technique exists and helps us at this point in deriving the regression line.)
As a result of this, the above sums of squares is at its minimum when:

$$b = \frac{SP}{SS_X} \text{ and } a = \overline{Y} - b\overline{X}$$

where $\overline{X}$ and $\overline{Y}$ are the means of the scores of the two variables, and SP is
the sums of products and SS_X the sums of squares for the scores on variable
X that we worked out in the calculation of r.

All we need to do now is work out a and b to produce the regression
line. For our example, looking back to the calculation of r, we have $SP =
971$, $SS_X = 1304$, $\overline{X} = 29$ and $\overline{Y} = 56$ so:

$$b = \frac{971}{1304} = 0.7446 \quad \text{and} \quad a = 56 - (0.7446 \times 29) = 34.4057$$

Finally, replacing a and b by their actual values in the formula for Y', we
are able to express the regression line by the following formula:

$$Y' = 34.41 + 0.74X \text{ (to two decimal places)}.$$

We can now use this formula to predict the values of Y (*examination performance*) from the values of X (*study time*). Below is a table of the predicted
values of Y based on the regression on X.[19]

Student	Study time	Examination mark	Predicted examination mark
	X	Y	Y'
1	40	58	64.01
2	43	73	66.23
3	18	56	47.73
4	10	47	41.81
5	25	58	52.91
6	33	54	58.83
7	27	45	54.39
8	17	32	46.99
9	30	68	56.61
10	47	69	69.19

We can also use the regression line to predict other values. For example, no one studied for 35 hours per week. What examination mark would we predict for someone who did study for this time? Using the formula for Y' we get: $Y' = 34.41 + (0.74 \times 35) = 60.31$. We would expect a student who studied for 35 hours per week to get a mark of 60.31 in the examination.

r and the slope of the regression line

We have found b, the slope of the regression line, and r, the correlation coefficient, which is the slope of the z scores regression line. There is a simple relationship between the two:

$$b = r \left(\frac{\text{standard deviation of } Y}{\text{standard deviation of } X} \right)$$

b takes account of the fact that the two variables are measured on two different scales, whereas r standardises them. In our example: $b = 0.72 \left(\dfrac{11.80}{11.42} \right) = 0.74$. So, whichever way we work out b we get the same value.[20]

Predicting X from Y

There is nothing in the logic of the regression analysis that prevents us from performing the regression the other way round, by assuming the Y values are correct and that it is the X values that deviate from a regression line due to error. The logic works in the same way to predict X from Y by the regression of X on Y. In this case we find $X' = a + bY$ (which is also a formula for a straight line), where $b = \dfrac{SP}{SS_Y}$ and $a = \bar{X} - b\bar{Y}$. In our example, we find $X' = 0.70Y - 10.06$. From this formula we can predict that someone who obtained a 60 in the examination studied for $(0.70 \times 60) - 10.06 = 31.94$ hours per week.

If we plot both the regression lines (Y on X, and X on Y) on the same graph we find, in our case, that they are close together (see Figure 20.4). This is because the stronger the correlation the closer the regression lines are to each other. With a perfect correlation the lines are the same. As the

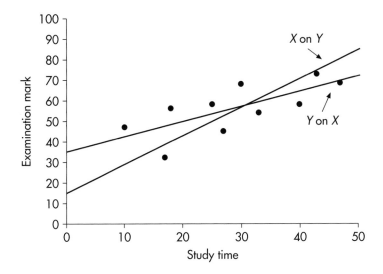

FIGURE 20.4 Regression of Y on X and the regression of X on Y

correlation gets weaker the regression lines separate until, when $r = 0$, the lines are orthogonal, that is at right angles to each other and have no predictive value as there is not a linear relationship between the variables.

The interpretation of correlation and regression

We must be careful when we interpret a significant correlation coefficient. The first point to note is that a smaller value of r is needed for significance as N increases. With a df of 70 for a one-tailed test, or a df of 100 for a two-tailed test, r is still significant (at $p = 0.05$) when it is as low as 0.2. With correlation coefficients we need to ask not just is it significant but is it big? One way of deciding the importance of the correlation is to consider how much of the variability of the scores in one variable can be explained (predicted) by the variability of the scores of the other variable. We might have a significant correlation but if it only explains a tiny amount of the variability then it may not be of much predictive worth.

Recall that $Y =$ Regression on $X +$ Error. We also find that the variability of the Y scores ($SS_Y = \Sigma(Y - \bar{Y})^2$) equals the variability due to the regression ($SS_{regression} = \Sigma(Y' - \bar{Y})^2$) plus the variability due to error ($SS_{error} = \Sigma(Y' - Y)^2$). It is reasonable to ask how much of the total variability of Y can be explained by that of the regression. We can express this as

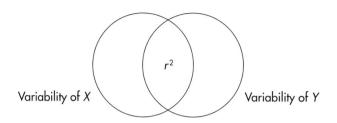

FIGURE 20.5 The coefficient of determination (r^2)

$SS_{regression}$ as a proportion of SS_Y. How much of the total Y sums of squares can be explained by the sums of squares of the regression on X? It turns out that:

$$\frac{SS_{regression}}{SS_Y} = \frac{SP^2}{SS_X SS_Y} = r^2$$

We find that the proportion of the variability in one set of scores that can be explained by the regression is actually the square of the regression coefficient, r^2, called the <u>coefficient of determination</u>. We can represent r^2 diagrammatically in Figure 20.5. A circle represents the total variability of the scores for one variable. The overlap of the two circles indicates the amount of variability of one variable that can be explained by the variability of the other variable, r^2.

With a perfect correlation of $r = +1$ or -1 then $r^2 = 1$ and all variability in the Y scores can be explained by the regression. The regression line is a perfect predictor of the Y scores. A high correlation, such as $r = 0.7$, yields an r^2 of 0.49 which tells us not quite half of the variability in Y can be explained by changes in X (and vice versa). With a correlation of 0.2 only 0.04 of the variability of the Y scores can be explained by the regression on X, so, in this case, despite the statistical significance we have every right to question the value of X as a predictor of Y.

Problems with correlation and regression

We must be careful to check that our data has homoscedasticity when we are undertaking a correlation. <u>Homoscedasticity</u> essentially means that the relationship between the two variables stays the same at all points, with the scores evenly spread along and around the regression line. Isolated points and clusters can both have a powerful influence on the correlation coefficient, and disguise the underlying relationship between the variables, particularly if we use a limited range of scores from the variables.

An example will illustrate these points. A researcher predicts that the more shop assistants smile at customers the more items are sold by the assistant. Each assistant in a store is videotaped during one day and the amount of smiling is calculated from the time an assistant greets a customer to the moment the customer decides to buy or not to buy an item. The researcher examined the correlation between the mean *smiling time* per customer for each assistant (in minutes) and the total number of *items sold* by each assistant during the day. The results for 9 assistants are shown below.

Assistant	Smiling time X	Items sold Y
1	0.4	16
2	0.8	12
3	0.8	20
4	1.2	16
5	1.4	34
6	1.8	30
7	2.2	26
8	2.6	22
9	3.0	38

When we take all 9 participants into account we find that $r = 0.69$ ($SP = 43.56$, $SS_X = 6.28$, $SS_Y = 627.56$, $df = 7$). This is significant at $p < 0.05$ (from Table A.9 in the Appendix we find that $r = 0.5822$, $p = 0.05$, $df = 7$, for a one-tailed test). However, looking at the scatterplot, Figure 20.6, we see that participant 9 is isolated from the rest. Without this participant $r = 0.52$ ($SP = 20.80$, $SS_X = 4.00$, $SS_Y = 400.00$, $df = 6$) which is no longer significant (as $r = 0.6215$, $p = 0.05$, $df = 6$, for a one-tailed test). Thus the effect of participant 9 is to make the correlation significant yet participant 9 is not typical, and so we should not take the result as practically useful despite its statistical significance. This shows how one 'outlier' can strongly affect the correlation.

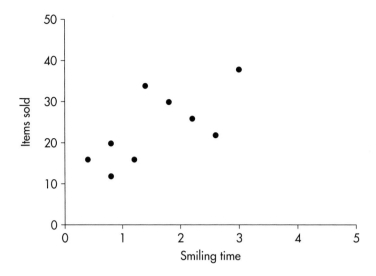

FIGURE 20.6 The scatterplot of smiling time by items sold

If we look at the scatterplot we can also see that the pattern of results is not the same for all participants: the relationship between smiling and items sold is not the same all along the regression line. If we limit our range to participants 1 to 4 we find that $r = 0$ ($SP = 0$, $SS_X = 0.32$, $SS_Y = 32.00$, $df = 2$). There is no correlation at all for these participants alone. If we now select only participants 5 to 8 we produce a correlation coefficient of $r = -1$ ($SP = -8.0$, $SS_X = 0.8$, $SS_Y = 80$, $df = 2$), which is a perfect negative correlation. These two clusters produce very different results which illustrates why we do not want a limited range in our study. The lack of homoscedasticity has resulted in a positive, zero and negative correlation dependent on which participants we select.

A similar spread of data along the regression line provides evidence that the correlation does in fact indicate a genuine underlying relationship between the variables. Isolated points, clusters and a limited range can all provide spurious correlations. We must look a little further than a statistically significant r when we are interpreting the meaning of a correlation.

The standard error of the estimate

We can always find a regression line for our data, regardless of the value of r, but just because we can calculate it does not mean that it is of theoretical significance. To be confident that our predictions are based on a genuine underling relationship we really want all the points to be close to the regression line. A way of determining how close the points are to the regression line is to calculate the standard error of the estimate, which, for the regression of Y on X, is the standard deviation of the Y scores from the regression line of Y on X. Recall that a variance is a sums of squares divided by a degrees of freedom. So the error variance, the amount by which the Y scores vary from the regression line, is $\frac{SS_{error}}{N-2}$. We find the square root to produce a standard deviation.

$$\text{Standard error of the estimate} = \sqrt{\frac{SS_{error}}{N-2}}$$

We also know from above that $SS_Y = SS_{regression} + SS_{error}$ and $r^2 = \frac{SS_{regression}}{SS_Y}$. From these two formulae we can show that $SS_{error} = (1 - r^2)SS_Y$. Replacing SS_{error} in the formula for the standard error of the estimate we get:

$$\text{Standard error of the estimate} = \sqrt{\frac{(1 - r^2)SS_Y}{N-2}}$$

For the study time/examination performance example we have $r^2 = 0.52$ and $SS_Y = 1392$, so the standard error of the estimate, the standard distance of a Y score from the regression line is: $\sqrt{\frac{(1 - r^2)SS_Y}{N-2}} = \sqrt{\frac{(1 - 0.52)1392}{10 - 2}}$
$= 9.14$.

The Spearman r_S correlation coefficient

There will be times when we wish to correlate data that is not measured on a interval scale. As long as the data are ordinal we can perform a correlation on the ranks using the Spearman r_S correlation coefficient. Each set of scores is ranked separately from lowest to highest. A Pearson's r is then calculated on the ranks. However, with ranks, as long as there are no ties, we can use a simpler formula. There will be the same ranks for both sets of scores so $SS_X = SS_Y$. If we replace SS_Y with SS_X in the formula for r we get:

$$r = \frac{SP}{\sqrt{SS_X \times SS_Y}} = \frac{SP}{SS_X}$$

It is also the case that with ranks $SP = SS_X - \frac{\sum D^2}{2}$, where D is the difference between a subject's ranks on the two variables. Furthermore, with ranks, $SS_X = \frac{N^3 - N}{12}$. Replacing SP and SS_X in the formula for r we get:

$$\text{Spearman's } r_S = 1 - \frac{6 \sum D^2}{N^3 - N}$$

All we have to do for ranked data is work out r_S. We then look up the figure in the tables for r_S at the chosen level of significance (Table A.10 in the Appendix). In this case we do not use the degrees of freedom to find the correct table value of r_S but N, the number of ranks. As with all analyses on ranks we have to be careful if there are many tied ranks and should consider employing a more sensitive measure of the variable to reduce them. Alternatively, the original Pearson formula can be used.

The Spearman coefficient is useful if we are concerned that the scores on two variables appear to correlate but not linearly. As long as the two variables vary monotonically, that is as one increases the other also increases consistently or as one increases the other decreases consistently, then the r_S coefficient can be used.

A worked example

Two teachers were asked to rate the same six teenagers on the variable *how likely to do well academically at University* on a 0–20 scale, from unlikely to highly likely. The results are shown below. Is there a positive correlation between the teachers' ranking?

Teenager	Teacher 1 ratings	Teacher 2 ratings	Teacher 1 ranks	Teacher 2 ranks	D	D^2
1	15	8	4	3	1	1
2	12	13	3	5	−2	4
3	18	16	6	6	0	0
4	4	5	1	2	−1	1
5	8	2	2	1	1	1
6	17	10	5	4	1	1
						$\sum D^2 = 8$

The ratings for each teacher are ranked separately. From these we produce the difference scores (D), showing the difference in ranks between the teachers, and the squared difference scores (D^2). The sum of the difference scores, $\sum D^2 = 8$. There are 6 participants so $N = 6$. We now work out r_S.

$$r_S = 1 - \frac{6 \sum D^2}{N^3 - N} = 1 - \frac{6 \times 8}{6^3 - 6} = 0.77$$

We have a one-tailed test as the prediction is for a positive correlation. From Table A.10 in the Appendix, $r_S = 0.829$, $p = 0.05$, $N = 6$ for a one-tailed test. The calculated value does not exceed the table value so we have not found a significant correlation in the rankings. (Notice how, with a small number of subjects, we need a high value of the coefficient for significance.)

Details on how to calculate a linear correlation and linear regression using the SPSS computer statistical package can be found in Chapter 15 of Hinton *et al.* (2004).

Chapter 21

Multiple correlation and regression

Introduction to multivariate analysis

Up to now we have looked at the correlation between two variables. Yet we can consider the correlation between three or more variables, say IQ, school grades, university grades and occupational performance. Dealing with many variables at the same time is referred to as multivariate analysis. In this chapter we shall be examining both correlation and regression with more than two variables as this is often an important form of analysis when we collect information about a number of factors (such as in a questionnaire or survey) and we want to investigate the relationships between them. For example, we might wish to study the relationship between housing quality, housing density, social support networks and pollution levels on health.

Partial correlation

In the previous chapter we analysed some example data to show a significant correlation between study time and examination performance. We might decide that a third variable, *intelligence*, could be influencing the correlation. If intelligence positively correlates with study time, that is, the more intelligent students spend the most time studying, and if it also positively correlates with examination performance, that is, the more intelligent students get the higher marks in the examination, then the correlation of study time and examination performance might simply be due to the third factor, intelligence. If this is the case then the relationship between study time and examination performance is not genuine, in that the reason they correlate is because they are both an outcome of *intelligence*. That is, the more intelligent students both study more and get higher marks in the examination. If we take out the effect of intelligence the relationship of study time to examination performance could disappear.

It is worth noting here that a correlation does not indicate a causal relationship. We might find that over a period of years the number of houses positively correlates with the amount of pollution in a town. It would be wrong to claim that the houses cause the pollution or that more pollution causes more houses. In this case, the correlation might arise due to a third factor *population*, which correlates with both. An increase in population (and human activity) might result in both more houses and also greater pollution. The correlation between houses and pollution is simply an outcome of a third factor rather than an important correlation in its own right.

To answer the question of the influence of intelligence on the study time/examination performance correlation we need to examine the correlation of study time and examination performance *after* removing the effects of intelligence. If the correlation disappears then we know it was due to the third factor. We do this by calculating a partial correlation. The first stage is to find out how well the factor intelligence correlates with study time and examination performance separately. To find this out we measure the students' intelligence on a standard test of intelligence. The results of this test along with the study times and examination marks are shown in the following table.

Student	Intelligence score	Study time	Examination mark
1	118	40	58
2	128	43	73
3	110	18	56
4	114	10	47
5	138	25	58
6	120	33	54
7	106	27	45
8	124	17	32
9	132	30	68
10	130	47	69
Mean	122	29	56
Standard deviation	9.72	11.42	11.80

Using the techniques outlined in the previous chapter we find the following correlation coefficients:

Study time and Examination performance $r = 0.72$
Study time and Intelligence $r = 0.37$
Examination performance and Intelligence $r = 0.48$

The correlations indicate that intelligence is positively correlated with the other two variables so there is reason to continue the investigation.

Recall from the previous chapter that the regression allows us to predict one variable from a second. If we perform a regression of study time on intelligence this will tell us what study time scores we would predict from intelligence. Thus, the difference between the actual study time scores and those predicted by intelligence should give us the study time scores with the effects of intelligence removed. These differences are termed residuals rather than 'error' here because, whilst the difference is an 'error' in the ability of intelligence to predict study time, in this case it is what we are interested in, that is, what is left (the residual variability in the scores) after taking out the effects of intelligence on study time.

Performing a regression of study time on intelligence we get the following equation: Study time = 0.44 × Intelligence − 24.50. From this we can work out the predicted study time scores and then subtract them from the actual scores to give the residuals. The following table shows this (see Note 19).

Student	Study time	Study time predicted by intelligence	Residual study time
1	40	27.42	12.58
2	43	31.82	11.18
3	18	23.90	−5.90
4	10	25.66	−15.66
5	25	36.22	−11.22
6	33	28.30	4.70
7	27	22.14	4.86
8	17	30.06	−13.06
9	30	33.58	−3.58
10	47	32.70	14.30

This has removed the effect of intelligence from study time. We now need to remove it from the examination performance. We follow the same method and perform a regression of examination performance on intelligence. This gives us the regression equation: Examination performance = 0.59 × Intelligence − 15.60. We use this equation to work out the residuals for examination performance.

Student	Examination mark	Examination mark predicted by intelligence	Residual examination mark
1	58	54.02	3.98
2	73	59.92	13.08
3	56	48.30	6.70
4	47	51.66	−4.66
5	58	65.82	−7.82
6	54	55.20	−1.20
7	45	46.94	−1.94
8	32	57.56	−25.56
9	68	62.28	5.72
10	69	61.10	7.90

We can now correlate the residual study time scores with the residual examination marks, having removed the effects of intelligence from the two factors. The correlation of these scores yields an r of 0.665. This is called a partial correlation as it is the correlation of study time and examination performance having partialled out the effect of intelligence. In this case the size of the correlation has been reduced but it is still significant (at $p = 0.05$), so the original correlation was not entirely due to the third variable, intelligence. There is still a significant relationship between the amount of time spent studying and performance in the examination *after* we have accounted for the effects of intelligence.

We can illustrate what we have done by representing the variability of the scores of each variable by a circle. As we can see from Figure 21.1 the three circles overlap. The area $SE + SIE$ is the portion of the examination performance variability explained by study time, the area $SI + SIE$ the portion of study time explained by intelligence and $IE + SIE$ the portion of examination performance explained by intelligence. The size of these areas can be found by calculating r^2 for each correlation. When we remove the effects of intelligence we take away the intelligence circle $(I + SI + SIE + IE)$ leaving $S + SE$ of the study time variability and $E + SE$ of the examination performance variability. The partial correlation of study time and examination performance, having removed the effect of intelligence, leaves us with the area SE as the residual variability of examination performance explained by the residual variability of study time.

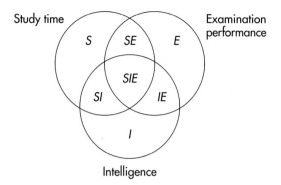

FIGURE 21.1 The variability of the scores on three variables

Fortunately, there is an easier method of calculating a partial correlation, than finding the residuals, when we know the three separate correlation coefficients. We label the variables as *1*, *2* and *3* (rather than *X* and *Y*) as it makes it easier to label additional variables. I will label examination performance as variable *1*, study time as variable *2* and intelligence as variable *3*. The correlation coefficients are labelled as r_{12} for the correlation of variables *1* and *2*, r_{13} for the correlation of variables *1* and *3* and r_{23} for the correlation of variables *2* and *3*. The partial correlation of variables *1* and *2* having removed the effects of variable *3* is termed $r_{12.3}$ and can be calculated with the following relatively simple formula.

$$r_{12.3} = \frac{r_{12} - r_{13}r_{23}}{\sqrt{1 - r_{13}^2}\sqrt{1 - r_{23}^2}}$$

For our example,

$$r_{12.3} = \frac{0.72 - (0.48 \times 0.37)}{\sqrt{1 - 0.48^2}\sqrt{1 - 0.37^2}} = 0.665$$

We are not restricted to finding just the one partial correlation. We can also find $r_{13.2}$ (the correlation between examination performance and intelligence having partialled out the effect of study time) and $r_{23.1}$ (the correlation of study time and intelligence having partialled out the effect of examination performance) by using the same formula with the correlation coefficients adjusted appropriately, so for $r_{13.2}$ we would replace r_{12} with r_{13} and so on. Notice that some of these are more meaningful to work out than others. Just because the statistical reasoning provides us with the possibility of an analysis it does not mean that we decide it is worthwhile undertaking.

We can extend the analysis to partial out the effects of more than one variable from a correlation. We can remove the effects of variable *4* if we wish by the following formula:

$$r_{12.34} = \frac{r_{12.3} - r_{14.3}r_{24.3}}{\sqrt{1 - r_{14.3}^2}\sqrt{1 - r_{24.3}^2}}$$

Notice that the formula contains the partial correlations of the variables having removed variable *3*. The logic allows us to go on to remove variables *5*, *6*, etc. However, the formulae make one key assumption, that is, the variables are <u>linearly correlated</u> with variables *1* and *2*. We are extending the linear model to all the variables. If this assumption is not valid we will only partial out the linear components of the variables, not all their effects.

Multiple correlation

We can use partial correlations to help us calculate a <u>multiple correlation</u>. A multiple correlation coefficient, R, gives us a measure of how well three or more variables correlate together. We do some relabelling again here. We specify a particular variable to label as Y. This is the dependent variable and we are calculating how it correlates with the rest. It is usually the variable we wish to predict (as we shall see in multiple regression later). I shall choose *examination performance* as this is an interesting one to predict. We call the other variables *1*, *2*, *3*, etc. We have only two others so I shall call *study time* variable *1* and *intelligence* variable *2*.

R is easier to explain if we work with R^2, the coefficient of determination for the multiple correlation. We take each of the variables *1*, *2*, *3*, etc. in turn and find out what proportion of the Y variability it can explain that has not already been explained by previous variables. Adding up these portions gives us a measure of how much of the Y variability can be explained by the combination of the other variables.

The first question we must ask is how much of the variability of the Y scores (examination performance) can be explained by variable *1*, study time? This is simply the coefficient of determination of the correlation of the two variables, r_{Y1}^2. Now we ask how much of the remaining variability of Y can be explained by variable *2*, intelligence? It is not r_{Y2}^2 as some of this area has already been explained. If we look back to the interlocking circles in Figure 21.1 we see that r_{Y2}^2 is the areas *SIE* and *IE*. Yet we have already explained the areas *SE* and *SIE* by r_{Y1}^2. We have already predicted the area *SIE* so we do not want to do it twice. Because intelligence and study time are correlated they both explain some of the *same* variability of examination performance (the area *SIE*). To overcome this we remove the effect of study time (variable *1*) before finding out what of the remaining variability in the examination performance can be explained by intelligence. The residual portion of examination performance after removing the effects of study time is $1 - r_{Y1}^2$ (that is, the whole area, *I*, minus that portion explained by study time, leaving $E + IE$). The amount of the area $1 - r_{Y1}^2$ explained by intelligence is the partial correlation of examination performance and intelligence having removed the effect of study time. This is $r_{Y2.1}^2$ (the area *IE*). Expressed as a portion of the residual *Y* variability this amount (*IE* as a portion of $E + IE$) is $r_{Y2.1}^2(1 - r_{Y1}^2)$. In conclusion we can say that the amount of *Y* variability explained by variables *1* and *2* is:

$$R_{Y.12}^2 = r_{Y1}^2 + r_{Y2.1}^2(1 - r_{Y1}^2)$$

(In terms of part of the examination performance circle in Figure 21.1, this is *SE* + *SIE* for variable *1* plus *IE* for variable *2*.)

The <u>multiple correlation coefficient</u>, $R_{Y.12}$, is simply the square root of this figure. In our example, $r_{Y1} = 0.72$ and $r_{Y2.1} = 0.33$, so $R_{Y.12}^2 = 0.72^2 + 0.33^2(1 - 0.72^2) = 0.57$, and the coefficient of multiple correlation, $R_{Y.12}$, is $\sqrt{0.57} = 0.75$. This tells us that more of the variability in *Y* (examination performance) can be explained by study time and intelligence ($R_{Y.12}^2 = 0.57$) than by study time alone ($r_{Y1}^2 = 0.52$), although not a lot more.

We can calculate a multiple correlation coefficient for any number of variables, with each new variable used to explain variability in *Y* unexplained by any previous variable. For four variables, $R_{Y.123}^2 = R_{Y.12}^2 + r_{Y3.12}^2(1 - R_{Y.12}^2)$ where the *R*s in the formula are themselves multiple correlation coefficients. The problem is that as each additional variable is brought in, we chip away at the variability of *Y* so that *R* becomes larger. Yet as each new variable is added we increase the risk of increasing *R* by random variation rather than by genuine relationships. Therefore multiple correlations should be undertaken with caution and when a large number of variables are used as 'predictor' variables then a correction should be made to *R* to compensate for the increased risk of error. (Statistical computer programs such as SPSS provide an 'Adjusted *R*' value to correct for this – see Hinton *et al.*, 2004.)

The significance of R^2

We can test the significance of a multiple correlation by using a variance ratio (F) test, comparing the estimated variance of the 'explained variability' to the estimated variance of the 'unexplained variability':

$$\frac{\dfrac{R^2}{k}}{\dfrac{1 - R^2}{N - k - 1}}$$

where N is the number of subjects and k is the number of predictor variables. Thus,

$$F = \frac{R^2(N - k - 1)}{k(1 - R^2)} \text{ with degrees of freedom } k, N - k - 1$$

In our example, with $R^2 = 0.57$, $N = 10$, $k = 2$, $F(2,7) = \dfrac{0.57(10 - 2 - 1)}{2(1 - 0.57)}$ = 4.64. From the tables of the F distribution, Table A.3 in the Appendix, $F(2,7) = 4.74$, $p = 0.05$, so the multiple correlation is not significant at $p = 0.05$. Note that if we had had the same value of R^2 but just one more participant ($N = 11$) the result would have been significant. This shows the importance of sample size when dealing with correlations.

Multiple regression

We can calculate a linear regression for more than two variables. Again we need to label one of the variables as Y because this will be the dependent variable. The other variables, the independent variables or predictor variables, will be used to predict it. Instead of having a single variable X for the linear regression we use a number of variables X_1, X_2, ..., X_k for the regression, where k is the number of predictor variables. To work out the regression line we calculate the following linear equation:

$$Y = a + b_1 X_1 + b_2 X_2 + \ldots + b_k X_k$$

I shall only consider the case of two predictor variables here, the simplest case, to illustrate multiple regression. The logic is the same for more predictor variables but the calculation becomes rather complex and will not be explained in this book.

With two predictor variables we wish to solve the equation:

$$Y = a + b_1 X_1 + b_2 X_2$$

Recall that with just one predictor variable, $Y = a + bX$, where $b = \left(\dfrac{s_Y}{s_X}\right) r_{YX}$ where s_Y and s_X are the standard deviations of the scores of the two variables.[20]

In the two variable case we *cannot* work out b_1 and b_2 by using $b_1 = \left(\dfrac{s_Y}{s_1}\right) r_{Y1}$ and $b_2 = \left(\dfrac{s_Y}{s_2}\right) r_{Y2}$ unless X_1 and X_2 are *not* correlated (where s_Y, s_1 and s_2 are the standard deviations of the three variables). The problem is that, as in multiple correlation, we will have some overlap in the variability of Y that the two predictor variables can explain. If we are not careful we will count this variability twice, once with X_1 and once with X_2 and our prediction will be distorted. The way to solve this problem is for the bs to be partial regression coefficients, that is, coefficients where the effect of one variable is partialled out when working out the b for the other. In the two predictor case:

$$b_1 = \beta_1 \left(\frac{s_Y}{s_1}\right) \quad \text{and} \quad b_2 = \beta_2 \left(\frac{s_Y}{s_2}\right)$$

where β_1 and β_2 are the standard partial regression coefficients:

$$\beta_1 = \frac{r_{Y1} - r_{Y2} r_{12}}{1 - r_{12}^2} \quad \text{and} \quad \beta_2 = \frac{r_{Y2} - r_{Y1} r_{12}}{1 - r_{12}^2}$$

Just as r is the slope of the line when we convert X and Y to z scores in the two variable case, β_1 and β_2 are the partial slopes of the regression of Y by the predictor variables when all the scores are converted to z scores.

To complete the linear regression we use the following formula to find a:

$$a = \bar{Y} - b_1 \bar{X}_1 - b_2 \bar{X}_2$$

We can illustrate the calculation by predicting examination performance (Y) using study time (X_1) and intelligence (X_2) as predictor variables. We first work out β_1 and β_2:

$$\beta_1 = \frac{0.72 - (0.48 \times 0.37)}{1 - 0.37^2} = 0.63 \quad \beta_2 = \frac{0.48 - (0.72 \times 0.37)}{1 - 0.37^2} = 0.25$$

Next we work out b_1 and b_2 using the values for the standard deviations of the variables (found from the table on p. 285):

$$b_1 = 0.63\left(\frac{11.80}{11.42}\right) = 0.65 \quad b_2 = 0.25\left(\frac{11.80}{9.72}\right) = 0.30$$

Finally we calculate a:

$$a = 56 - (0.65 \times 29) - (0.30 \times 122) = 0.55$$

We now have the equation for the multiple regression:[19]

$$Y' = 0.55 + 0.65X_1 + 0.30X_2$$

Replacing the symbols with the variable names gives us the formula for predicting examination performance using study time and intelligence:

Examination mark = 0.55 + 0.65 Study time + 0.30 Intelligence

From this we can predict, for example, a student with an intelligence score of 110 and who studies for 30 hours per week will obtain the following examination mark:

Examination mark = 0.55 + (0.65 × 30) + (0.30 × 110) = 53.05

Thus, on the basis of the linear multiple regression we predict that the student would get an examination mark of 53.05.

Multicollinearity

When our predictor variables are highly correlated with each other we have what is referred to as multicollinearity. This can be a problem for multiple regression. First, the predictors are explaining much the same variability in the dependent variable Y. Consider the case of two predictor variables. When the two variables are not correlated then the Y variability explained by one is different to the Y variability explained by the other but when they are correlated there is an overlap in the Y variability they explain. Second, we do not know which of the predictor variables is the more important due to the common variability explained. With many predictor variables this problem can arise quite easily. A solution to multicollinearity is to combine variables into a single variable or to leave one out if it is essentially predicting the same variability as another. As an example, imagine that you were predicting a person's height from other bodily dimensions, such as foot length, forearm length, index finger length, etc. If you had included the length of the left foot and the length of the right foot as two separate variables then you might find that these two measurements are so highly correlated that you really do not need or want both in your regression due to multicollinearity. You might decide to include only the right foot length or even the average of the two feet lengths for each person.

Calculating multiple regression

In our example we have included all the predictor variables in the regression, not surprisingly since there were only two, and this is called direct regression. When there are more predictor variables, the researcher might start by calculating the multiple regression by working out the equation using the predictor variable that correlated most highly with the dependent variable. Predictor variables are then added into the regression on the basis of the additional variance they can explain. The process is terminated when a variable no longer significantly increases R^2. This is called forward regression. An alternative is to include all the predictor variables initially but to remove variables one at a time, taking out the one that contributes the least to R^2, until removing a variable would significantly reduce R^2. At which point the regression calculation stops. This is called backward regression. Stepwise regression combines the above two methods, adding variables and taking others away at the same time. The reason why we use alternatives to the direct method is that the most predictive regression is where few variables explain lots of the variability in the dependent variable. Not only is it parsimonious, it also means that we are not including a lot of additional variables which contribute little to the prediction.

Details on how to calculate a multiple correlation and multiple regression using the SPSS computer statistical package can be found in Chapter 16 of Hinton *et al.* (2004).

Chapter 22

Complex analyses
and computers

Undertaking data analysis by computer

Throughout this book I have been explaining how to perform a range of statistical analyses. So the next piece of advice may seem a little unexpected: don't use up your valuable time undertaking statistical analysis when you can get a computer to do it for you! There are many excellent statistics programs, such as SPSS (see Hinton *et al.*, 2004), the calculations are done quickly with a degree of consistent accuracy that we can rarely match as human beings. The key point I hope to have made in the book is that it is important to know why and how statistical analysis operates, the reasoning behind it, the assumptions made and the types of data that particular analyses can deal with. This knowledge not only allows you to perform the calculations with a calculator but it is also invaluable when using a computer. If you do not understand what you are doing then using a computer simply compounds the problem. When performing, say, a *t* test by hand you might learn something about the operation and logic of the test but with a computer the test gets 'magically' done and the result appears like a rabbit out of a hat. If you didn't know what you were doing beforehand, you certainly will not be any the wiser afterwards. It is only when we know what we are doing that the computer comes into its own. The person who understands statistical analysis can appreciate what the computer is doing, and more importantly, know when it is NOT DOING what is really wanted.

A key thing to remember when using a computer is the acronym GIGO – garbage in, garbage out. If you put a lot of nonsense into the computer you will get a lot of nonsense out! Computers do not know when you have made a mistake, in fact they do not 'know' anything, they simply do as they are told. If you choose the wrong analysis, or type in the wrong data, the computer program will still perform the analysis on that data. If you do not realise your mistake then you can unknowingly take away the results of an incorrect or inappropriate analysis. If this is for an important research programme with much depending on the results then the ramifications of your mistake may be profound.

Errors in data input

There are a number of checks you can perform to make sure that you have input the data correctly into a computer program or computer file for subsequent analysis. The first thing to do is to obtain a printout of the data <u>after</u> it has been input into the computer. You will then be able to make a check on the data that was actually analysed rather than the data you hoped was analysed. Look at the printout and ask yourself the following questions.

1   Are there any large numbers where you did not expect them? If you leave your finger on a key for too long you might input that digit twice by mistake. Check that numbers that should be 2 are not 22 or even 222.

2   Are there missing values where there should not be? When reading down a list of numbers to input, it is quite possible to miss one out. Check that the correct number of figures have been input.

3   Does the pattern of data look correct? Often with a large amount of data you can see patterns on the page of numbers, such as all 1s in a particular column. As you scan down the data is there an unusual figure somewhere? If so, check that it is correct rather than an error on input.

4   Has the data been input in the correct order for the analysis? This can be a very important question. If the analysis is complex such as a two factor mixed design ANOVA the data must be input in the correct order. If not, the computer might analyse the data for the independent factor as though it were the repeated measures factor and vice versa.

Interpreting output

Once the computer has performed the analysis the program will present a display or a printout of the results of the analysis. When interpreting this analysis keep in mind one question: is this what you expected when you input the data? If not then why were your expectations out? This illustrates why knowledge of statistical analysis is so useful. If you know that a certain analysis cannot produce what you have obtained then you know there is an error somewhere, whereas someone who has no knowledge of statistical analysis might simply accept the result as correct.

The first area to check is the means, totals, standard deviations, etc. You may already have worked out the means of the various conditions before performing the analysis. Does the computer come up with the same values? Has it the correct means in the correct conditions? A basic check of the simple calculations can confirm that the data has been input correctly and the correct numbers are in the appropriate conditions.

Next check that the statistical analysis is the one you wanted. Often the name of the analysis will appear on the output. Does it say 'related or repeated measures' when you really wanted independent? Does it say 'completely randomised or independent measures' when you wanted to perform a repeated measures analysis? Simply looking at the information at the top of the output can often be the most useful. But always make sure you know what analysis you want to perform before you ask the computer to do it!

Occasionally the computer program will have an error in it. The chances of a commercially available one containing a 'bug' are very small but if you are using a helpful little program you downloaded from the Internet (often written by academics then generously offered to others for free) then make sure that the results match your expectations. Recall that there are certain results you should never get, such as a negative value for a sums of squares in an ANOVA summary table. Always check the data first but do not always trust the program.

There are differences between the ways computer programs present the results and the ways it is done when working out the analysis by hand. The most common difference is in the presentation of the significance of a finding. Computer programs often give the actual probability of the result occurring by chance rather than whether it exceeds the significance level or not. For example, rather than stating '$p < 0.05$' or 'significant at $p = 0.05$' the computer might display '$p = 0.034215$', which is the actual probability of the result under the null hypothesis. It is up to you to decide whether this is significant at the significance level you have chosen. A result with a probability 0.034215 is less than 0.05 so is significant at the $p = 0.05$ level of significance but not at $p = 0.01$. Sometimes the computer will output the probability as $p = 0.000000$. This appears to indicate that the result could never occur under the null hypothesis, which is obviously impossible. The true explanation lies in the way the computer displays numbers. As there can never be a probability of zero that the data occurred by chance it must be that the probability is so small that there is not enough space for the computer to display enough decimal places. Therefore we should replace the last zero with a 1 so that we read 0.000000 as 0.000001.

We know that the probability is smaller than this so we are erring on the side of safety in reporting this probability. If we incorrectly reported a probability of zero other researchers would spot the error immediately whereas more correctly reporting a probability of 0.000001 clearly indicates a highly significant result. If you get a probability this low then check that your calculated value of the statistic under test is very large (or very small depending on the test) as we would expect with such a small probability value.

Always be wary of unusual figures, especially ones you did not expect. It is tempting to believe that a highly significant result must be true, particularly if it is a 'better' result than you were hoping for. Do not be seduced by the computer output. Is this really the result you would have expected by looking at the data? In this book, mainly for illustration purposes most of the statistical analyses have been found to be significant. It does not work like this in research. Often there are many non-significant findings. A significant finding is often cherished, particularly as it is more likely to be published than a non-significant finding. Yet we should still treat significant results with some scepticism as, if there is an error, the cost will be that much greater.

Complex analyses

There are a number of statistical analyses that are commonly used today which would have only been undertaken by a statistician in the past. This is due to the development of sophisticated computer programs for statistical analyses and the advance of computer technology. The computing power required to undertake complex analysis would have been owned only by major institutions (such as universities) only two decades ago. And prior to the advent of computers a statistician would have possibly taken days to carry out certain calculations. Now a standard personal computer can undertake these complex analyses in just a few seconds or less. The major time-consuming activity is inputting the data rather than carrying out the analysis. Thus it is outside the scope of this book to provide worked examples for complex analyses that would take forever by hand but which the modern computer can perform in considerably less time than it takes to boil a kettle!

However, the reason why certain complex analyses are now popular is that researchers are able to collect large amounts of data and then examine these data for underlying relationships between the various variables under study. This is particularly the case when a number of participants are asked to provide scores on a wide range of variables. This might be a study in the laboratory where a group of people are tested on a number of skilled tasks such as logic, mathematical, spatial and verbal tasks. The research aim here is to find out which tasks are related, with the implication that they might rely on the same cognitive processing systems. Alternatively, a consumer questionnaire might be constructed where the questions ask for both a range of background information as well as finding out about the participants' product use and product preference. Indeed, the data layout in statistical computer programs often reflects this format:

	Variable 1	Variable 2	. . .	Variable k
Participant 1				
Participant 2				
⋮				
Participant n				

An example data input table

In the following analyses I am going to use the data in the table below for illustration purposes. In many real cases – for example questionnaire data – a researcher will have a lot more data, often hundreds if not thousands of data points. This is one reason why we usually would not contemplate undertaking these analyses by hand. However, to demonstrate the analyses the dataset will be small. I am also describing the data in rather a general way, labelling the variables Question 1, Question 2, etc. to again illustrate the wide applicability of the analyses. As long as the data satisfy the assumptions of the test then we can see that the analyses are very versatile and can be used in a number of different instances with a range of research topics.

Participant	Question 1	Question 2	Question 3	Question 4	Question 5
1	1	1	7	8	6
2	3	4	3	3	5
3	3	3	8	7	8
4	4	2	2	1	2
5	5	5	2	2	2
6	7	5	4	5	6
7	7	7	7	7	4
8	6	8	9	9	8
9	9	7	5	5	4
10	8	10	10	9	7
Mean	5.30	5.20	5.70	5.60	5.20
Stand.dev.	2.54	2.82	2.91	2.88	2.20
Variance	6.4556	7.9556	8.4556	8.2667	4.8444

Reliability

When we develop a questionnaire or other measure of a construct (such as 'honesty' or 'verbal ability') we want that measure to be both valid and reliable. A valid measure is one that genuinely measures the underlying construct. This is not always easy to achieve and often there is debate in the literature on the validity of a test, for example, do IQ tests really examine intelligence? Deciding on the validity of a measure is an academic issue rather than one for statistical analysis. However, reliability can be examined statistically.

When data are collected on a number of different measures we may be interested in examining their reliability. Reliability is defined as the ability of a measuring instrument to measure the concept in a consistent manner. Imagine I had a tape measure and recorded a person's height as 1 metre 65 centimetres. It would be most odd if I measured them a second time with the same tape measure ten minutes later and read off a height of 1 metre 42 centimetres. The tape measure would be a highly unreliable measuring device. Similarly we want a questionnaire to be reliable across people and occasions. One way of testing reliability is to examine the 'test–retest' reliability. Does the test give the same results on different occasions? All we need to do is to give the test twice and correlate the findings. A high correlation indicates a high level of reliability. However, it is not quite as simple as that, as the participants may have remembered their answers from the first test and this might influence the way they respond on the second test. To avoid this some researchers construct two measures (version A and version B of their questionnaire) with slightly different questions which they hope are equivalent. However, this may double the work.

Within a questionnaire (or indeed similarly structured dataset) we can examine the internal reliability of the items within it. If the five questions in the above questionnaire are measuring different aspects of the concept of 'happiness' then we can examine whether participants are responding to the different items in a consistent manner. I have used the term item here rather than question as it is a more general term and the item could be a question or a score on any specific task. Thus, we can examine the internal reliability of our questionnaire by looking at the relationships between the answers to the different questions.

One measure of reliability is called 'split-half' reliability, where the answers on the first half of the questionnaire are compared to the answers on the second half of the questionnaire. So, if there is a high correlation between the two halves of the questionnaire we can argue that there is internal consistency in the questionnaire.

The most popular measure of internal consistency is Cronbach's alpha, which is a more sophisticated test of reliability than the split-half analysis as it examines the average inter-item correlation of the items in the questionnaire. It also takes into account the number of items in the questionnaire:

$$\text{Cronbach's } \alpha = \frac{k}{(k-1)} \left[1 - \frac{\sum \text{var}(i)}{\text{var}(sum)} \right]$$

where k is the number of items, $\text{var}(i)$ is the variance of an item, and $\text{var}(sum)$ is the variance of the totals for each participant. (In the above example participant 1 has a total of 23, and participant 2 has a total of 18).

Essentially, if all the items are measuring exactly the same thing (without any error), we can refer to this as the 'true score', and the scores will reflect this in the following way: all the individual item variances will be identical and var(sum) will simply be $k \times$ var(i). This will result in $\alpha = 1$. However, at the other extreme, if there is no shared variance in the items, then they are reflecting only 'error' rather than an underlying true score, resulting in var(sum) = $\sum$ var(i) and $\alpha = 0$.

In our example:

$$\alpha = \frac{5}{(5-1)}\left[1 - \frac{6.4556 + 7.9556 + 8.4556 + 8.2667 + 4.8444}{107.7778}\right]$$

$$= 0.8327$$

It is conventional to view an α of 0.7 or greater as indicating a reliable scale, so we would view this limited questionnaire data as reliable.

Interestingly, we can argue that if the items are measuring the same underlying dimension on the same scale then they should have the same variance. If we make this assumption then we can calculate a slightly different Cronbach's alpha, called the standardised Chronbach's alpha, based on the inter-item correlations rather than on item variances. This is expressed as follows:

$$\text{Standardised Cronbach's } \alpha = \frac{k\bar{r}}{1 + \bar{r}(k-1)}$$

where k is the number of items and $\bar{r}$ is the average inter-item correlation. The inter-item correlations for the questionnaire example are shown in the table below, referred to as the <u>correlation matrix</u>.

	Question 1	Question 2	Question 3	Question 4	Question 5
Question 1	1	0.8434	0.1790	0.1551	−0.0517
Question 2	0.8434	1	0.4958	0.4494	0.2434
Question 3	0.1790	0.4958	1	0.9675	0.8090
Question 4	0.1551	0.4494	0.9675	1	0.8217
Question 5	−0.0517	0.2434	0.8090	0.8217	1

There are 10 different correlations (of each question with another question), giving the average iter-item correlation $\bar{r}$, as 0.4913. Thus for our example:

$$\text{Standardised } \alpha = \frac{5 \times 0.4913}{1 + 0.4913 \times (5 - 1)} = 0.8284$$

Notice that there is a small difference between our two alpha values. This is due to the difference in the variances of the items rather than one alpha being 'better' than the other. We would use the standardised alpha when we have comparable items (i.e. measured on the same scale as in the example here) or we have standardised the data, but otherwise we would report the 'raw' value based on the item variances.

A further reason why we undertake the analysis by computer is that we can get a printout of the alpha value when a particular item is removed from the analysis. If we do this for each item in turn then we can see which combination of items gives the highest alpha value, and hence highest reliability. This allows us to refine a questionnaire and maximise its reliability.

Details on how to perform a reliability analysis using the SPSS computer statistical package can be found in Chapter 18 of Hinton *et al.* (2004).

Factor analysis

In the above example we found a high level of reliability of our items in the questionnaire ($\alpha = 0.83$) so we might wish to employ the questionnaire as it is. However, if we had found a low reliability then it would have informed us that the scores on the different items were not varying in a consistent manner. The reason for this might be that different questions are 'tapping' different underlying factors. For example in developing a cognitive test battery where a group of children are given four tests, of arithmetic, geometry, verbal reasoning and story comprehension, we might find that there is a high correlation between the scores on the arithmetic and geometry and a high correlation between the verbal reasoning and story comprehension scores but low correlations between the scores on arithmetic and verbal reasoning, arithmetic and story comprehension, geometry and verbal reasoning, geometry and story comprehension. Thus, arithmetic and geometry scores are correlated and verbal reasoning and story comprehension are correlated indicating (possibly) two underlying factors that we might label 'mathematical ability' and 'language ability'.

Factor analysis is a procedure that examines the relationship between the scores on the different items and uses the correlations between them to specify where the relationships are strong enough to indicate underlying factors. This is not a procedure that we would wish to undertake by hand. In the past factor analysis would be the domain of statisticians who would take many hours of calculation in order to determine the factors underlying a dataset.

A factor analysis is essentially a data reduction technique as it is used to see whether there is a set of factors that can explain the variation of the variables under study. It is only useful if we can find fewer factors than variables which are able to explain the variation in the data. It can be undertaken for two reasons: exploratory (to discover underlying factors) or confirmatory (to confirm factors already proposed). We shall look at exploratory factor analysis in this example.

The first thing we need to consider is whether the data is suitable for a factor analysis. Essentially we need samples large enough to ensure that the correlations are a good representation of their population values. There are a number of 'rules of thumb' proposed to indicate what constitutes a large enough dataset: there should be at least 200 scores overall, with at least 10 scores per item and at least five times as many subjects as items. There clearly are not enough scores in our example data to satisfy these criteria but we shall continue for the purpose of illustration.

Two useful tests on the data are often carried out before a factor analysis. The Kaiser–Meyer–Olkin (KMO) test examines the data for sampling adequacy. This gives a measure of the common variance amongst the variables that the factors will be able to account for. The KMO statistic ranges from 0 to 1. In our example, the KMO value is 0.655. Any value over 0.6 is regarded as acceptable for a factor analysis as values below this would mean that the factor analysis will not be able to account for much of the variability in the data and so is not worth undertaking.

The second test is the Bartlett's test of sphericity. This examines the correlation matrix (see above). If there was no correlation at all between any of the variables then the values in the correlation matrix would have 1s down the diagonal with all the other values as zero. This is called an identity matrix. Our example gives a Bartlett $\chi^2 = 38.11$, $df = 10$, $p < 0.001$. This indicates that our correlation matrix is significantly different from an identity matrix so there are correlations worth investigating.

Now that we are confident that it is worth proceeding with the factor analysis we undertake a principal component analysis to find the factors. The scores on each item are standardised to a mean of 0 and a standard deviation of 1. Thus, the variance of every item becomes 1. With 5 items the total variance to explain is 5. Factors are then identified. Each factor has an eigenvalue which gives a value or 'weight' of each factor, in terms of the variance explained. These are shown in the following table.

Component	Eigenvalue	Percentage of overall variance	Cumulative percentage of variance
1	3.0838	61.6750	61.6750
2	1.5896	31.7925	93.4675
3	0.1956	3.9113	97.3789
4	0.1020	2.0393	99.4182
5	0.0291	0.5818	100.0000
Total	5.0000	100.0000	

We can see from the table that 5 components or factors have been identified. It is conventional to select only those factors with eigenvalues greater than 1 as an eigenvalue of 1 indicates that a factor can only explain as much variance as a single item. Only the first two factors are selected as their eigenvalues are greater than 1. Notice also that they can explain 61.6750 per cent and 31.7925 per cent of the variance in the items, so 2 factors can explain over 93 per cent of the total variability in the five items.

An alternative way of selecting the important factors is to produce a 'scree plot' of the components against eigenvalues. Imagine the profile of a mountain. If it was a real mountainside the scree falling down the slope would settle at a point where the slope flattens out. In Figure 22.1 this would be at component 3. We then take factors before this 'elbow' in the graph. So, in Figure 22.1, we can identify two factors as important from the scree plot, supporting the choice of factors from the table of eigenvalues.

We can now look at the correlation of each of the items with our two selected factors (shown in the following table, part (a), referred to as the

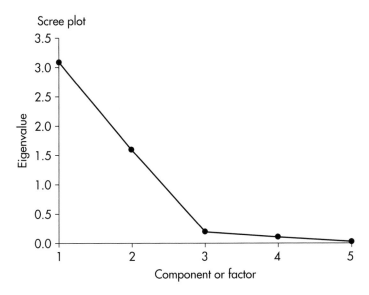

Scree plot

FIGURE 22.1 Scree plot of the eigenvalues

component matrix). Notice that Question 1 correlates 0.4105 with Factor 1 and 0.8850 with Factor 2.

(a)	Unrotated		(b)	Rotated	
	Factor 1	Factor 2		Factor 1	Factor 2
Question 1	0.4105	0.8850		0.0349	0.9750
Question 2	0.6893	0.6858		0.3040	0.9236
Question 3	0.9498	−0.2239		0.9482	0.2306
Question 4	0.9395	−0.2617		0.9561	0.1922
Question 5	0.8096	−0.4663		0.9330	−0.0491

The unrotated values give us some idea of the relationship between items and factors but we can make this much clearer by a procedure called rotation. This rotates our factors to 'line them up' better with the variables. Imagine placing a painting on a wall. You notice it is a little skewed so you rotate it to line it up straight. Rotating factors is a little like this: we are not changing the relationships – simply making them clearer. There are different methods of rotation, with the second version of the component matrix, (b) above, showing the effect of a <u>varimax rotation</u> which endeavours to produce 1s and 0s in the Factor columns of the component matrix. Now we have a clearer picture with Questions 1 and 2 'loading' onto Factor 2 and Questions 3, 4, and 5 loading onto Factor 1. Question 2 does load onto both Factors but the rotation indicates that Factor 2 is the more important.

Finally we can ask how much of the variance in each of our items can be explained by the two factors we have produced. We can answer this by squaring the correlations in the component matrix and adding them for each item. Should we take the unrotated or the rotated correlations? The answer is that it does not matter: the rotation does not change the factors. I will take the rotated values but you can work them out for the unrotated values if you wish.

$$\text{Question 1: Variance explained} = (-0.0349)^2 + 0.9750^2 \quad = 0.9518$$
$$\text{Question 2: Variance explained} = \quad 0.3040^2 + 0.9236^2 \quad = 0.9455$$
$$\text{Question 3: Variance explained} = \quad 0.9482^2 + 0.2306^2 \quad = 0.9522$$
$$\text{Question 4: Variance explained} = \quad 0.9561^2 + 0.1922^2 \quad = 0.9511$$
$$\text{Question 5: Variance explained} = \quad 0.9330^2 + (-0.0491)^2 = 0.8728$$

Remember that the variance in each item has been standardised to 1, so our factors are able to explain a very large amount of the variability in the data. The figures in the final column above are referred to as the <u>communalities</u>, which provide a measure of the variability in that item shared with other items, in our case supporting the factors we have produced.

In conclusion factor analysis examines the correlations between the items in the dataset and produces a set of underlying factors. If we find factors that can explain a lot of the variability in the items then we can argue that our items can be reduced to the fewer factors we have elicited. In our example, the factor analysis revealed two factors, one underlying Questions 3, 4, and 5 and the second factor underlying Questions 1 and 2.

> Details on how to perform a factor analysis using the SPSS computer statistical package can be found in Chapter 17 of Hinton *et al.* (2004).

Multivariate analysis of variance (MANOVA)

In many instances of data analysis we wish to compare different groups of participants on our measuring device, such as a questionnaire, to examine hypotheses such as, 'Are younger adults going to score higher on happiness than older adults?' If we obtain an overall score on our measuring device then the data is suitable for a <u>univariate</u> analysis: that is, analysing a single dependent variable – the participant's score on the test. We can then undertake a univariate test such as a *t* test (if we have two groups of participants) or an analysis of variance (if we have more). However, we may not produce a composite score for the questionnaire but wish to analyse the different questions as separate dependent variables. In this case we could do lots and lots of univariate tests on each separate dependent variable. The problem with this is that we will undertake lots of tests and increase the risk of a Type I error. A solution to this is to perform a multivariate analysis of variance (MANOVA) which allows the analysis of more than one dependent variable. In the table below I have added an additional question from the questionnaire where participants indicate their income level.

Participant	Income	Question 1	Question 2	Question 3	Question 4	Question 5
1	Low	1	1	7	8	6
2	Low	3	4	3	3	5
3	Low	3	3	8	7	8
4	Low	4	2	2	1	2
5	Low	5	5	2	2	2
Group mean		3.20	3.00	4.40	4.20	4.60
6	High	7	5	4	5	6
7	High	7	7	7	7	4
8	High	6	8	9	9	8
9	High	9	7	5	5	4
10	High	8	10	10	9	7
Group mean		7.40	7.40	7.00	7.00	5.80
Overall mean		5.30	5.20	5.70	5.60	5.20

We now have a single independent variable of 'income' and we could examine the effect of this on the responses to each question by five separate *t* tests. However, an alternative is to analyse the data employing a MANOVA with the five questions as five dependent variables in the analysis.

Like the ANOVA the MANOVA requires the assumptions of normally distributed populations and homogeneity of variances. However, as we have a multivariate design we also have the assumption of homogeneity of covariance, that is, the intercorrelations are similar across the conditions of the variables.

The logic of the MANOVA follows that of the ANOVA but the calculations involve matrix algebra which is beyond the scope of this book (although see the end of Chapter 23). Our data table is actually a matrix of responses. In a MANOVA we analyse the dependent variables in combination to provide a composite dependent variable to test for the effect of the independent variable. In an ANOVA we work out the sums of squares for the 'treatment' and a sums of squares for the 'error'. We then calculate the mean square (or variance) for the treatment and the mean square for the error to produce a variance ratio (or F value). In a MANOVA we still work out the sums of squares but we also work out <u>cross-products</u>. With one dependent variable Y, the sums of squares is $\sum(Y - \overline{Y})^2$. When there is more than one dependent variable (Y_1, Y_2, etc.) we can still work out sums of squares for each one, i.e. $\sum(Y_1 - \overline{Y}_1)^2$ for Y_1, but we can also work out the cross-products, with the cross product of Y_1 and Y_2 being $(Y_1 - \overline{Y}_1)(Y_2 - \overline{Y}_2)$ and then we work out a sums of cross-products. We have seen this type of product before in the description of the Pearson correlation coefficient. Essentially a cross-product is a measure of how much two variables covary. A matrix called the 'sums of squares and cross-products' (SSCP) is at the heart of the MANOVA just as the sums of squares is at the heart of the ANOVA. So the MANOVA analyses the covariation of the dependent variables. Thus, it is able to determine the effect of the independent variable on the composite dependent variables.

Just like in an ANOVA, where we divide the total sums of squares into the sums of squares between groups and the sums of squares within groups, the total SSCP matrix ($\mathbf{T}$) is calculated as well as an SSCP matrix for the treatment effect between groups ($\mathbf{B}$) and for the 'error' or within groups ($\mathbf{E}$). Now we would like to compare these last two: $\mathbf{B}$ and $\mathbf{E}$ in the same way as we compare the sums of squares in an ANOVA. (Actually we compare the mean squares in the ANOVA rather than the sums of squares but the principle is the same.) Unfortunately, $\mathbf{B}$ and $\mathbf{E}$ are not single values but matrices. However, there is a mathematical way of finding out the variation of the values in a matrix and this is referred to as the <u>determinant</u> of the matrix, with the notation $|\mathbf{B}|$ for the determinant of $\mathbf{B}$, which returns a single figure. This now allows us to work out a statistic to evaluate the significance of the effect under investigation. (I appreciate that matrix mathematics may be a new concept but I think you can appreciate from the above description the similarity in the logic of MANOVA and ANOVA.)

A number of different statistics have been produced for MANOVA but the most commonly used is Wilks' lambda which is calculated as follows:

$$\text{Wilks' lambda } \Lambda = \frac{|\mathbf{E}|}{|\mathbf{B} + \mathbf{E}|}$$

This will range from 0 when there is no error (and all the variation is due to the treatment effect) to 1 when the variation is due to error and there is no treatment effect. So we are looking for a small value of Λ to indicate a significant effect.

In comparison to the variance ratio (F) in an ANOVA, where the F value is the treatment effect plus error divided by the error, Λ is like an upside down F ratio. Indeed, Λ can be converted to an F value quite easily and so you will usually see an F value as well as a Λ value in a computer printout for a MANOVA. In the above example, with income as the independent factor and the five questions as the five dependent variables we obtain $\Lambda = 0.0542$, $p < 0.05$ (which converts to $F(5,4) = 13.9675$). Thus we have found an effect of income on the dependent variables.

We can then undertake separate one factor independent measures ANOVAs on each question to examine the effect of income on them individually. These give the following results:

Question 1 $F(1,8) = 25.20$ $p < 0.01$
Question 2 $F(1,8) = 16.69$ $p < 0.01$
Question 3 $F(1,8) = 2.28$ $p > 0.05$
Question 4 $F(1,8) = 2.86$ $p > 0.05$
Question 5 $F(1,8) = 0.72$ $p > 0.05$

From this array we can see that income is having a significant effect on the first two questions but not the remaining three.

When we undertake a number of tests on the same data we often correct the significance level for the increased risk of Type I errors. This is called a Bonferroni correction and involves dividing the significance level by the number of tests, so with five tests, instead of choosing the $p = 0.05$ level of significance we would choose $p = 0.01$ (see Chapter 12). In this example the pattern of results of the univariate ANOVAs remains the same even with the stricter criterion for significance.

Details on how to perform a MANOVA using the SPSS computer statistical package can be found in Chapter 12 of Hinton *et al*. (2004).

Discriminant function analysis

Whereas a MANOVA examines the effect of an independent variable or variables on a number of dependent variables, a discriminant function analysis works in the opposite direction by examining which combination of independent variables is best able to predict a dependent variable. Interestingly, a discriminant function analysis is a useful follow-up analysis after a significant independent measures MANOVA as it is actually employing the same sums of squares and cross-products matrices as the MANOVA calculations. For this reason it requires the same assumptions as a MANOVA.

Essentially the discriminant function analysis produces functions of the independent variables that discriminate between the conditions of the dependent variable. To undertake this analysis on the example the independent and dependent variables are swapped round. The five questions are treated as the independent variables in this analysis and income becomes the dependent variable. Can we find functions of our five questions that are able to predict a person's income level? With only two income levels (low and high) there will only be one function produced. If we had three or more income levels then more than one function might emerge. With more than one function each will explain a certain percentage of the variation in the data and the functions (like factors in factor analysis) can be examined to see how much variation they can explain (and whether this is a significant amount). Conventionally functions are seen as worthy of further consideration if their eigenvalue is over 1 and the canonical correlation is over 0.6. A canonical correlation is essentially the correlation of the function with the dependent variable – in this case the multiple correlation coefficient (R – see Chapter 21). In the current example there is evidence of the strength of the discrimination as the eigenvalue of the function is 17.4594 and the canonical correlation is 0.9725, both high values. The significance of the function is shown by Wilks' lambda, in this case 0.0542, $p < 0.01$, so the function is highly significant in being able to discriminate the two income conditions. Notice also that this is exactly the same value of Wilks' lambda we produced in the MANOVA above, illustrating the link between the two analyses.

As we have only one function, this function is actually the multiple regression equation. The unstandardised canonical discriminant function coefficients (produced in this analysis) provide the regression coefficients, so the function for our example can be expressed as:

Discriminant function = $a + b_1X_1 + b_2X_2 + b_3X_3 + b_4X_4 + b_5X_5$

Discriminant function

$= -10.6089 + 1.4508 \times \text{Question1} - 0.0639 \times \text{Question2}$
$- 1.1093 \times \text{Question3} + 1.5500 \times \text{Question4} + 0.1721 \times \text{Question5}$

The point about this function is that when we input the values of questions 1–5 for a participant in the equation it should provide us with an outcome that we can use to classify the person into the categories of the dependent variable (i.e. predict their income level). You can see from the following table that the function is able to classify all the participants correctly: by producing a negative value for all low income participants and a positive value for all the high income participants.

Participant	Income group	Function
1	Low	−3.5545
2	Low	−4.3295
3	Low	−3.0958
4	Low	−5.2579
5	Low	−2.4488
6	High	3.5726
7	High	2.8727
8	High	2.9278
9	High	4.8929
10	High	4.4202

The mean values of the function for each group, referred to as the group centroids, provide information to make a classification. In this case the group centroids are −3.7373 and +3.7373. As we have equal numbers of participants in each group we can choose our cut-off point at the middle position between them (i.e. their average = zero). (With unequal sample sizes we would weight them by their sample size to find a weighted average position for the cut-off point.) We can now use the function to predict the income group of a new participant once we have their results for Questions 1–5. If the function gives a negative value we classify them as 'low income' and if the function produces a positive value we classify them as 'high income'. A person who scores 7, 4, 8, 3, 5 on Questions 1–5 will score −4.0728 on the function and hence we predict them to be in the low income group.

Finally, we can examine the structure matrix (the table below) that shows the correlation of each variable with the function which, as in factor analysis, allows us to see which variables correlate highly with the function. The structure matrix has the correlation coefficients for each of the questions in order of size, with Questions 1 and 2 showing the highest values, echoing what we showed above in the MANOVA analysis.

Question	Function
1	0.4284
2	0.3457
4	0.1431
3	0.1279
5	0.0718

In this particular example, we saw a simple case of discriminant function analysis. With a more complex design we might find two or more functions and therefore reveal a pattern of the underlying relationship between variables responsible for a significant Wilks' lambda.

Conclusion

The advent of fast computers, available to all, has meant that even the most complicated statistical analysis can be undertaken on research data at the touch of a button. However, the crucial point is not whether an analysis can be done but whether it should be undertaken. The question for the researcher is whether they have enough understanding of the analysis to decide if it is appropriate for their data and whether they are able to correctly interpret the output of the analysis when it is produced. It may well be that a relatively simple analysis is able to properly demonstrate the key findings of a piece of research in a clear and comprehensible manner.

An introduction
to the general
linear model

FOR SOME PEOPLE it a surprise to learn that the basic principles underlying the *t* test, the analysis of variance, correlation and regression, plus the multivariate tests considered in the previous chapter, are the same – they all are examples of the general linear model. The tests seem to have different aims, the calculations appear to be different, the outcomes produce different statistics, such as *t*, *F* or *r*, so that superficially they appear not the same at all. However, underlying these different tests is a model of how we expect the data to behave in order for us to perform the tests. Indeed, you may have observed that the assumptions underlying the tests are very much the same.

Now it is quite possible that you find this all very interesting but not relevant to you. Just as a person can happily drive a car without understanding the workings of the engine we can undertake statistics without knowing about the general linear model. However, if the car breaks down and you know the basics of the engine you might be able to get it going again (especially if it's a simple blockage or a lack of fuel) whereas not knowing might lead to a costly wait for the breakdown truck. Similarly, a basic understanding of the general linear model provides an awareness of what is happening in a test and whether the data are appropriate to that test. Understanding the general linear model can lead to an understanding of why we have the assumptions of the statistical tests and what it means if those assumptions are not met.

Models

In everyday conversation, when we think of a model (and not a fashion model) we often think of a small object such as a model car or a model of the Eiffel Tower. Notice that these models are representations of the thing they are modelling. Some models are very good representations, such as a detailed scale model of the Eiffel Tower, and some are not, such as the fluffy pink models of the Eiffel Tower you can buy in the souvenir shops of Paris. Yet even the poor models have to resemble the original to some extent – even the fluffy models of the Eiffel Tower have four feet and a

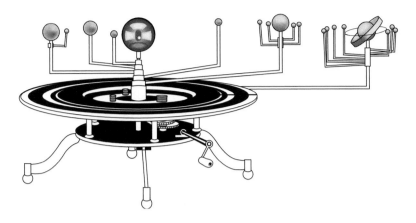

FIGURE 23.1 An orrery

pointed top. So models seek to represent the essential pattern of the thing they are modelling.

A classic example of a model is an orrery. This is a model of the solar system and you may have seen them in museums and collections of antiques. The first one was made by the clockmaker John Rowley in 1712 for Charles Boyle, the 4th Earl of Orrery (from whence it got its name). The one in Figure 23.1 is based on an orrery in the Smithsonian Institution in Washington DC.

To operate the model you turn the handle and the planets rotate around the sun. Notice that the model had the extremely useful function of being able to demonstrate in a simple manner the workings of the solar system – how the planets move relative to each other, what a year means and so on. In fact it is an extremely helpful teaching aid. However, at another level it is a very poor model. The objects are not to scale – the sun at the centre would need to be much, much bigger – and the real planets do not go round the sun in circular orbits but in ellipses. It is certainly not a model you could use to guide an astronaut in space.

Yet men have been to the moon and spacecraft have landed on other planets and the space centres have needed models of the solar system to get them there successfully. Clearly these models are enormously more complicated than the simple orrery but more importantly these models are no longer built by clockmakers in their workshops but are constructed by using mathematics. They are no longer physical objects but mathematical formulae, written down and stored on computer. If we want to estimate where Mars and Venus will be in six months time we no longer turn the handle on the orrery and look at the new positions of the planets but input the time data into the mathematical model on the computer and print out the details of the new positions of the planets <u>predicted</u> by the model. If it is a good model then the positions will be accurate predictions.

Models share the same features in that they attempt to represent the relationships within a particular system (such as the movement of the planets). As soon as we decide a system is not random we can seek out a model to represent the pattern we observe. From the beginning of time people have noted the rising and setting of the sun and the change of the seasons and tried to make sense of the patterns they observe. Our current mathematical models are quite impressive as we can use them to land a spacecraft on another planet. But, who knows, in three hundred years time they may look as crude and simplistic to the people of the future as the orrery does to us today.

An example of a linear model

When we collect data we are not interested in the specific scores produced at a specific time but what the collection of scores can tell us about the relationships between variables in order to make predictions. The way we do this is by assuming that there is an underlying relationship between the variables and then we attempt to model that relationship. And, like the orrery, we can decide if the model is any good or not.

One specific type of model that is central to statistical analysis is referred to as a <u>linear model</u>. As we saw in Chapter 20, in its simplest case, with only the relationship between two variables, a linear model is a straight line. The mathematical formula for a straight line is $Y = a + bX$, where X and Y are the variables, 'a' is a constant (the value of Y when X is zero, the point at which the line crosses the Y axis) and 'b' is the slope of the line.

Imagine that you give a person a pack of playing cards and ask them to sort the pack as quickly as they can (but without making mistakes) into 2 piles, one of red cards and one of black cards. You shuffle the pack thoroughly and accurately measure the time it takes them to complete the task. It takes them 20.8 seconds. Now you shuffle the pack again and, this time, ask them to sort the cards into the four suits. This takes 31.2 seconds. Finally you ask them to sort the pack into 8 piles: low hearts (ace to seven), high hearts (8 to king), low diamonds, high diamonds, etc. This takes 41.6 seconds. We now plot these figures on a graph (Figure 23.2).

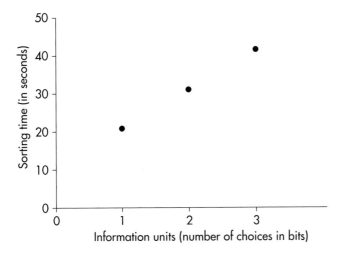

FIGURE 23.2 A graph of card sorting times

You can see that the X-axis is labelled 'information units' rather than 'number of piles'. A single choice (two options: e.g. on/off or red/black) contains one information unit (one 'bit' of information). Four choices involve two information units (two bits) and eight choices involve three information units (3 bits). The reason we use information units rather than number of choices is that the researchers who first did this study in the early 1950s noticed that the pattern of results when plotted on a graph in this way followed a straight line. They obviously collected considerably more data (which was much more varied) than the simple example I have given above. The resulting model, a linear relationship between amount of information and speed of processing, has immortalised the researchers who found it, and it is referred to as the Hick–Hyman Law.

For our participant, we can work out the formula for the straight line that passes through these three points, by putting the three points into the formula $Y = a + bX$ and working out 'a' and 'b' to give: $Y = 10.40 + 10.40X$, which states that:

Sorting time $= 10.40 + (10.40 \times$ Information units$)$

We can now use this model to predict what we do not know. If the person had to sort the pack into the high, middle and low numbers of each suit (12 choices or 3.585 bits) we would expect them to take $10.40 + (10.40 \times 3.585) = 47.68$ seconds.

Modelling data

Underlying most of our statistical techniques is the assumption that a linear model represents the pattern of the relationship between variables. Without this model we would not be able to draw the conclusions we do from our statistical analysis. Just as the space scientists need their models to land a spacecraft on Mars we need a model to make a statistical decision. In this example we shall be taking a more complex case than the three points considered in the card sorting example above, and in this new example our points will not all lie neatly along a straight line.

A researcher is interested in the relationship between a child's age and their general knowledge. We shall assume, for the sake of argument, that the researcher is able to appropriately select a suitable school and randomly selects 6 children from classes across three school years: Class 1 (roughly 8 years old), Class 2 (roughly 9 years old) and Class 3 (roughly 10 years old). Each child is given the same test of general knowledge and the scores are recorded. The results are shown in the table below.

Class	Child's age in months	General knowledge score
1	91	6
1	93	9
1	95	8
1	96	10
1	98	9
1	100	12
2	103	11
2	105	14
2	107	13
2	108	15
2	110	14
2	112	17
3	115	16
3	117	19
3	119	18
3	120	20
3	122	19
3	124	22

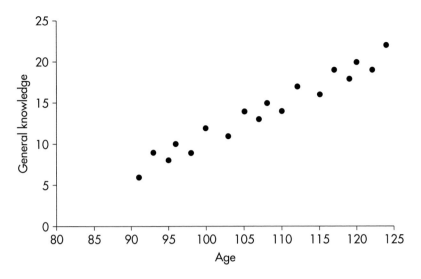

FIGURE 23.3 A plot of the children's general knowledge scores by age

Are the results random or is there a systematic relationship between age and general knowledge score? Certainly it looks from the table that the scores get larger as age increases. We can see this rather better if we plot the results, as in Figure 23.3.

I could look at the data in the graph and say that these are the results and that is that: what do we need a model for? I could claim that each point is a true representation of the child's age and score. However, this does not tell us anything we really want to know. We are not really interested in the finding that on Thursday February 21st John Peterson aged 8 years 4 months scored 12 on a general knowledge test. What we really wish to learn is whether there is an underlying relationship between age and general knowledge. If there is then we can use this relationship to make predictions about what level of general knowledge we can expect in children we have not tested. We can generalise our findings to a wider population.

When we look closely at the data it does look as though the scores more or less follow a straight line. Notice that they are all contained within a narrow band going from the bottom left to the top right of Figure 23.3 – with no scores in the top left or bottom right. So I could propose that the relationship between the general knowledge scores and age is linear (a straight line in this case) and that the underlying model for the data is a linear model. So, if the relationship between the variables really is a straight line, then that line should lie somewhere in the middle of the points, as in Figure 23.4.

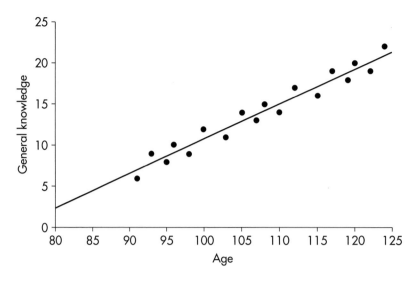

FIGURE 23.4 A proposed linear relationship between general knowledge and age

Now there is a problem here. None of the points actually lie on the line! Does this mean that this straight line is a poor model of the relationship between the general knowledge scores and age? Not necessarily. First the points seem pretty close to the line (which surely indicates that the model is not that bad). Second I could argue, the points would lie on the line had it been a perfect world but we live in a world of error and chance. Maybe one child under-performed due to having a cold and another did better than usual because they guessed an answer correctly. There are a number of factors in our everyday lives that make it messy rather than well ordered. Maybe if we took away the messiness (or random errors) then the underlying pattern would emerge (if there is one). I am suggesting that in an ideal world all the points would lie along the line. In this example, it could be that the scores have not quite fallen on the line due to these random errors that occur in any human activity, such as research, despite our best efforts at control (see Chapter 10 for a related argument).

I, therefore, argue that the underlying model of the relationship between the general knowledge scores and age is a straight line and that the reason the scores have not fallen exactly on the straight line is due to random error. Hence each observed score is made up of that predicted by the model ('explained variation') plus a random error ('unexplained variation').

Each point in Figure 23.5 shows a child's general knowledge score. Notice that a very large proportion of each general knowledge score can be

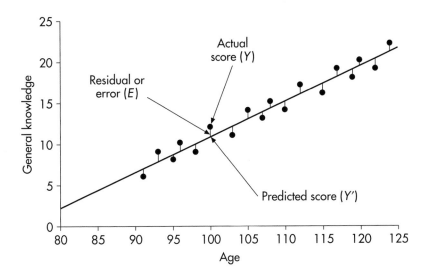

FIGURE 23.5 Separating each score into predicted score plus residual

accounted for by the model (the sloping line) as the points more or less follow the line. The 'error' scores – that is the difference between the actual score and that predicted by the model – seem quite small. The size of the error score is shown by the vertical bar joining the point to the line.

If we take one child's general knowledge score, that I will call Y, then we can explain most of that score by our model (i.e. a point on the straight line where we would predict the score would be) which we can call Y'. But, because the score does not lie on the straight line, Y is not equal to Y'. As a result I argue that E, the difference between Y and Y', is the 'error', as I believe that this is a result of random error, and cannot be explained by my model. Another term for E is <u>residual</u> as each of these values is the residual amount of the general knowledge score after we have taken away the amount explained by the model. So for each score:

Actual score (Y) = Predicted score (Y') + Residual (E)

The model: the regression equation

I predicted a straight line as a model for the relationship between age and general knowledge score. The problem is: which line? We can begin to work out the answer to this by looking at Figure 23.6.

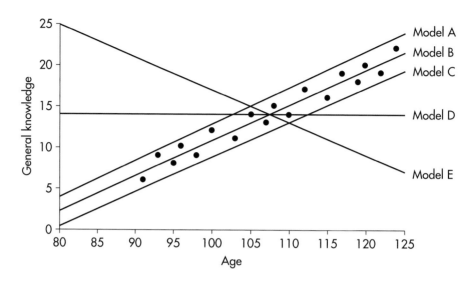

FIGURE 23.6 Different linear models

Model C is clearly not a good model as the line is way below the actual data points. We can demonstrate this mathematically as the residuals will all be positive values and their sum will be a large positive number. Similarly Model A does not fit the data very well as, again, the residuals will add to a large negative number. Adding them up will give us a large but negative sum. Model B not only looks to be the best model as it lies amongst the data points but also has smaller residual values than both Models A and C. With some of the residuals positive (the point lies above the line) and some negative (the point lies below the line), when we add up the residuals they will cancel each other out. So our best fitting model will be the straight line where the residuals add up to zero.

Another way of putting this is that the residuals have a <u>mean of zero</u> for our best fitting line. This makes sense as, in this case, the 'average' amount of error will be zero. Looking back to Models A and C on the above graph we can see that the residuals will not have a mean of zero as the models are not a good fit for the data, with their mean values telling us how far they are from the best model we can produce for the data. A mean of zero also indicates that the line passes through the mean values for age and general knowledge.

Unfortunately, if we now look at Models B, D and E we see all three pass through the mean values for age and general knowledge (107.5 months and a score of 14). All three models will have residuals that add up to zero (you can work them out if you wish) and the mean of their residuals will also be zero. However, it does not require much observation to see that both Models D and E are a very poor fit to the data. The difference between Model B and Models D and E is that Model B is the model with the smallest residuals.

We now need to find the equation of the line with the smallest residual values, which add up to zero (Model B). We do this by working out the regression of age on the general knowledge scores (described in Chapter 20), which gives us the model of 'best fit' to the data. The linear regression technique is built upon the assumption of a linear model and relies on the in-built assumptions of linearity in order for it to produce its analysis. In this case it finds the linear model that minimises the size of the residuals and hence explains more variation in the data than any other linear model.

We are assuming that the observed general knowledge scores (Y) are a combination of the linear model (the regression line Y') plus the errors or residuals (E) then:

$$Y = Y' + E$$

As we know the formula for a straight line we have: $Y' = a + bX$ (where Y' is the predicted general knowledge score and X is the child's age), so:

$$Y = a + bX + E$$

This gives us a formula for E:

$$E = Y - a - bX$$

Now we can add up all the residuals:

$$\sum E = \sum (Y - a - bX)$$

This sum needs to be zero for the 'best fit' line. But we also need to find the values of 'a' and 'b' that result in the smallest residuals to get the best fitting model (Model B rather than Model D or E). There is no point simply adding up the residuals as they will cancel each other out to give a total of zero. So to find the smallest residuals we square all the residual values to get rid of the pluses and minuses and then find the line that gives us the smallest value for the sum of the squared residuals (the 'least squares method' – see Chapter 20 – that finds the minimised value for $\sum (Y - a - bX)^2$).

The outcome of this analysis gives us the following formula for the straight line that provides the best fitting straight line for the data:

$$Y' = -31.77 + 0.43X \qquad \text{(To be more accurate,}$$
$$a = -31.7665 \text{ and } b = 0.4257)$$

This formula, our model, predicts:

General knowledge = $-31.77 + (0.43 \times \text{Age})$

We can now use this model to work out the values of the residuals by putting the age values in the equation and finding the predicted general knowledge scores. These are shown in the table below.

Child's age in months	General knowledge score from the test	General knowledge score predicted by model	Residuals	Squared residuals
91	6	6.98	−0.98	0.96
93	9	7.83	1.17	1.37
95	8	8.68	−0.68	0.46
96	10	9.10	0.90	0.81
98	9	9.96	−0.96	0.92
100	12	10.81	1.19	1.42
103	11	12.08	−1.08	1.17
105	14	12.94	1.06	1.12
107	13	13.79	−0.79	0.62
108	15	14.21	0.79	0.62
110	14	15.06	−1.06	1.12
112	17	15.92	1.08	1.17
115	16	17.19	−1.19	1.42
117	19	18.04	0.96	0.92
119	18	18.90	−0.90	0.81
120	20	19.32	0.68	0.46
122	19	20.17	−1.17	1.37
124	22	21.02	0.98	0.96
Total	252	252	0	17.71

The first point to note is that the residuals add up to zero, with some positive residuals and some negative residuals that cancel each other out when added up. Furthermore, the sum of the squared residuals (17.71) is smaller for this line than any other.

Selecting a good model

There are two qualities of a good model. The first is that the model follows the pattern of the data. If we plot the data on a graph and it follows an S-shaped curve then a straight line might not be a very good model to apply. We want to be convinced that a linear model is the appropriate model for the data. This is where the residuals come into play. The decision on what makes a good model and whether it is a good fit to the data is determined first by the characteristics of the residuals.

Second the model needs to explain as much of the data as possible. If the model can explain only 10 per cent of the variation in the scores we might not consider it as good a model as one that can explain 90 per cent of the variation. We shall be examining this second aspect later but first we consider the characteristics of the residuals.

Characteristics of the residuals

A good model is one where the error or residual values are random. If our model leaves systematic variation in the residuals then the implication is that there is a better model than the one we proposed that is able to take account of this systematic variation as well.

We want the model to explain the data equally well regardless of where we examine the data. If the model is a close fit to the data for the first few points (leaving small residuals) but then is a poor fit to subsequent points (resulting in large residuals) then it is not a good model. This is where the equality of variance assumption (or homoscedasticity) is required: the residuals should be randomly spread out at whichever point of the model we examine. Thus, we predict that the variance of the residuals at any point on the model should be the same – as there is no systematic reason why they should be larger or smaller at one point or another.

To be certain that our model is a good model and the residuals are truly random we make three further assumptions about them:

- they add to zero and have a mean of zero;
- they are from a normally distributed population; and
- they are independent of each other.

Characteristics of the residuals: they add up to zero

We have seen from the above analysis that only a model where the residuals add up to zero can provide an appropriate linear model for the data. Taking the reverse position, if the residuals do not add up to zero then we know that there is a better fitting model for the data. With the residuals summing to zero we guarantee that the model maps onto the mean values of the data.

Characteristics of the residuals: they are drawn from a normally distributed population

Given that we are assuming that the linear model underlies the data then the errors (i.e. the residuals) should be random with a normal distribution. Think about what a normal distribution means. If the errors are occurring randomly then we should occasionally get a large positive residual and occasionally we should get a large negative residual; however, most residuals should cluster round zero. So the assumption that the residuals are drawn from a normal distribution is the assumption that the residuals are indeed random (and there are no systematic patterns in the data that the model has not accounted for). If the residuals were not from a normally distributed population then the model we are proposing may be an inappropriate model for these data.

Characteristics of the residuals: they are independent of each other

If the sizes of the residuals were related to the order that the children were tested or the class they were in, then there would be a non-random element in the residuals. If the residuals got larger with increasing age of the child then the residuals would not be independent of each other. This is a concern because it demonstrates a relationship in the data not accounted for by the model.

However, if the residuals are independent of each other then there is no relationship between them and hence the 'error' remaining after we have imposed the model is random, leaving no systematic variation to be explained. Thus a good model explains all the systematic variation in the data, leaving only random variation.

Conclusion

If we do not meet these assumptions then it is quite possible that the residuals are not completely random and there is still some systematic variation within them that could be accounted for by an alternative model. Indeed the common assumptions we make with our statistical tests (homogeneity of variance, etc.) arise from these assumptions concerning the residuals.

The variation in the data explained by the model

We have found, in our example, the linear model that best fits the data. No other linear model is as good as the one we have worked out. The characteristics of the residuals satisfy the assumptions. Now that we have found the best linear model we can ask a second question: how good is it? To explain what I mean, I'll rephrase the question: how much of the data is now explained by the model and how much of the data remains unexplained as error data (shown by the residuals)?

If we look at Figure 23.7 we can see that the same model (the same line) fits both sets of data (one indicated by the crosses + and the second indicated by the dots •). However, the crosses are more spread out around the line compared to the dots. We can restate this by saying that the residuals are larger for the first dataset than in the second. We can restate this again by saying that for the first dataset there is more data unexplained by the model than in the second.

This leads us on to the second judgement of a good model. A good model takes into account the variation in the data. From the data we see that as the children get older the general knowledge scores get higher. The model should predict this. There are two related methods for examining the amount of data explained by a linear model: linear correlation and the analysis of variance. Both make the assumption that the underlying model is linear, so they require the above assumptions concerning the residuals to be met.

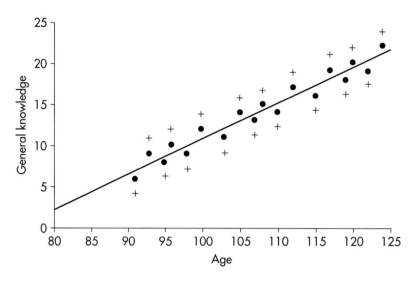

FIGURE 23.7 The same linear model for two sets of data

The linear model and correlation

We can examine whether a linear model is able to explain a lot or only a little of the variation in the data by working out the linear correlation coefficient. The technique it employs (described in Chapter 20) examines the variation in the data measured on one variable in relationship to variation on the second variable. However, it can only do that by assuming that the relationship between the two variables is linear, and then testing the strength of that relationship. It cannot detect a complex non-linear correlation – it will simply tell us that the data follows a linear relationship very badly.

In our example, the linear correlation of age and general knowledge scores is $r = 0.975$, which is an extremely high correlation ($p < 0.01$, for a two-tailed prediction, $df = 16$). Essentially, this is telling us that, assuming the relationship to be linear, the variation in the general knowledge scores can be accounted for by the variation in age to a large extent. Recall from Chapter 20 that r^2 tells us the amount of the variation in one variable explained by the other, so $r^2 = 0.951$, which means that 95.1 per cent of the variation in the general knowledge scores is explained by the variation in age.

Put simply, the linear correlation undertakes the following analysis: assuming an underlying linear relationship between the variables, how much of the variation in the data can be attributed to that relationship and how much cannot? With 95.1 per cent of the variation in the data accounted for we can be confident that there is a linear relationship between these two variables.

Interestingly, the correlation coefficient is the slope of the 'best fit' regression line for the z scores for general knowledge and age (see Chapter 20 on z scores in the correlation calculation). A z score standardises a score so that the mean becomes zero and the standard deviation becomes 1. So instead of producing a regression for the actual scores we can produce a regression line for the z scores. This will have $a = 0$, as the line passes through $(0, 0)$ because the means of the z scores will both be 0. It will have $b = 0.975$, as r is the slope of the line.

For the z scores:

$$z_Y = 0 + 0.975z_X$$

So:

The z score of general knowledge $= 0.975 \times$ the z score of age

The good thing about this is that it shows a strong linear relationship. However, the formula is not very useful in making predictions about general knowledge scores from age, as it is couched in terms of z scores, which is why we use the standard regression equation.

The linear model and the analysis of variance

We can also provide an answer to the question about how much of the variation in the data is explained by the model by employing an analysis of variance. The analysis of variance technique is built on the assumption of a linear model. The ANOVA proportions the data into variance explained by the model and the variance that remains unexplained (the error variance). In the ANOVA we consider the variation of the scores from the mean to give a measure of the variation in the general knowledge scores. The mean general knowledge score is 14. If we take the first child's score of 6 we find that the model would predict 6.98 for this child. Thus, the model can explain $6.98 - 14 = -7.02$ of the variation of this child's score from the mean. We then square this difference (we always do this to give us a measure of the size of a difference and to get rid of the awkward minus signs at the same time). For the first child this value is 49.35. Finally we add up these squared differences to give us a 'sums of squares' for the amount of variation in the data explained by our model. These figures are shown in the table below.

Class	Child's age in months	General knowledge score	General knowledge score predicted by model	Explained variation from mean	Explained variation squared	Residuals: unexplained variation	Squared residuals: unexplained variation squared
1	91	6	6.98	−7.02	49.35	−0.98	0.96
1	93	9	7.83	−6.17	38.11	1.17	1.37
1	95	8	8.68	−5.32	28.32	−0.68	0.46
1	96	10	9.10	−4.90	23.97	0.90	0.81
1	98	9	9.96	−4.04	16.36	−0.96	0.92
1	100	12	10.81	−3.19	10.20	1.19	1.42
2	103	11	12.08	−1.92	3.67	−1.08	1.17
2	105	14	12.94	−1.06	1.13	1.06	1.12
2	107	13	13.79	−0.21	0.05	−0.79	0.62
2	108	15	14.21	0.21	0.05	0.79	0.62
2	110	14	15.06	1.06	1.13	−1.06	1.12
2	112	17	15.92	1.92	3.67	1.08	1.17
3	115	16	17.19	3.19	10.20	−1.19	1.42
3	117	19	18.04	4.04	16.36	0.96	0.92
3	119	18	18.90	4.90	23.97	−0.90	0.81
3	120	20	19.32	5.32	28.32	0.68	0.46
3	122	19	20.17	6.17	38.11	−1.17	1.37
3	124	22	21.02	7.02	49.35	0.98	0.96
Total		252	252	0	342.29	0	17.71

(I have given the accurate total for the sixth column. If you added up the figures to only two decimal places you would get a figure of 342.32 due to rounding errors.)

Now we have both the 'sums of squares' for the general knowledge scores explained by age (342.29) plus the 'sums of squares' for the error term (the sum of the squared residuals: 17.71). Thus, of the total variation in the data (total sums of squares = 360.00) we can explain 342.29 of it by the linear model, leaving 17.71 unexplained. It is a simple matter to complete an ANOVA summary table – we just need to supply the degrees of freedom to finalise the calculations.

THE ANOVA SUMMARY TABLE

Source of variation	Degrees of freedom	Sums of squares	Mean square	F	Significance
Model (linear regression)	1	342.29	342.29	309.25	$p < 0.01$
Residual (error)	16	17.71	1.11		
Total	17	360.00			

The results of the analysis of variance tell us that the model can explain a highly significant amount of the variation in the data.

We have employed a regression, correlation and analysis of variance on our data. Each of these analyses assumes that there is a linear relationship between the two variables we have measured. In the example of age and general knowledge all three statistical techniques have supported a linear relationship between the two variables. A linear model is a good fit to the data and it can explain a considerable amount of the variation in the scores.

Comparing samples (the analysis of variance once again)

It is relatively easy to see the underlying assumption of a linear model in a linear regression and linear correlation. However, it is not always so clear that this assumption is also inherent in the analysis when we are comparing samples (e.g. in a *t* test or ANOVA). We can illustrate this assumption by once again looking at the general knowledge and age data. We can use a one factor independent measures ANOVA to compare the general knowledge scores for the different Classes (Class 1, Class 2 and Class 3). By placing them in the category of Class rather than taking their age we are placing all of the 6 children in each class at the same position on the X-axis. But the same logic that we employed above when looking at age still applies. We can see a plot of the data in Figure 23.8.

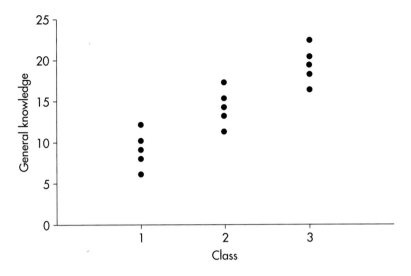

FIGURE 23.8 Plot of general knowledge scores for each class

Now we can do exactly as we did before with the scatterplot of general knowledge scores and age. Is there a linear model that underlies Figure 23.8? Although we do not normally think of undertaking a correlation with category data like this, computer statistical programmes will often print out the correlation coefficient r, or r^2, with the ANOVA summary table.

Correlating the general knowledge scores with Class produces a high linear relationship between the two variables ($r = 0.913$, $p < 0.01$ for a two-tailed prediction, $df = 16$) with $r^2 = 0.833$, indicating that the variable Class can explain 83.3 per cent of the variation in the general knowledge scores. Even though we are comparing the categories Class 1, Class 2, and Class 3, we are still examining the fit of a linear model.

We can find the best linear model to fit these data by performing a regression analysis. The result of this gives us the following formula:

$$Y = 4 + 5X$$

So our 'best fit' linear model predicts:

General knowledge = $4 + 5 \times$ Class

This model is shown in Figure 23.9.

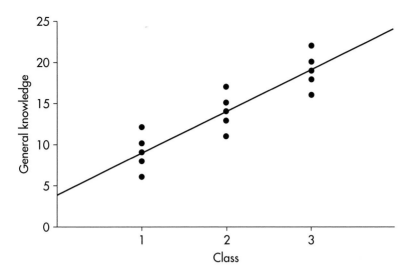

FIGURE 23.9 A linear model for the class data

Interestingly you can see, from Figure 23.9, why we have the equality of variance assumption with comparisons and the homoscedasticity assumption with correlations. We are assuming that the data is evenly spread around the regression line in both cases.

Now that we have our model we can work out the general knowledge scores as predicted by the model and the 'error' scores or residuals. Notice, from the third column in the following table, that the scores predicted by the model are the category means, so the predicted score for all the children in Class 1 is the mean of Class 1 (a score of 9). The residuals are shown in the sixth column. Just as we did in the previous analysis of variance, we work out the variation from the mean for each data point predicted by the model (as this is the variation the model is able to explain). We square these values to produce a measure of explained variation. If we add these up we get a 'sums of squares' for the explained variation. We also square the residuals to get a value for the size of the unexplained variation. Adding these up gives us the 'sums of squares' for the error variation. These are also listed in the table below.

Class	General knowledge score	General knowledge score predicted by model	Explained variation from mean	Explained variation squared	Residuals: unexplained variation	Squared residuals: unexplained variation squared
1	6	9	−5	25	−3	9
1	9	9	−5	25	0	0
1	8	9	−5	25	−1	1
1	10	9	−5	25	1	1
1	9	9	−5	25	0	0
1	12	9	−5	25	3	9
2	11	14	0	0	−3	9
2	14	14	0	0	0	0
2	13	14	0	0	−1	1
2	15	14	0	0	1	1
2	14	14	0	0	0	0
2	17	14	0	0	3	9
3	16	19	5	25	−3	9
3	19	19	5	25	0	0
3	18	19	5	25	−1	1
3	20	19	5	25	1	1
3	19	19	5	25	0	0
3	22	19	5	25	3	9
Total	252	252	0	300	0	60

We now have all the information to draw up the analysis of variance summary table:

THE ANOVA SUMMARY TABLE

Source of variation	Degrees of freedom	Sums of squares	Mean square	F	Significance
Model (linear regression)	2	300.00	150.00	37.50	$p < 0.01$
Residual (error)	15	60.00	4.00		
Total	17	360.00			

Analysing the data by Class rather than age divides the total sums of squares (360.00) into that explained by the model (300.00) and the remainder not explained by the model (60.00). It is clear that our underlying model can account for a significantly large proportion of the variation in the data ($p < 0.01$). Hence we can reject the null hypothesis that the means are drawn from the same population distribution.

Explaining variations in the data

You may have wondered why in both of the above analyses of variance we worked out the explained variation relative to the mean value. The answer arises from the way we calculate variation in the data. If we simply square the general knowledge scores and add them up we get a total of 3888. This value would only be a measure of the total variability of the scores in the data *if* the mean equals zero. Consider two scores 99 and 101. These scores vary by 2, with 99 one below their mean of 100, and 101 one above their mean of 100. Now consider two other scores 25 and 35. These vary by 10 with 25 five below their mean of 30, and 35 five above their mean of 30. It is obvious that there is greater variation in the second two scores compared to the first, despite the fact that 25 and 35 are smaller than 99 and 101. So when considering the variation of scores in our data we are not interested in their actual values but the amount of variation between them so that is why we compare them to the mean. Sometimes you will see, in the output of statistical computer programs, the sum of the squared scores referred to as the 'total' and the sum of the squared scores-minus-the-mean as the 'corrected total' as it is the second of these two sums that gives us the correct measurement of the total variability in the data. In our example the corrected total is 360 (the value we have used in the above calculations for the total variability in the scores). The difference between the total and the corrected total, $3888 - 360 = 3528$, is simply an indication of how far the mean value differs from zero.

We now have undertaken two analyses of variance on the general knowledge data. The first looked at the relationship between the general knowledge scores and age and the second compared the general knowledge scores across the three classes. In both cases the analyses were only possible because we had postulated an underlying linear model for the data. The models that best fitted the data were different in the two cases as the first analysis included the age information whereas the second included only the class information. However, given that the analysis was undertaken on the same general knowledge scores it is no surprise to see that the total variation in the data (the 'sums of squares') added up to 360 in both cases. With the assumption of a linear model we were able to separate this into the 'variability explained by the model' and the unexplained variability in the data. In our first analysis the 'explained sums of squares' was 342.29 and the 'unexplained sums of squares' was 17.71. In the second analysis these figures were 300 and 60 respectively.

The general linear model

Up to now we have deal with the simplest case of a linear model, that is, a straight line relationship between two variables, shown by the formula $Y = a + bX$. However, this is the simplest case of a much more general model that can include not just one independent or X variable but many independent variables (indeed we have seen two independent variables in the two factor ANOVAs in Chapter 15). Furthermore, it also allows for multiple Y or dependent variables. To illustrate this we need first to display our model in terms of matrix representation.

Our two variable example using matrix representation

Consider once again the general knowledge and age data. To find our linear model we minimised the error for $Y = a + bX + E$, where Y is the test score and X the age and E the error or residual. So for our children we can put each of their scores into the formula, one at a time:

$$Y_1 = a + bX_1 + E_1 \qquad \blacktriangleright \qquad \text{or with the} \qquad \blacktriangleright \qquad 6 = a + b \times 91 + E_1$$
$$Y_2 = a + bX_2 + E_2 \qquad\qquad\qquad \text{values of general} \qquad\qquad 9 = a + b \times 93 + E_2$$
$$Y_3 = a + bX_3 + E_3 \qquad\qquad\qquad \text{knowledge and} \qquad\qquad 8 = a + b \times 95 + E_3$$
$$\vdots \qquad\qquad\qquad\qquad\qquad \text{age inserted} \qquad\qquad\qquad \vdots$$
$$Y_{16} = a + bX_{16} + E_{16} \qquad\qquad\qquad\qquad\qquad\qquad\qquad 20 = a + b \times 120 + E_{16}$$
$$Y_{17} = a + bX_{17} + E_{17} \qquad\qquad\qquad\qquad\qquad\qquad\qquad 19 = a + b \times 122 + E_{17}$$
$$Y_{18} = a + bX_{18} + E_{18} \qquad\qquad\qquad\qquad\qquad\qquad\qquad 22 = a + b \times 124 + E_{18}$$

(I have used the small dots to indicate that the rest of the values need to be included here, otherwise I would have had to list out the formulae for all eighteen children.)

We can represent this in matrix terms as follows:

$$
\begin{bmatrix} Y_1 \\ Y_2 \\ Y_3 \\ \vdots \\ Y_{16} \\ Y_{17} \\ Y_{18} \end{bmatrix} = \begin{bmatrix} 1 & X_1 \\ 1 & X_2 \\ 1 & X_3 \\ \vdots & \vdots \\ 1 & X_{16} \\ 1 & X_{17} \\ 1 & X_{18} \end{bmatrix} \begin{bmatrix} a \\ b \end{bmatrix} + \begin{bmatrix} E_1 \\ E_2 \\ E_3 \\ \vdots \\ E_{16} \\ E_{17} \\ E_{18} \end{bmatrix}
$$

▶ or with the ▶ values of general knowledge and age inserted

$$
\begin{bmatrix} 6 \\ 9 \\ 8 \\ \vdots \\ 20 \\ 19 \\ 22 \end{bmatrix} = \begin{bmatrix} 1 & 91 \\ 1 & 93 \\ 1 & 95 \\ \vdots & \vdots \\ 1 & 120 \\ 1 & 122 \\ 1 & 124 \end{bmatrix} \begin{bmatrix} a \\ b \end{bmatrix} + \begin{bmatrix} E_1 \\ E_2 \\ E_3 \\ \vdots \\ E_{16} \\ E_{17} \\ E_{18} \end{bmatrix}
$$

Using large bold characters to represent matrices rather than the smaller letters we have been using to represent individual values we can replace the matrices as follows:

$$
Y = \begin{bmatrix} Y_1 \\ Y_2 \\ Y_3 \\ \vdots \\ Y_{16} \\ Y_{17} \\ Y_{18} \end{bmatrix}, X = \begin{bmatrix} 1 & X_1 \\ 1 & X_2 \\ 1 & X_3 \\ \vdots & \vdots \\ 1 & X_{16} \\ 1 & X_{17} \\ 1 & X_{18} \end{bmatrix}, B = \begin{bmatrix} a \\ b \end{bmatrix}, E = \begin{bmatrix} E_1 \\ E_2 \\ E_3 \\ \vdots \\ E_{16} \\ E_{17} \\ E_{18} \end{bmatrix}
$$

(We have a column of 1s in the **X** matrix to represent the intercept, 'a', in our model. If we did not put in this column then our line would be forced to go through zero.)

So, in matrix terms:

Y = XB + E

Employing matrix algebra (which is a little too complicated for this book) we can find the values of 'a' and 'b' that minimise the error quite easily as:

B = (X′X)$^{-1}$X′Y

where **X′** is the transpose of **X** and is worked out by swapping the rows and columns of **X**, and the inverse matrix (a matrix raised to the power of −1) can be calculated by a mathematical formula.

I hope you will appreciate that we are able work out the appropriate values of 'a' and 'b' using matrix algebra (which I am not expecting you to know about) using the information we already have. And it turns out that:

$$\mathbf{B} = \begin{bmatrix} \overline{Y} - b\overline{X} \\ \\ \dfrac{SP}{SS_x} \end{bmatrix}$$

(You can see from Chapter 20 on regression that these are the formulae for '*a*' and '*b*'.)

Hopefully, even for readers not familiar with matrix algebra, it is clear that all we have done is represent the same model but in a different way.

Multiple X variables

We can extend the linear model by looking at more than two variables. If you refer back to Chapter 21 on multiple regression, we see that the formula we employ is of the form:

$$Y = a + b_1 X_1 + b_2 X_2 + b_3 X_3 + \ldots$$

This is still a linear model as it still contains the intercept '*a*' plus the slope '*b*' but here we have a *b*-value for each of the *X* variables. Essentially the linear model means that there are no squared or higher values of *X* in the formula. As we are no longer working with only two variables the linear model is no longer a straight line but a multidimensional space. However, we can use the same logic to examine as many independent or *X* variables as we wish in our analysis and perform multiple correlation and regression operations as well as performing multifactorial analyses of variance, such as a two factor analysis of variance.

This is still a linear model of the form:

$$\mathbf{Y} = \mathbf{XB} + \mathbf{E}$$

In this case the **X** matrix is now

$$\begin{bmatrix} 1 & X_{11} & X_{21} & \cdots & X_{k1} \\ 1 & X_{12} & X_{22} & \cdots & X_{k2} \\ \vdots & \vdots & \vdots & \vdots & \vdots \\ 1 & X_{1n} & X_{2n} & \cdots & X_{kn} \end{bmatrix} \quad \text{and} \quad \mathbf{B} = \begin{bmatrix} a \\ b_1 \\ b_2 \\ \vdots \\ b_k \end{bmatrix}$$

where *n* is the number of participants and *k* is the number of independent variables so, for example, X_{12} is the value of participant 2 on the first independent variable.

The general linear model and multivariate analysis

We can generalise the linear model further to allow more than one Y variable as well as more than one X variable. We refer to analysis involving multiple dependent variables as multivariate analysis as compared to the single Y variable or univariate analysis (as we saw in Chapter 22). But the matrix notation does not change. We still have:

$Y = XB + E$

But in this case the **Y** matrix is now

$$\begin{bmatrix} Y_{11} & Y_{21} & \cdots & Y_{m1} \\ Y_{12} & Y_{22} & \cdots & Y_{m2} \\ \vdots & \vdots & \vdots & \vdots \\ Y_{1n} & Y_{2n} & \cdots & Y_{mn} \end{bmatrix}$$

where m is the number of dependent variables and Y_{21} is the score of the first participant on the second dependent variable.

Thus, the model is now referred to as the General Linear Model as it can include multiple independent and multiple dependent variables. You may have noticed that in Chapter 22 on multivariate analyses there is mention of matrices at various points in the discussions of complex analyses (such as factor analysis and MANOVA).

The important point here is that, regardless of whether we are dealing with one independent and one dependent variable or many of them, we can map our data onto a linear model and, as long as we satisfy the assumptions of the model, we have a powerful tool for making sense of research findings. Just as scientists use their models of the solar system to predict the movements of the planets, we can use a linear model to predict the relationships between our variables. We may be excited by the prospect of exploring other planets but we need to get there safely first and we can only do that with a good model. Similarly we may wish to discover exciting relationships between variables in our own field of study and it is well worth appreciating the role of the general linear model in the processes of quantitative data analysis and how it helps us to reach conclusions to our studies.

I hope this brief account of the underlying linear model in statistical analysis has given you some insight into the construction and application of many statistical tests. In particular an awareness of the importance of residuals is crucial to understanding the assumptions required for these tests. Unfortunately, further explanation requires a deeper foray into matrix algebra, which is beyond the scope of this book.

Notes

1 There is a possible problem when accurately calculating the median when the same score is obtained by the positions that surround the median position. In our case 55 is the score obtained by six positions: 48, 49, 50, 51, 52 and 53. The 47th score is 54 and the 54th score is 56. The median, between positions 50 and 51, is halfway between positions 48 and 53. To be completely accurate, a score of 55 could actually be anything ranging between 54.5 and 55.5 (as we would round the decimal points up or down respectively to the nearest whole number, so the score at position 48 in reality could be as low as 54.5 and the score at position 53 as high as 55.5). As our median value is halfway along the six positions scoring 55, it is also halfway along the range 54.5 to 55.5, and is 55. This might seem a convoluted way of demonstrating what appears obvious, but imagine that the positions scoring 55 were 47, 48, 49, 50, 51 and 52. Here the median is not halfway but 4/6ths of the way along the positions scoring 55. Now, again, a score of 55 could be as low as 54.5 and as high as 55.5 so our median, in this second example, is actually 4/6ths of the way between 54.5 and 55.5, and hence turns out to be 55.167.

2 If we have the same score at positions surrounding a quartile then we have to do the same sort of calculation we did with the median (see Note 1 above) to produce an accurate value. Interestingly, there are different ways to calculate quartiles depending on the method used. The technique suggested here is a simple method. However, statistical programs (such as SPSS) may give you a different result such as 48.25 instead of 48.5 for the first quartile

and 59.75 rather than 59.5 for the third quartile due to the way they weight the values when they divide the set of numbers into four quartiles.

3   The formula for the normal distribution is: $f(X) = \dfrac{1}{\sqrt{2\pi\sigma^2}} e^{\frac{-(X-\mu)^2}{2\sigma^2}}$ where μ and σ are the mean and standard deviation of the population and π and e are constants. You may be more familiar with π than e but they are both known fixed values. We can plot the function $f(X)$ by putting values of X into the formula and we get the familiar bell-shaped curve of the normal distribution.

4   Cyadmine is a purely fictitious name that I made up for this example. Any similarity of the name with a real chemical is purely coincidental.

5   Sometimes 'the critical t value' is referred to as $t_{\alpha/2, df}$ as we want the t value from the tables that cuts off $\alpha/2$ of each end of the distribution for a confidence of $(1 - \alpha)\%$ and df is the degrees of freedom.

6   The reference for GPOWER is Faul and Erdfelder (1992). It can be found at the following web page: http://www.psycho.uni-duesseldorf.de/aap/projects/gpower/index.html. Interested readers are referred to the paper by Thomas and Krebs (1997) which reviews a number of different software packages that perform power calculations.

7   When we have the same subjects in each condition we only use part of the within conditions variance as an estimate of the error variance as we are able to produce a more sensitive measure of the systematic differences between conditions. This is explained in Chapter 13.

8   The formula here is a sums of squares as $\sum(X - \overline{X})^2$ can be also be expressed by the alternative formula that does not require us to work out the mean first:

$$\sum X^2 - \frac{\left(\sum X\right)^2}{N}.$$

9   $F = t^2$ when $df = 1$. In the calculation we introduce some minor 'rounding errors' when we round to two decimal places. This is why the square of the t of 1.82 (producing $t^2 = 3.31$) is not quite the same as the F of 3.30. If we had performed all calculations to more decimal places we would have found them to be identical.

10   One disadvantage of the repeated measures ANOVA is that it also requires a further assumption called 'sphericity'. Essentially this means that the effects of the factor are consistent across the participants and the conditions. When analysing data by a computer program (e.g. SPSS) we can employ a test of sphericity to check our data. See Hinton *et al.* (2004) for a fuller discussion of this topic.

11   Laying out data for analysis by hand or for a report needs to be done in a manner that is clear and easy to read, so it minimises the possibility of misinterpretation. However, when inputting data into computer statistical analysis programs there are a few simple rules. Each row contains the data from a single subject. Independent measures variables are often referred to as 'grouping variables' and the different conditions are organised by rows. For example, if you had the scores for ten men and ten women on a task, you would not input two columns of ten results with one column labelled 'men' and the second labelled 'women'. You would put the scores in one column of 20 rows and distinguish between the men and women by a second column (the grouping variable) with a category label for men (i.e. 1) and a category label for the women (i.e. 2), so the second column would contain 10 ones

and 10 twos. Thus, when you read along a row you would know whether it was a man or a women by the category label in the appropriate column. A repeated measures variable does have each condition as a separate column. For example, if 20 people performed a task on Monday and then again on Tuesday, the results would be input in two columns the first headed 'Monday' and the second headed 'Tuesday'. Each row would have two values in it – the score for a participant on Monday and the same person's score for Tuesday.

12   I have followed Keppel (1973) in the choice of error term here. The reader is referred to this text for a discussion of the choice of error terms for the simple main effect in this case. The text also provides further details of the simple main effects for all the two factor ANOVAs.

13   Keppel (1973) contains further details of the simple main effects (see Note 12 above).

14   From Winer (1971).

15   If we wish to use a correction for ties we can work out SE using the following formula:

$$\sqrt{\frac{N(N+1)}{12} - \frac{\sum t}{12(N-1)}\left(\frac{1}{n_i} + \frac{1}{n_j}\right)}$$

16   From Zar (1996) with permission.

17   See Winer (1971) for further details of χ_r^2.

18   The correlation coefficient r uses z scores in its analysis. The z score requires the population mean and standard deviation. Due to this the scores are viewed as a population and the formula for calculating the standard deviation is the population standard deviation formula given in Chapter 2. Also, as we are working out means and standard deviations the scores must be measured on interval scales.

19   I am working to two decimal places here to aid the clarity of the explanation and the simplicity of the workings out. More usually we would employ more decimal places to improve the accuracy of the calculation. Most statistical analysis computer programs work to an accuracy of many decimal places.

20   With the same number of subjects for X and Y, $\dfrac{s_Y}{s_X}$ will be the same regardless of whether we use the formula for a population standard deviation for both s_X and s_Y or a sample standard deviation for both s_X and s_Y as the degrees of freedom will cancel out in the calculation.

Glossary

absolute deviation   When we subtract the mean value from a score the result (the deviation from the mean) is positive (+) if the score is larger than the mean and negative (−) if it is smaller. If we ignore the sign of the deviation and always treat it as positive we produce the absolute deviation.

ANOVA   An acronym for the **AN**alysis **O**f **VA**riance.

between subjects   Also known as independent measures. In this design, the samples we select for each condition of the independent variable are *independent*, in that the samples come from different subjects.

causal relationship   A relationship where variation in one variable causes variation in another. Statistical tests can show a relationship between variables but not that it is causal. Other factors might be involved in the relationship. We might find that it snows more when the leaves have fallen from the trees, but we cannot claim the fallen leaves cause the snow. Factors such as the season and temperature are involved.

component   The term used in the principal components method of factor analysis for a potential underlying factor.

condition   A researcher chooses levels or categories of the independent variable to observe its effect on the dependent variable. These are referred to as conditions, levels, treatments or groups. For example, 'morning' and 'afternoon' might be chosen as the conditions for the independent variable of time of day.

confidence interval In statistics we use samples to estimate population values, such as the mean or the difference in means. The confidence interval provides a range of values within which we predict lies the population value (to a certain level of confidence). The 95 per cent confidence interval of the mean worked out from a sample indicates that the estimated population mean would fall between the upper and lower limits for 95 per cent of the samples chosen.

confounding factor An independent variable (in addition to the one under test) that has a systematic influence on the dependent variable.

control group A group of subjects or participants matched with the experimental group on all relevant factors except the experimental manipulation. For example, a placebo group (who do not take a particular drug) could be used as a control group for a drug group (who do) to examine the effect of the drug on performance.

correlation The degree to which the scores (from a set of subjects) on two variables co-relate. That is, the extent to which a variation in the scores on one variable results in a corresponding variation in the scores on the second variable. Usually the relationship we are looking for is linear. A multiple correlation examines the relationship between a combination of predictor variables with a dependent variable.

critical value We reject the null hypothesis after a statistical test if the probability of the calculated value of the statistic (under the null hypothesis) is lower than the significance level (e.g. 0.05). Textbooks print tables of the critical values of the statistic, which are the values of the statistic at a particular significance level (e.g. 0.05). We then compare our calculated value with the critical value from the table. For example, if the calculated value of a t statistic is 4.20 and the critical value is 2.31 (at the 0.05 level of significance) then clearly the probability of the test statistic is less than 0.05 and the result is significant. Computer programs do not give a critical value but print out the actual probability of the calculated value (e.g. 0.023765) and we can examine this to see if it is higher or lower than the significance level for the significance of the result.

degrees of freedom When calculating a statistic we use information from the data (such as the mean or total) in the calculation. The degrees of freedom is the number of scores we need to know before we can work out the rest using the information we already have. It is the number of scores that are free to vary in the analysis.

dependent variable   The variable measured by the researcher and predicted to be influenced by (that is, depend on) the independent variable.

descriptive statistics   Usually we wish to describe our data before conducting further analysis or comparisons. Descriptive statistics such as the mean and standard deviation enable us to summarise a set of data.

deviation   The difference of a score from the mean. When we subtract the mean value from a score the result is the deviation.

discriminant function   A discriminant function is one derived from a set of independent (or predictor) variables that can be used to discriminate between the conditions of a dependent variable.

distribution   The range of possible scores on a variable and their frequency of occurrence. In statistical terms we refer to a distribution as a 'probability density function'. We use the mathematical formulae for known distributions to work out the probability of finding a score as high as or as low as a particular score.

effect size   The size of the difference between the means of two populations, usually expressed in standard deviation units.

eigenvalue   In a factor analysis an eigenvalue provides a measure of the amount of variance that can be explained by a proposed factor. If a factor has an eigenvalue of 1 then it can explain as much variance as one of the original independent variables.

equality of variance   see homogeneity of variance.

factor   Another name for 'variable', used commonly in the analysis of variance to refer to an independent variable. In factor analysis we analyse the variation in the data to see if it can be explained by fewer factors (i.e. 'new' variables) than the original number of independent variables.

general linear model   The underlying mathematical model employed in parametric statistics. When there are only two variables, X and Y, the relationship between them is linear when they satisfy the formula $Y = a + bX$ (where a and b are constants). The general linear model is a general form of this equation allowing as many X and Y variables as we wish in our analysis.

frequency   The number of times a score, a range of scores, or a category is obtained in a set of data is referred to as its frequency.

frequency data   The data collected is simply the number of scores that fall into each of certain specified categories. See also 'nominal data'.

histogram   A plot of data on a graph, where vertical bars are used to represent the frequency of the scores, range of scores or categories under study.

homogeneity of variance   Underlying parametric tests is the assumption that the populations from which the samples are drawn have the same variance.

We can examine the variances of the samples in our data to see whether this assumption is appropriate with our data or not.

homoscedasticity   The scores in a scatterplot are evenly distributed along and about a regression line. This is the assumption made in linear correlation and regression. (This is the correlation and regression equivalent of the homogeneity of variance assumption.)

hypothesis   A predicted relationship between variables. For example: 'As sleep loss increases so the number of errors on a specific monitoring task will increase'.

independent measures   A term used to indicate that there are different subjects in each condition of an independent variable.

independent variable   A variable chosen by the researcher for testing, predicted to influence the dependent variable.

inferential statistics   Statistics that allow us to make inferences about the data – for example whether samples are drawn from different populations or whether two variables correlate.

interaction   When there are two or more factors in an analysis of variance then we can examine the interactions between the factors. An interaction indicates that the effect of one factor is not the same at each condition of another factor. For example, if we find that more cold drinks are sold in summer and more hot drinks sold in winter then we have an interaction of 'drink temperature' and 'time of year'.

intercept   A linear regression finds the best fit linear relationship between two variables. This is a straight line based on the formula $Y = a + bX$, where b is the slope of the line and a is the intercept, or point where the line crosses the Y-axis.

interval data   Data produced by the use of an interval scale. Parametric tests require interval data.

interval scale   A scale of measurement where the interval between consecutive numbers is always the same. Most measuring devices, such as timers, thermometers, tape measures, employ interval scales.

item   When we employ a test with a number of variables (such as questions in a questionnaire) we refer to these variables as items, particularly in reliability analysis where we are interested in the correlation between items in the test.

linear correlation   The extent to which two variables correlate in a linear manner. That is, how close their scatterplot is to a straight line.

main effect   The effect of a factor on the dependent variable in an analysis of variance measured separately from other factors in the analysis.

MANOVA   A **M**ultivariate **AN**alysis **O**f **VA**riance. An analysis of variance technique where there can be more than one dependent variable in the analysis.

matching subjects Subjects are matched on relevant criteria across the conditions of the independent variable to control for possible confounding variables. For example, participants may be matched on intelligence or experience to control for these factors.

mean A measure of the 'average' score in a set of data. The mean is found by adding up all the scores and dividing by the number of scores.

mean square A term used in the analysis of variance to refer to the variance in the data due to a particular source of variation.

median If we order a set of data from lowest to highest the median is the point that divides the scores into two, with half the scores below and half above the median.

mixed design A mixed design is one that includes both independent measures factors and repeated measures factors. For example, a group of men and a group of women are tested in the morning and the afternoon. In this test 'gender' is an independent measures variable (also known as 'between subjects') and time of day is a repeated measures factor (also known as 'within subjects'), so we have a mixed design.

mode The score which has occurred the highest number of times in a set of data.

multiple comparisons The results of a statistical test with more than two conditions will often show a significant result but not where that difference lies. We need to undertake a comparison of conditions to see which ones are causing the effect. If we compare them two at a time this is known as pairwise comparisons. Multiple comparisons are either 'planned' and a specific comparison is planned in advance of the main test or 'unplanned' where comparisons are undertaken after discovering the significant finding.

multiple correlation The correlation of one variable with a combination of other variables.

multivariate Literally this means 'many variables' but is most commonly used to refer to a test with more than one dependent variable (as in the MANOVA).

nominal data When we use numbers as labels for categories we refer to the data collected as nominal (names). We cannot perform mathematical operations on these numbers: for example if we label the category 'men' as 1 and 'women' as 2 we cannot add up two men and claim it equals one woman! The data are usually the frequency of responses in each category.

nonparametric test Statistical tests that do not use, or make assumptions about, the characteristics (parameters) of populations.

normal distribution A bell-shaped frequency distribution that appears to underlie many human variables. The normal distribution can be worked out mathematically using the population mean and standard deviation.

null hypothesis   A prediction that there is no relationship between the independent and dependent variables.

one-tailed test   A prediction that two samples come from different populations, specifying the direction of the difference: that is, which of the two populations will have the larger mean value.

opportunity sample   An available sample, which is neither randomly chosen nor chosen to be representative of the population.

ordinal data   When we cannot assume that the intervals between consecutive numbers on a scale of measurement are of equal size we have ordinal data and can only use the data to rank order the subjects. Ratings are assumed to be ordinal data. We perform nonparametric tests on ordinal data.

outlier   An extreme value in a scatterplot – in that it lies outside the main cluster of scores. When calculating a linear correlation or regression an outlier will have a disproportionate influence on the statistical calculations.

parameter   A characteristic of a population, such as the population mean.

parametric tests   Statistical tests that use the characteristics (parameters) of populations or estimates of them (when assumptions are also made about the populations under study).

partial correlation   The correlation of two variables after having removed the effects of a third variable from both.

participant   A person taking part as a 'subject' in a study. The term 'participant' is preferred to 'subject' as it acknowledges the person's agency: i.e. that they have consented to take part in the study.

population   A complete set of objects or events. In statistics this usually refers to the complete set of subjects or scores we are interested in, from which we have drawn a sample.

post hoc tests   When we have more than two conditions of an independent variable a statistical test (such as an ANOVA) may show a significant result but not the source of the effect. We can perform post hoc tests (literally post hoc means 'after this') to see which conditions are showing significant differences. Post hoc tests should correct for the additional risk of Type I errors when performing multiple tests on the same data.

power of a test   The probability that, when there is a genuine effect to be found, the test will find it (that is, correctly reject a false null hypothesis). As an illustration, one test might be like a stopwatch that gives the same time for two runners in a race but a more powerful test is like a sensitive electronic timer that more accurately shows the times to differ by a fiftieth of a second.

probability   The chance of a specific event occurring from a set of possible events, expressed as a proportion. For example, if there were 4 women and 6 men in a room the probability of meeting a woman first on entering the room is 4/10 or 0.4 as there are 4 women out of 10 people in the room. A probability of 0 indicates an event will never occur and a probability of 1 that it will always occur. In a room of only 10 men there is a probability of 0 (0/10) of meeting a woman first and a probability of 1 (10/10) of meeting a man.

quartile If we order a set of scores from the lowest to the highest the quartiles are the points that divide the scores into four equal groups, with a quarter of the scores in each group. The second quartile is the median.

random error There will always be random factors influencing subjects' scores in an experiment. Random error is the influence of these random factors on the data. Statistical tests take account of random factors.

random sample A sample of a population where each member of the population has an equal chance of being chosen for the sample.

range The difference between the highest and lowest scores in a set of data.

rank When a set of data is ordered from lowest to highest the rank of a score is its position in this order.

rank order A method of ordering scores, listing them from lowest to highest.

ratio data Data measured on a ratio scale.

ratio scale An interval scale with an absolute zero. A stopwatch has an absolute zero as 0 indicates 'no time' and so we can make ratio statements: 20 seconds is twice as long as 10 seconds. The Celsius and Fahrenheit scales of temperature are interval but not ratio scales and indeed have 0 at different temperatures.

regression The prediction of subjects' scores on one variable by their scores on a second variable. This prediction is usually based on the relationship between the variables being linear and hence the prediction can be made using the formula $Y = a + bX$. The larger the correlation between the variables the more accurate the prediction. A multiple regression predicts the variation in a variable by a number of predictor variables.

reliability A reliable test is one that that will produce the same result when repeated (in the same circumstances). We can investigate the reliability of the items in a test (such as the questions in a questionnaire) by examining the relationship between each item and the overall score on the test.

repeated measures A term used to indicate that the same subjects are providing data for all the conditions of an independent variable.

representative sample A subset of a population that shares the same key characteristics of the population. For example, the sample has the same ratio of men to women as the population.

residual A linear regression provides a prediction of the subjects' scores on one variable by their scores on a second. The residual is the difference between a subject's actual score and their predicted score on the first variable. (A linear regression predicts that the data follow a linear model. The residuals indicate the extent to which the data do not fit the model, so are often referred to as 'errors'.)

scatterplot A graph of subjects' scores on one variable plotted against their scores on a second variable. The graph shows how the scores are 'scattered'.

significance level The risk (probability) of erroneously claiming a relationship between an independent and a dependent variable when there is not one. Statistical tests are undertaken so that this probability is chosen to be small, usually set at 0.05 indicating that this will occur no more than 5 times in 100. This sets the probability of making a Type I error.

simple main effects A significant interaction in a two factor analysis of variance indicates that the effect of one variable is different at the various conditions of the other variable. Calculating simple main effects tell us what these different effects are. A simple main effect is the effect of one variable at a single condition of a second variable.

standard deviation A measure of the standard ('average') difference (deviation) of a score from the mean in a set of scores. It is the square root of the variance. (There is a different calculation for standard deviation when the set of scores are a population as opposed to a sample.)

standard error of the estimate A measure of the 'average' distance (standard error) of a score from the regression line.

standard error of the mean The standard deviation of the distribution of sample means. It is a measure of the standard ('average') difference of a sample mean from the mean of all sample means of samples of the same size from the same population.

standard normal distribution A normal distribution with a mean of 0 and a standard deviation of 1.

standard score The position of a score within a distribution of scores. It provides a measure of how many standard deviation units a specific score falls above or below the mean. It is also referred to as a z score.

statistic Specifically, a characteristic of a sample, such as the sample mean. More generally, statistic and statistics are used to describe techniques for summarising and analysing numerical data.

subject The term used for the source of data in a sample. If people are the subjects of the study it is viewed as more respectful to refer to them as participants, which acknowledges their role as helpful contributors to the investigation.

sums of squares The sum of the squared deviations of scores from their mean value.

systematic error   Data that has been systematically influenced by another variable in addition to the independent variable under test is said to contain systematic error. The additional variable is said to confound the experiment.

two-tailed test   A prediction that two samples come from different populations, but not stating which population has the higher mean value.

Type I error   The error of rejecting the null hypothesis when it is true. The risk of this occurring is set by the significance level.

Type II error   The error of accepting the null hypothesis when it is false.

univariate   A term used to refer to a statistical test where there is only one dependent variable. ANOVA is a univariate analysis as there can be more than one independent variable but only one dependent variable.

variance   A measure of how much a set of scores vary from their mean value. Variance is the square of the standard deviation.

within subjects   Also known as repeated measures. We select the same subjects for each condition of an independent variable for a within-subjects design.

References

Cohen, J. (1988) *Statistical Power Analysis for the Behavioral Sciences*. 2nd edition. Hillsdale, NJ: Lawrence Erlbaum Associates.

Faul, F. and Erdfelder, E. (1992) GPOWER: A priori, post-hoc, and compromise power analysis of MS-DOS (Computer program). Bonn: Bonn University, Dept of Psychology.

Hinton, P.R., Brownlow, C., McMurray, I. and Cozens, B. (2004) *SPSS Explained*. Hove: Routledge.

Keppel, G. (1973) *Design and Analysis: A Researcher's Handbook*. Englewood Cliffs, NJ: Prentice Hall Inc.

Siegel, S. (1956) *Nonparametric Statistics*. New York: McGraw-Hill.

Thomas, L. and Krebs, C.J. (1997) A review of statistical power analysis software. *Bulletin of the Ecological Society of America*, 78(2), 126–139. Web page: http://www.zoology.ubc.ca/~krebs/power.html, accessed 01.10.2003.

Wilkinson, L. and Task Force on Statistical Inference (1999) Statistical methods in psychology journals: Guidelines and explanations. *American Psychologist*, 54(8), 594–604.

Winer, B.J. (1971) *Statistical Principles in Experimental Design*. 2nd edition. Tokyo: McGraw-Hill Kogakusha Ltd.

Zar, J.H. (1996) *Biostatistical Analysis*. 3rd edition. Upper Saddle River, NJ: Prentice Hall.

Appendix

Acknowledgements

I am grateful to the following sources for allowing me to reprint or adapt the following statistical tables:

A.1 The standard normal distribution tables

From: Table IIi of of R.A. Fisher and F. Yates (1974) *Statistical Tables for Biological, Agricultural, and Medical Research*, 6th edition. London: Pearson Education Limited (previously published by Oliver and Boyd Ltd, Edinburgh).

A.2 Critical values of the *t* distribution

From: Table III of of R.A. Fisher and F. Yates (1974) *Statistical Tables for Biological, Agricultural, and Medical Research*, 6th edition. London: Pearson Education Limited (previously published by Oliver and Boyd Ltd, Edinburgh).

A.3 Critical values of the *F* distribution

From: M. Merrington and C.M. Thompson (1943) Tables of percentage points of the inverted Beta (*F*) distribution, *Biometrika*, 33 (1943–6), 73–88, by permission of the *Biometrika* Trustees and Oxford University Press.

A.4 Critical values of the Studentized range statistic, q

From: Tables 2 and 3 in J. Pachares (1959) Table of the upper 10% points of the studentized range, Biometrika, 46, 461–6, by permission of the *Biometrika* Trustees and Oxford University Press.

A.5 Critical values of the Mann–Whitney U statistic

From: Table K of S. Siegel (1956) *Nonparametric Statistics for the Behavioral Sciences*, New York: McGraw-Hill. Reproduced with the permission of The McGraw-Hill Companies.

A.6 Critical values of the Wilcoxon T statistic

From: Table J of R.P. Runyan and A. Haber (1991) *Fundamentals of Behavioral Statistics*, 7th edition. New York: McGraw-Hill. Reproduced with the permission of The McGraw-Hill Companies.

A.7 Critical values of the chi-square (χ^2) distribution

From: Table IV of R.A. Fisher and F. Yates (1974) *Statistical Tables for Biological, Agricultural, and Medical Research*, 6th edition. London: Pearson Education Limited (previously published by Oliver and Boyd Ltd, Edinburgh).

A.8 Table of probabilities for χ_r^2 when k and n are small

From: M. Friedman (1937) The use of ranks to avoid the assumption of normality implicit in the analysis of variance, *Journal of the American Statistical Association*, 32, 200, 675–701. Reprinted with permission. Copyright (1937) by the American Statistical Association. All rights reserved.

A.9 Critical values of the Pearson r correlation coefficient

From: Table VII of R.A. Fisher and F. Yates (1974) *Statistical Tables for Biological, Agricultural, and Medical Research*, 6th edition. London: Pearson Education Limited (previously published by Oliver and Boyd Ltd, Edinburgh).

A.10 Critical values of the Spearman r_s ranked correlation coefficient

From: E.G. Olds (1949) The 5% significance levels for sums of squares of rank differences and a correction, *Annals of Mathematical Statistics*, volume 9, pages 133–48. With the permission of The Institute of Mathematical Statistics.

Table on page 240 – extract from the larger table of the Q Statistic in Zar, J., BIO-STATISTICAL ANALYSIS, 3/e, copyright © 1996. Adapted by permission of Pearson Education, Inc., Upper Saddle River, New Jersey.

I am grateful to Pearson Education Limited, on behalf of the Literary Executor of the late Sir Ronald Fisher, FRS, and Dr Frank Yates, FRS for permission to reprint Tables Ili, III, IV, V and VII from their book *Statistical Tables for Biological, Agricultural, and Medical Research*, 6th edition, 1974.

A.1 The standard normal distribution tables

z	0	1	2	3	4	5	6	7	8	9
0.0	0.5000	0.4960	0.4920	0.4880	0.4840	0.4801	0.4761	0.4721	0.4681	0.4641
0.1	0.4602	0.4562	0.4522	0.4483	0.4443	0.4404	0.4364	0.4325	0.4286	0.4247
0.2	0.4207	0.4168	0.4129	0.4090	0.4052	0.4013	0.3974	0.3936	0.3897	0.3859
0.3	0.3821	0.3783	0.3745	0.3707	0.3669	0.3632	0.3594	0.3557	0.3520	0.3483
0.4	0.3446	0.3409	0.3372	0.3336	0.3300	0.3264	0.3228	0.3192	0.3156	0.3121
0.5	0.3085	0.3050	0.3015	0.2981	0.2946	0.2912	0.2877	0.2843	0.2810	0.2776
0.6	0.2743	0.2709	0.2676	0.2643	0.2611	0.2578	0.2546	0.2514	0.2483	0.2451
0.7	0.2420	0.2389	0.2358	0.2327	0.2296	0.2266	0.2236	0.2206	0.2177	0.2148
0.8	0.2119	0.2090	0.2061	0.2033	0.2005	0.1977	0.1949	0.1922	0.1894	0.1867
0.9	0.1841	0.1814	0.1788	0.1762	0.1736	0.1711	0.1685	0.1660	0.1635	0.1611
1.0	0.1587	0.1562	0.1539	0.1515	0.1492	0.1469	0.1446	0.1423	0.1401	0.1379
1.1	0.1357	0.1335	0.1314	0.1294	0.1271	0.1251	0.1230	0.1210	0.1190	0.1170
1.2	0.1151	0.1131	0.1112	0.1093	0.1075	0.1056	0.1038	0.1020	0.1003	0.0985
1.3	0.0968	0.0951	0.0934	0.0918	0.0901	0.0885	0.0869	0.0853	0.0838	0.0823
1.4	0.0808	0.0793	0.0778	0.0764	0.0749	0.0735	0.0721	0.0708	0.0694	0.0681
1.5	0.0668	0.0655	0.0643	0.0630	0.0618	0.0606	0.0594	0.0582	0.0571	0.0559
1.6	0.0548	0.0537	0.0526	0.0516	0.0505	0.0495	0.0485	0.0475	0.0465	0.0455
1.7	0.0446	0.0436	0.0427	0.0418	0.0409	0.0401	0.0392	0.0384	0.0375	0.0367
1.8	0.0359	0.0351	0.0344	0.0336	0.0329	0.0322	0.0314	0.0307	0.0301	0.0294
1.9	0.0287	0.0281	0.0274	0.0268	0.0262	0.0256	0.0250	0.0244	0.0239	0.0233
2.0	0.0228	0.0222	0.0217	0.0212	0.0207	0.0202	0.0197	0.0192	0.0188	0.0183
2.1	0.0179	0.0174	0.0170	0.0166	0.0162	0.0158	0.0154	0.0150	0.0146	0.0143
2.2	0.0139	0.0136	0.0132	0.0129	0.0125	0.0122	0.0119	0.0116	0.0113	0.0110
2.3	0.0107	0.0104	0.0102	0.0099	0.0096	0.0094	0.0091	0.0089	0.0087	0.0084
2.4	0.0082	0.0080	0.0078	0.0075	0.0073	0.0071	0.0069	0.0068	0.0066	0.0064
2.5	0.0062	0.0060	0.0059	0.0057	0.0055	0.0054	0.0052	0.0051	0.0049	0.0048
2.6	0.0047	0.0045	0.0044	0.0043	0.0041	0.0040	0.0039	0.0038	0.0037	0.0036
2.7	0.0035	0.0034	0.0033	0.0032	0.0031	0.0030	0.0029	0.0028	0.0027	0.0026
2.8	0.0026	0.0025	0.0024	0.0023	0.0023	0.0022	0.0021	0.0021	0.0020	0.0019
2.9	0.0019	0.0018	0.0018	0.0017	0.0016	0.0016	0.0015	0.0015	0.0014	0.0014
3.0	0.0013	0.0013	0.0013	0.0012	0.0012	0.0011	0.0011	0.0011	0.0010	0.0010
3.1	0.0010	0.0009	0.0009	0.0009	0.0008	0.0008	0.0008	0.0008	0.0007	0.0007
3.2	0.0007	0.0007	0.0006	0.0006	0.0006	0.0006	0.0006	0.0005	0.0005	0.0005
3.3	0.0005	0.0005	0.0005	0.0004	0.0004	0.0004	0.0004	0.0004	0.0004	0.0003
3.4	0.0003	0.0003	0.0003	0.0003	0.0003	0.0003	0.0003	0.0003	0.0003	0.0002
3.5	0.0002	0.0002	0.0002	0.0002	0.0002	0.0002	0.0002	0.0002	0.0002	0.0002
3.6	0.0002	0.0002	0.0001	0.0001	0.0001	0.0001	0.0001	0.0001	0.0001	0.0001
3.7	0.0001	0.0001	0.0001	0.0001	0.0001	0.0001	0.0001	0.0001	0.0001	0.0001
3.8	0.0001	0.0001	0.0001	0.0001	0.0001	0.0001	0.0001	0.0001	0.0001	0.0001
3.9	0.0000	0.0000	0.0000	0.0000	0.0000	0.0000	0.0000	0.0000	0.0000	0.0000

To look up the probability of a z score use the first column, headed 'z', to find the first decimal place of the z score. The other columns represent the second decimal place. For example, if we wish to look up the probability of a z score of 1.8641 we first round it to two decimal places: 1.86. We go down the z column until we find 1.8. We move along the 1.8 row until we are in the column headed '6' (as the second decimal place is 6) and we find the probability of 0.0314. The probability of finding a score as high or higher than 1.86 is 0.0314.

Notice that there are no z scores in the table greater than 3.99 even though we might calculate them in our analyses. Observe also that the probability values of 3.9 or greater are given as 0.0000. The probability of a z score of 3.9 or larger is not actually zero but is so small that we cannot represent it in a table with only four decimal places.

A.2 Critical values of the *t* distribution

	0.05 Level of significance		0.01 Level of significance	
df	One-tailed test	Two-tailed test	One-tailed test	Two-tailed test
1	6.314	12.706	31.821	63.657
2	2.920	4.303	6.965	9.925
3	2.353	3.182	4.541	5.841
4	2.132	2.776	3.747	4.604
5	2.015	2.571	3.365	4.032
6	1.943	2.447	3.143	3.707
7	1.895	2.365	2.998	3.499
8	1.860	2.306	2.896	3.355
9	1.833	2.262	2.821	3.250
10	1.812	2.228	2.764	3.169
11	1.796	2.201	2.718	3.106
12	1.782	2.179	2.681	3.055
13	1.771	2.160	2.650	3.012
14	1.761	2.145	2.624	2.977
15	1.753	2.131	2.602	2.947
16	1.746	2.120	2.583	2.921
17	1.740	2.110	2.567	2.898
18	1.734	2.101	2.552	2.878
19	1.729	2.093	2.539	2.861
20	1.725	2.086	2.528	2.845
21	1.721	2.080	2.518	2.831
22	1.717	2.074	2.508	2.819
23	1.714	2.069	2.500	2.807
24	1.711	2.064	2.492	2.797
25	1.708	2.060	2.485	2.787
26	1.706	2.056	2.479	2.779
27	1.703	2.052	2.473	2.771
28	1.701	2.048	2.467	2.763
29	1.699	2.045	2.462	2.756
30	1.697	2.042	2.457	2.750
40	1.684	2.021	2.423	2.704
60	1.671	2.000	2.390	2.660
120	1.656	1.980	2.358	2.617
∞	1.645	1.960	2.326	2.576

The values indicate the size of *t* that cuts off either 0.05 or 0.01 of the *t* distribution at the different degrees of freedom. For example, for a one-tailed test with $df = 20$, a value of $t = 1.725$ cuts off 0.05 of the distribution. Thus, for a calculated value of *t* to be significant it must be greater than or equal to the appropriate table value. That is to say, if the calculated value of *t* is greater than the table value then the probability that such a result occurred by chance is less than 0.05.

When you have calculated a degrees of freedom that is not in the table (i.e. $df = 32$) use the next lowest value in given the table (i.e. $df = 30$ for a calculated $df = 32$). If you really want to you can use linear interpolation if you wish to be a little more accurate. When the degrees of freedom is very large (into the hundreds) use the infinity (∞) value.

A.3 Critical values of the *F* distribution

0.05 Level of significance

df2	1	2	3	4	5	6	7	8	9	10	20	∞
1	161.45	199.50	215.71	224.58	230.16	233.99	236.77	238.88	240.54	241.88	248.01	254.32
2	18.51	19.00	19.16	19.25	19.30	19.33	19.35	19.37	19.38	19.40	19.45	19.50
3	10.13	9.55	9.28	9.12	9.01	8.94	8.89	8.85	8.81	8.79	8.66	8.53
4	7.71	6.94	6.59	6.39	6.26	6.16	6.09	6.04	6.00	5.96	5.80	5.63
5	6.61	5.79	5.41	5.19	5.05	4.95	4.88	4.82	4.77	4.74	4.56	4.36
6	5.99	5.14	4.76	4.53	4.39	4.28	4.21	4.15	4.10	4.06	3.87	3.67
7	5.59	4.74	4.35	4.12	3.97	3.87	3.79	3.73	3.68	3.64	3.44	3.23
8	5.32	4.46	4.07	3.84	3.69	3.58	3.50	3.44	3.39	3.35	3.15	2.93
9	5.12	4.26	3.86	3.63	3.48	3.37	3.29	3.23	3.18	3.14	3.07	3.01
10	4.96	4.10	3.71	3.48	3.33	3.22	3.14	3.07	3.02	2.98	2.77	2.54
11	4.84	3.98	3.59	3.36	3.20	3.09	3.01	2.95	2.90	2.85	2.65	2.40
12	4.75	3.89	3.49	3.26	3.11	3.00	2.91	2.85	2.80	2.75	2.54	2.30
13	4.67	3.81	3.41	3.18	3.03	2.92	2.83	2.77	2.71	2.67	2.46	2.21
14	4.60	3.74	3.34	3.11	2.96	2.85	2.76	2.70	2.65	2.60	2.39	2.13
15	4.54	3.68	3.29	3.06	2.90	2.79	2.71	2.64	2.59	2.54	2.33	2.07
16	4.49	3.63	3.24	3.01	2.85	2.74	2.66	2.59	2.54	2.49	2.28	2.01
17	4.45	3.59	3.20	2.96	2.81	2.70	2.61	2.55	2.49	2.45	2.23	1.96
18	4.41	3.55	3.16	2.93	2.77	2.66	2.58	2.51	2.46	2.41	2.19	1.92
19	4.38	3.52	3.13	2.90	2.74	2.63	2.54	2.48	2.42	2.38	2.16	1.88
20	4.35	3.49	3.10	2.87	2.71	2.60	2.51	2.45	2.39	2.35	2.12	1.84
21	4.32	3.47	3.07	2.84	2.68	2.57	2.49	2.42	2.37	2.32	2.10	1.81
22	4.30	3.44	3.05	2.82	2.66	2.55	2.46	2.40	2.34	2.30	2.07	1.78
23	4.28	3.42	3.03	2.80	2.64	2.53	2.44	2.37	2.32	2.27	2.05	1.76
24	4.26	3.40	3.01	2.78	2.62	2.51	2.42	2.36	2.30	2.25	2.03	1.73
25	4.24	3.39	2.99	2.76	2.60	2.49	2.40	2.34	2.28	2.24	2.01	1.71
26	4.23	3.37	2.98	2.74	2.59	2.47	2.39	2.32	2.27	2.22	1.99	1.69
27	4.21	3.35	2.96	2.73	2.57	2.46	2.37	2.31	2.25	2.20	1.97	1.67
28	4.20	3.34	2.95	2.71	2.56	2.45	2.36	2.29	2.24	2.19	1.96	1.65
29	4.18	3.33	2.93	2.70	2.55	2.43	2.35	2.28	2.22	2.18	1.94	1.64
30	4.17	3.32	2.92	2.69	2.53	2.42	2.33	2.27	2.21	2.16	1.93	1.62
40	4.08	3.23	2.84	2.61	2.45	2.34	2.25	2.18	2.12	2.08	1.84	1.51
60	4.00	3.15	2.76	2.53	2.37	2.25	2.17	2.10	2.04	1.99	1.75	1.39
120	3.92	3.07	2.68	2.45	2.29	2.18	2.09	2.02	1.96	1.91	1.66	1.25
∞	3.84	3.00	2.60	2.37	2.21	2.10	2.01	1.94	1.88	1.83	1.57	1.00

The calculated value of *F* must be larger than or equal to the table value for significance.

A.3 Critical values of the *F* distribution (continued)

0.01 Level of significance

						df 1						
df 2	1	2	3	4	5	6	7	8	9	10	20	∞
1	4052.2	4999.5	5403.3	5624.6	5763.7	5859.0	5928.3	5981.6	6022.5	6055.8	6208.7	6366.0
2	98.50	99.00	99.17	99.25	99.30	99.33	99.36	99.37	99.39	99.40	99.45	99.50
3	34.12	30.82	29.46	28.71	28.24	27.91	27.67	27.49	27.34	27.23	26.69	26.12
4	21.20	18.00	16.69	15.98	15.52	15.21	14.98	14.80	14.66	14.55	14.02	13.46
5	16.26	13.27	12.06	11.39	10.97	10.67	10.46	10.29	10.16	10.05	9.55	9.02
6	13.74	10.92	9.78	9.15	8.75	8.47	8.26	8.10	7.98	7.87	7.40	6.88
7	12.25	9.55	8.45	7.85	7.46	7.19	6.99	6.84	6.72	6.62	6.16	5.67
8	11.26	8.65	7.59	7.01	6.63	6.37	6.18	6.03	5.91	5.81	5.36	4.86
9	10.56	8.02	6.99	6.42	6.06	5.80	5.61	5.47	5.35	5.26	4.81	4.31
10	10.04	7.56	6.55	5.99	5.64	5.39	5.20	5.06	4.94	4.85	4.41	3.91
11	9.65	7.21	6.22	5.67	5.32	5.07	4.89	4.74	4.63	4.54	4.10	3.60
12	9.33	6.93	5.95	5.41	5.06	4.82	4.64	4.50	4.39	4.30	3.86	3.36
13	9.07	6.70	5.74	5.21	4.86	4.62	4.44	4.30	4.19	4.10	3.66	3.17
14	8.86	6.51	5.56	5.04	4.70	4.46	4.28	4.14	4.03	3.94	3.51	3.00
15	8.68	6.36	5.42	4.89	4.56	4.32	4.14	4.00	3.89	3.80	3.37	2.87
16	8.53	6.23	5.29	4.77	4.44	4.20	4.03	3.89	3.78	3.69	3.26	2.75
17	8.40	6.11	5.18	4.67	4.34	4.10	3.93	3.79	3.68	3.59	3.16	2.65
18	8.29	6.01	5.09	4.58	4.25	4.01	3.84	3.71	3.60	3.51	3.08	2.57
19	8.18	5.93	5.01	4.50	4.17	3.94	3.77	3.63	3.52	3.43	3.00	2.49
20	8.10	5.85	4.94	4.43	4.10	3.87	3.70	3.56	3.46	3.37	2.94	2.42
21	8.02	5.78	4.87	4.37	4.04	3.81	3.64	3.51	3.40	3.31	2.88	2.36
22	7.95	5.72	4.82	4.31	3.99	3.76	3.59	3.45	3.35	3.26	2.83	2.31
23	7.88	5.66	4.76	4.26	3.94	3.71	3.54	3.41	3.30	3.21	2.78	2.26
24	7.82	5.61	4.72	4.22	3.90	3.67	3.50	3.36	3.26	3.17	2.74	2.21
25	7.77	5.57	4.68	4.18	3.86	3.63	3.46	3.32	3.22	3.13	2.70	2.17
26	7.72	5.53	4.64	4.14	3.82	3.59	3.42	3.29	3.18	3.09	2.66	2.13
27	7.68	5.49	4.60	4.11	3.78	3.56	3.39	3.26	3.15	3.06	2.63	2.10
28	7.64	5.45	4.57	4.07	3.75	3.53	3.36	3.23	3.12	3.03	2.60	2.06
29	7.60	5.42	4.54	4.04	3.73	3.50	3.33	3.20	3.09	3.00	2.57	2.03
30	7.58	5.39	4.51	4.02	3.70	3.47	3.30	3.17	3.07	2.98	2.55	2.01
40	7.31	5.18	4.31	3.83	3.51	3.29	3.12	2.99	2.89	2.80	2.37	1.80
60	7.08	4.98	4.13	3.65	3.34	3.12	2.95	2.82	2.72	2.63	2.20	1.60
120	6.85	4.79	3.95	3.48	3.17	2.96	2.79	2.66	2.56	2.47	2.03	1.38
∞	6.63	4.61	3.78	3.32	3.02	2.80	2.64	2.51	2.41	2.32	1.88	1.00

The calculated value of *F* must be larger than or equal to the table value for significance.

A.4 Critical values of the Studentized range statistic, *q*

0.05 Level of significance

Error	Number of conditions (*k*)										
df	2	3	4	5	6	7	8	9	10	11	12
5	3.64	4.60	5.22	5.67	6.03	6.33	6.58	6.80	6.99	7.17	7.32
6	3.46	4.34	4.90	5.30	5.63	5.90	6.12	6.32	6.49	6.65	6.79
7	3.34	4.16	4.68	5.06	5.36	5.61	5.82	6.00	6.16	6.30	6.43
8	3.26	4.04	4.53	4.89	5.17	5.40	5.60	5.77	5.92	6.05	6.18
9	3.20	3.95	4.41	4.76	5.02	5.24	5.43	5.59	5.74	5.87	5.98
10	3.15	3.88	4.33	4.65	4.91	5.12	5.30	5.46	5.60	5.72	5.83
11	3.11	3.82	4.26	4.57	4.82	5.03	5.20	5.35	5.49	5.61	5.71
12	3.08	3.77	4.20	4.51	4.75	4.95	5.12	5.27	5.36	5.51	5.61
13	3.06	3.73	4.15	4.45	4.69	4.88	5.05	5.19	5.32	5.43	5.53
14	3.03	3.70	4.11	4.41	4.64	4.83	4.99	5.13	5.25	5.36	5.46
15	3.01	3.67	4.08	4.37	4.59	4.78	4.94	5.08	5.20	5.31	5.40
16	3.00	3.65	4.05	4.33	4.56	4.74	4.90	5.03	5.15	5.26	5.35
17	2.98	3.63	4.02	4.30	4.52	4.70	4.86	4.99	5.11	5.21	5.31
18	2.97	3.61	4.00	4.28	4.49	4.67	4.82	4.96	5.07	5.17	5.27
19	2.96	3.59	3.98	4.25	4.47	4.65	4.79	4.92	5.04	5.14	5.23
20	2.95	3.58	3.96	4.23	4.45	4.62	4.77	4.90	5.01	5.11	5.20
24	2.92	3.53	3.90	4.17	4.37	4.54	4.68	4.81	4.92	5.01	5.10
30	2.89	3.49	3.85	4.10	4.30	4.46	4.60	4.72	4.82	4.92	5.00
40	2.86	3.44	3.79	4.04	4.23	4.39	4.52	4.63	4.73	4.82	4.90
60	2.83	3.40	3.74	3.98	4.16	4.31	4.44	4.55	4.65	4.73	4.81
120	2.80	3.36	3.68	3.92	4.10	4.24	4.36	4.47	4.56	4.64	4.71
∞	2.77	3.31	3.63	3.86	4.03	4.17	4.29	4.39	4.47	4.55	4.62

A.4 Critical values of the Studentized range statistic, *q* (continued)

0.01 Level of significance

Error	Number of conditions (*k*)										
df	2	3	4	5	6	7	8	9	10	11	12
5	5.70	6.98	7.80	8.42	8.91	9.32	9.67	9.97	10.24	10.48	10.70
6	5.24	6.33	7.03	7.56	7.97	8.32	8.61	8.87	9.10	9.30	9.48
7	4.95	5.92	6.54	7.01	7.37	7.68	7.94	8.17	8.37	8.55	8.71
8	4.75	5.64	6.20	6.62	6.96	7.24	7.47	7.68	7.86	8.03	8.18
9	4.60	5.43	5.96	6.35	6.66	6.91	7.13	7.33	7.49	7.65	7.78
10	4.48	5.27	5.77	6.14	6.43	6.67	6.87	7.05	7.21	7.36	7.49
11	4.39	5.15	5.62	5.97	6.25	6.48	6.67	6.84	6.99	7.13	7.25
12	4.32	5.05	5.50	5.84	6.10	6.32	6.51	6.67	6.81	6.94	7.06
13	4.26	4.96	5.40	5.73	5.98	6.19	6.37	6.53	6.67	6.79	6.90
14	4.21	4.89	5.32	5.63	5.88	6.08	6.26	6.41	6.54	6.66	6.77
15	4.17	4.84	5.25	5.56	5.80	5.99	6.16	6.31	6.44	6.55	6.66
16	4.13	4.79	5.19	5.49	5.72	5.92	6.08	6.22	6.35	6.46	6.56
17	4.10	4.74	5.14	5.43	5.66	5.85	6.01	6.15	6.27	6.38	6.48
18	4.07	4.70	5.09	5.38	5.60	5.79	5.94	6.08	6.20	6.31	6.41
19	4.05	4.67	5.05	5.33	5.55	5.73	5.89	6.02	6.14	6.25	6.34
20	4.02	4.64	5.02	5.29	5.51	5.69	5.84	5.97	6.09	6.19	6.28
24	3.96	4.55	4.91	5.17	5.37	5.54	5.69	5.81	5.92	6.02	6.11
30	3.89	4.45	4.80	5.05	5.24	5.40	5.54	5.65	5.76	5.85	5.93
40	3.82	4.37	4.70	4.93	5.11	5.26	5.39	5.50	5.60	5.69	5.76
60	3.76	4.28	4.59	4.82	4.99	5.13	5.25	5.36	5.45	5.53	5.60
120	3.70	4.20	4.50	4.71	4.87	5.01	5.12	5.21	5.30	5.37	5.44
∞	3.64	4.12	4.40	4.60	4.76	4.88	4.99	5.08	5.16	5.23	5.29

A.5 Critical values of the Mann–Whitney *U* statistic

The calculated value of *U* must be smaller than or equal to the table value for significance. Dashes in the table indicate that no value is possible for significance.

0.05 Level of significance: One-tailed test

n_1

n_2	1	2	3	4	5	6	7	8	9	10	11	12	13	14	15	16	17	18	19	20
1	–	–	–	–	–	–	–	–	–	–	–	–	–	–	–	–	–	–	0	0
2	–	–	–	–	0	0	0	1	1	1	1	2	2	2	3	3	3	4	4	4
3	–	–	0	0	1	2	2	3	3	4	5	5	6	7	7	8	9	9	10	11
4	–	–	0	1	2	3	4	5	6	7	8	9	10	11	12	14	15	16	17	18
5	–	0	1	2	4	5	6	8	9	11	12	13	15	16	18	19	20	22	23	25
6	–	0	2	3	5	7	8	10	12	14	16	17	19	21	23	25	26	28	30	32
7	–	0	2	4	6	8	11	13	15	17	19	21	24	26	28	30	33	35	37	39
8	–	1	3	5	8	10	13	15	18	20	23	26	28	31	33	36	39	41	44	47
9	–	1	3	6	9	12	15	18	21	24	27	30	33	36	39	42	45	48	51	54
10	–	1	4	7	11	14	17	20	24	27	31	34	37	41	44	48	51	55	58	62
11	–	1	5	8	12	16	19	23	27	31	34	38	42	46	50	54	57	61	65	69
12	–	2	5	9	13	17	21	26	30	34	38	42	47	51	55	60	64	68	72	77
13	–	2	6	10	15	19	24	28	33	37	42	47	51	56	61	65	70	75	80	84
14	–	2	7	11	16	21	26	31	36	41	46	51	56	61	66	71	77	82	87	92
15	–	3	7	12	18	23	28	33	39	44	50	55	61	66	72	77	83	88	94	100
16	–	3	8	14	19	25	30	36	42	48	54	60	65	71	77	83	89	95	101	107
17	–	3	9	15	20	26	33	39	45	51	57	64	70	77	83	89	96	102	109	115
18	–	4	9	16	22	28	35	41	48	55	61	68	75	82	88	95	102	109	116	123
19	0	4	10	17	23	30	37	44	51	58	65	72	80	87	94	101	109	116	123	130
20	0	4	11	18	25	32	39	47	54	62	69	77	84	92	100	107	115	123	130	138

0.05 Level of significance: Two-tailed test

n_1

n_2	1	2	3	4	5	6	7	8	9	10	11	12	13	14	15	16	17	18	19	20
1	–	–	–	–	–	–	–	–	–	–	–	–	–	–	–	–	–	–	–	–
2	–	–	–	–	–	–	–	0	0	0	0	1	1	1	1	1	2	2	2	2
3	–	–	–	–	0	1	1	2	2	3	3	4	4	5	5	6	6	7	7	8
4	–	–	–	0	1	2	3	4	4	5	6	7	8	9	10	11	11	12	13	13
5	–	–	0	1	2	3	5	6	7	8	9	11	12	13	14	15	17	18	19	20
6	–	–	1	2	3	5	6	8	10	11	13	14	16	17	19	21	22	24	25	27
7	–	–	1	3	5	6	8	10	12	14	16	18	20	22	24	26	28	30	32	34
8	–	0	2	4	6	8	10	13	15	17	19	22	24	26	29	31	34	36	38	41
9	–	0	2	4	7	10	12	15	17	20	23	26	28	31	34	37	39	42	45	48
10	–	0	3	5	8	11	14	17	20	23	26	29	33	36	39	42	45	48	52	55
11	–	0	3	6	9	13	16	19	23	26	30	33	37	40	44	47	51	55	58	62
12	–	1	4	7	11	14	18	22	26	29	33	37	41	45	49	53	57	61	65	69
13	–	1	4	8	12	16	20	24	28	33	37	41	45	50	54	59	63	67	72	76
14	–	1	5	9	13	17	22	26	31	36	40	45	50	55	59	64	67	74	78	83
15	–	1	5	10	14	19	24	29	34	39	44	49	54	59	64	70	75	80	85	90
16	–	1	6	11	15	21	26	31	37	42	47	53	59	64	70	75	81	86	92	98
17	–	2	6	11	17	22	28	34	39	45	51	57	63	67	75	81	87	93	99	105
18	–	2	7	12	18	24	30	36	42	48	55	61	67	74	80	86	93	99	106	112
19	–	2	7	13	19	25	32	38	45	52	58	65	72	78	85	92	99	106	113	119
20	–	2	8	13	20	27	34	41	48	55	62	69	76	83	90	98	105	112	119	127

A.5 Critical values of the Mann–Whitney U statistic (continued)

The calculated value of U must be smaller than or equal to the table value for significance. Dashes in the table indicate that no value is possible for significance.

0.01 Level of significance: One-tailed test

n_1

n_2	1	2	3	4	5	6	7	8	9	10	11	12	13	14	15	16	17	18	19	20
1	–	–	–	–	–	–	–	–	–	–	–	–	–	–	–	–	–	–	–	–
2	–	–	–	–	–	–	–	–	–	–	–	–	0	0	0	0	0	0	1	1
3	–	–	–	–	–	–	0	0	1	1	1	2	2	2	3	3	4	4	4	5
4	–	–	–	–	0	1	1	2	3	3	4	5	5	6	7	7	8	9	9	10
5	–	–	–	0	1	2	3	4	5	6	7	8	9	10	11	12	13	14	15	16
6	–	–	–	1	2	3	4	6	7	8	9	11	12	13	15	16	18	19	20	22
7	–	–	0	1	3	4	6	7	9	11	12	14	16	17	19	21	23	24	26	28
8	–	–	0	2	4	6	7	9	11	13	15	17	20	22	24	26	28	30	32	34
9	–	–	1	3	5	7	9	11	14	16	18	21	23	26	28	31	33	36	38	40
10	–	–	1	3	6	8	11	13	16	19	22	24	27	30	33	36	38	41	44	47
11	–	–	1	4	7	9	12	15	18	22	25	28	31	34	37	41	44	47	50	53
12	–	–	2	5	8	11	14	17	21	24	28	31	35	38	42	46	49	53	56	60
13	–	0	2	5	9	12	16	20	23	27	31	35	39	43	47	51	55	59	63	67
14	–	0	2	6	10	13	17	22	26	30	34	38	43	47	51	56	60	65	69	73
15	–	0	3	7	11	15	19	24	28	33	37	42	47	51	56	61	66	70	75	80
16	–	0	3	7	12	16	21	26	31	36	41	46	51	56	61	66	71	76	82	87
17	–	0	4	8	13	18	23	28	33	38	44	49	55	60	66	71	77	82	88	93
18	–	0	4	9	14	19	24	30	36	41	47	53	59	65	70	76	82	88	94	100
19	–	1	4	9	15	20	26	32	38	44	50	56	63	69	75	82	88	94	101	107
20	–	1	5	10	16	22	28	34	40	47	53	60	67	73	80	87	93	100	107	114

0.01 Level of significance: Two-tailed test

n_1

n_2	1	2	3	4	5	6	7	8	9	10	11	12	13	14	15	16	17	18	19	20
1	–	–	–	–	–	–	–	–	–	–	–	–	–	–	–	–	–	–	–	–
2	–	–	–	–	–	–	–	–	–	–	–	–	–	–	–	–	–	–	0	0
3	–	–	–	–	–	–	–	–	0	0	0	1	1	1	2	2	2	2	3	3
4	–	–	–	–	–	0	0	1	1	2	2	3	3	4	5	5	6	6	7	8
5	–	–	–	–	0	1	1	2	3	4	5	6	7	7	8	9	10	11	12	13
6	–	–	–	0	1	2	3	4	5	6	7	9	10	11	12	13	15	16	17	18
7	–	–	–	0	1	3	4	6	7	9	10	12	13	15	16	18	19	21	22	24
8	–	–	–	1	2	4	6	7	9	11	13	15	17	18	20	22	24	26	28	30
9	–	–	0	1	3	5	7	9	11	13	16	18	20	22	24	27	29	31	33	36
10	–	–	0	2	4	6	9	11	13	16	18	21	24	26	29	31	34	37	39	42
11	–	–	0	2	5	7	10	13	16	18	21	24	27	30	33	36	39	42	45	48
12	–	–	1	3	6	9	12	15	18	21	24	27	31	34	37	41	44	47	51	54
13	–	–	1	3	7	10	13	17	20	24	27	31	34	38	42	45	49	53	56	60
14	–	–	1	4	7	11	15	18	22	26	30	34	38	42	46	50	54	58	63	67
15	–	–	2	5	8	12	16	20	24	29	33	37	42	46	51	55	60	64	69	73
16	–	–	2	5	9	13	18	22	27	31	36	41	45	50	55	60	65	70	74	79
17	–	–	2	6	10	15	19	24	29	34	39	44	49	54	60	65	70	75	81	86
18	–	–	2	6	11	16	21	26	31	37	42	47	53	58	64	70	75	81	87	92
19	–	0	3	7	12	17	22	28	33	39	45	51	56	63	69	74	81	87	93	99
20	–	0	3	8	13	18	24	30	36	42	48	54	60	67	73	79	86	92	99	105

A.6 Critical values of the Wilcoxon *T* statistic

The calculated value of *T* must be lower than or equal to the table value for significance.
Dashes in the table indicate that no value is possible for significance.

n	0.05 Level of significance One-tailed test	0.05 Level of significance Two-tailed test	0.01 Level of significance One-tailed test	0.01 Level of significance Two-tailed test
5	0	–	–	–
6	2	0	–	–
7	3	2	0	–
8	5	3	1	0
9	8	5	3	1
10	10	8	5	3
11	13	10	7	5
12	17	13	9	7
13	21	17	12	9
14	25	21	15	12
15	30	25	19	15
16	35	29	23	19
17	41	34	27	23
18	47	40	32	27
19	53	46	37	32
20	60	52	43	37
21	67	58	49	42
22	75	65	55	48
23	83	73	62	54
24	91	81	69	61
25	100	89	76	68
26	110	98	84	75
27	119	107	92	83
28	130	116	101	91
29	140	126	110	100
30	151	137	120	109
31	163	147	130	118
32	175	159	140	128
33	187	170	151	138
34	200	182	162	148
35	213	195	173	159
36	227	208	185	171
37	241	221	198	182
38	256	235	211	194
39	271	249	224	207
40	286	264	238	220
41	302	279	252	233
42	319	294	266	247
43	336	310	281	261
44	353	327	296	276
45	371	343	312	291
46	389	361	328	307
47	407	378	345	322
48	426	396	362	339
49	446	415	379	355
50	466	434	397	373

A.7 Critical values of the chi-square (χ^2) distribution

df	0.05 Level of significance	0.01 Level of significance
1	3.84	6.64
2	5.99	9.21
3	7.82	11.34
4	9.49	13.28
5	11.07	15.09
6	12.59	16.81
7	14.07	18.48
8	15.51	20.09
9	16.92	21.67
10	18.31	23.21
11	19.68	24.72
12	21.03	26.22
13	22.36	27.69
14	23.68	29.14
15	25.00	30.58
16	26.30	32.00
17	27.59	33.41
18	28.87	34.80
19	30.14	36.19
20	31.41	37.57
21	32.67	38.93
22	33.92	40.29
23	35.17	41.64
24	36.42	42.98
25	37.65	44.31
26	38.88	45.64
27	40.11	46.97
28	41.34	48.28
29	42.56	49.59
30	43.77	50.89

The calculated value of χ^2 must be larger than or equal to the table value for significance.

A.8 Table of probabilities for χ_r^2 when k and n are small

k	n	0.05 Level of significance χ_r^2	Probability	0.01 Level of significance χ_r^2	Probability
3	2	–	–	–	–
		–	–	–	–
3	3	6.00	0.028	–	–
		4.67	0.194	–	–
3	4	6.50	0.042	8.00	0.005
		6.00	0.069	6.50	0.042
3	5	6.40	0.039	8.40	0.009
		5.20	0.093	7.60	0.024
3	6	7.00	0.029	9.00	0.008
		6.33	0.052	8.33	0.012
3	7	7.14	0.027	8.86	0.008
		6.00	0.052	8.00	0.016
3	8	6.25	0.047	9.00	0.010
		5.25	0.079	7.75	0.018
3	9	6.22	0.048	8.67	0.010
		6.00	0.057	8.22	0.016
4	2	6.00	0.042	–	–
		5.40	0.167	–	–
4	3	7.40	0.033	9.00	0.002
		7.00	0.054	8.20	0.017

When k and n are small χ_r^2 can only take a few values. For each combination of k and n there are two values given for χ_r^2. The table gives the two values closest to the significance level with their actual probabilities. For example, when k = 3 and n = 6, χ_r^2 = 7.00 or greater with a probability of 0.029. This is less than 0.05 and so is significant. The next value below 7.00 that χ_r^2 can be is 6.33, with a probability of 0.052, which is not quite significant at 0.05. Dashes in the table indicate that no value is possible for significance.

A.9 Critical values of the Pearson *r* correlation coefficient

	0.05 Level of significance		0.01 Level of significance	
df	One-tailed test (directional)	Two-tailed test (non-directional)	One-tailed test (directional)	Two-tailed test (non-directional)
1	0.9877	0.9969	0.9995	0.9999
2	0.9000	0.9500	0.9800	0.9900
3	0.8054	0.8783	0.9343	0.9587
4	0.7293	0.8114	0.8822	0.9172
5	0.6694	0.7545	0.8329	0.8745
6	0.6215	0.7067	0.7887	0.8343
7	0.5822	0.6664	0.7498	0.7977
8	0.5494	0.6319	0.7155	0.7646
9	0.5214	0.6021	0.6851	0.7348
10	0.4973	0.5760	0.6581	0.7079
11	0.4762	0.5529	0.6339	0.6835
12	0.4575	0.5324	0.6120	0.6614
13	0.4409	0.5139	0.5923	0.6411
14	0.4259	0.4973	0.5742	0.6226
15	0.4124	0.4821	0.5577	0.6055
16	0.4000	0.4683	0.5425	0.5897
17	0.3887	0.4555	0.5285	0.5751
18	0.3783	0.4438	0.5155	0.5614
19	0.3687	0.4329	0.5034	0.5487
20	0.3598	0.4227	0.4921	0.5368
25	0.3233	0.3809	0.4451	0.4869
30	0.2960	0.3494	0.4093	0.4487
35	0.2746	0.3246	0.3810	0.4182
40	0.2573	0.3044	0.3578	0.3932
45	0.2428	0.2875	0.3384	0.3721
50	0.2306	0.2732	0.3218	0.3541
60	0.2108	0.2500	0.2948	0.3248
70	0.1954	0.2319	0.2737	0.3017
80	0.1829	0.2172	0.2565	0.2830
90	0.1726	0.2050	0.2422	0.2673
100	0.1638	0.1946	0.2301	0.2540

The calculated value of *r* must be larger than or equal to the table value for significance.

A.10 Critical values of the Spearman r_s ranked correlation coefficient

N	0.05 Level of significance		0.01 Level of significance	
	One-tailed test (directional)	Two-tailed test (non-directional)	One-tailed test (directional)	Two-tailed test (non-directional)
5	0.900	1.000	1.000	–
6	0.829	0.886	0.943	1.000
7	0.714	0.786	0.893	0.929
8	0.643	0.738	0.833	0.881
9	0.600	0.683	0.783	0.833
10	0.564	0.648	0.746	0.794
12	0.506	0.591	0.712	0.777
14	0.456	0.544	0.645	0.715
16	0.425	0.506	0.601	0.665
18	0.399	0.475	0.564	0.625
20	0.377	0.450	0.534	0.591
22	0.359	0.428	0.508	0.562
24	0.343	0.409	0.485	0.537
26	0.329	0.392	0.465	0.515
28	0.317	0.377	0.448	0.496
30	0.306	0.364	0.432	0.478

The calculated value of r_s must be larger than or equal to the table value for significance.

Index